FORMS OF TRUTH
AND THE
UNITY OF KNOWLEDGE

FORMS OF TRUTH
AND THE
UNITY OF KNOWLEDGE

Edited by

VITTORIO HÖSLE

University of Notre Dame Press

Notre Dame, Indiana

Manufactured in the United States of America

The Press gratefully acknowledges the support of the Institute for Scholarship in the Liberal Arts, University of Notre Dame, in the publication of this book.

Library of Congress Cataloging-in-Publication Data

Forms of truth and the unity of knowledge / edited by Vittorio Hösle.
pages   cm
Includes bibliographical references and index.
ISBN 978-0-268-03111-4 (pbk. : alk. paper) —
ISBN 0-268-03111-8 (pbk. : alk. paper)
1. Knowledge, Theory of.   2. Truth.   3. Science—Philosophy.
4. Humanities—Philosophy.   5. Art and religion.
I. Hösle, Vittorio, 1960– editor.
BD161.F587   2014
121—dc23

2014022434

° *The paper in this book meets the guidelines for permanence and durability of the Committee on Production Guidelines for Book Longevity of the Council on Library Resources.*

CONTENTS

PART III
EXPLANATION IN THE NATURAL SCIENCES

PART IV
INTROSPECTION AND UNDERSTANDING
IN THE HUMANITIES

CHAPTER TWELVE

PART V

ART AND RELIGION

CHAPTER THIRTEEN

CHAPTER FOURTEEN

Introduction

————————

VITTORIO HÖSLE

The Notre Dame Institute for Advanced Study was founded in 2008 in the belief that every research university needs a place where scholars come together so as to be inspired by colleagues in disciplines different from their own. There is no doubt that the subdivision of universities into departments is reasonable: given the increase of knowledge in every discipline, controlling the quality of work in a given academic field presupposes expertise in that field. At the same time, the dangers connected with this departmentalization of knowledge are various. For example, people may simply ignore what occurs outside of their own fields. Sometimes this may not affect the quality of their research; sometimes, however, this leads them to miss opportunities to connect their own studies with those of others and thus achieve more general insights. This danger is particularly menacing whenever basic insights are ignored that have repercussions for more applied research. As physics cannot progress without mathematics, so also the humanities, to give only one example, inevitably operate with basic philosophical categories, such as meaning or value; the lack of an explicit reflection on these concepts does not mean that they are not presupposed. On the contrary, the less reflection occurs, the more likely the concepts used are imprecise and

1

perhaps even inconsistent. But the disconnect of philosophy from the other disciplines is due not only to the specialization of those disciplines: philosophy itself has, to a considerable degree, given up its ambition to address a larger audience and withdrawn into very technical problems that are of interest only to "specialists of the universal," as one could call such philosophers. The decline of public intellectuals, the topic of the Institute's 2013 annual conference, which was organized by Michael Desch, who will edit the corresponding volume, is a necessary consequence of this development—one with dangerous consequences for politics: without the advocacy of public intellectuals, the political system is far more likely to be manipulated by populists and those *terribles simplificateurs* in the mass media who care more for advertising revenue than the truth.

Its three inaugural conferences in 2010, 2011, and 2012 were, together with the residential life of scholars working on research projects that deal with questions both interdisciplinary and normative, the two foci of the Notre Dame Institute for Advanced Study. These three conferences addressed the three concepts that have often been considered by the philosophical tradition the most fundamental—namely, beauty, goodness, and truth—by bringing together scholars from as many disciplines as could fruitfully interact in three days. The first two volumes, *The Many Faces of Beauty* and *Dimensions of Goodness*, appeared in 2013 with the University of Notre Dame Press and Cambridge Scholar Publishers respectively; this volume on conceptions of truth and the unity of knowledge completes the trilogy. The participants of the three conferences did not overlap—with the exception of myself: as founding director of the Institute from 2008 to 2013, I contributed to these three volumes three essays that complement one another. Those invited to the conference on truth were chosen to represent philosophy—including epistemology, logic, and ethics—theology, mathematics, chemistry, biology, psychology, literary criticism, historiography, and architecture. They hailed not only from the United States but also from Israel and various European countries such as France, Germany, Italy, Poland, Spain, and the United Kingdom, and one essay deals with the Chinese contribution to the concept of history. The essays in this volume are collected in five parts, the first dealing with the historical development of the tree of knowledge; the second with the foundational disciplines of epistemology, logic, and mathematics; the third with explanation in the natural sciences; the fourth with introspection and understanding in those disciplines dealing with humans; and the fifth with the contribution of art and religion.

Some of the common, overarching questions that the contributors to this volume address are these: By which different methods do the various disciplines achieve knowledge of truth? What is common to their methods, and what distinguishes them? Are some disciplines more foundational than others, that is, can they be understood on their own while the others presuppose them? Which forms of knowledge influence each other, and which disciplines have very little overlap? Are there different ontological realms connected with the various epistemological activities? And since it is impossible to give up the belief that the various disciplines contribute to an ultimately coherent vision of reality, how should we imagine this tree of knowledge?

Vittorio Hösle's essay, "How Did the Western Culture Subdivide Its Various Forms of Knowledge and Justify Them? Historical Reflections on the Metamorphoses of the Tree of Knowledge," gives an overview of how Western culture has grouped its various disciplines from antiquity to the present, often under the metaphor of the tree of knowledge, which points to the common roots and thus to the underlying unity of all knowledge. It starts with reflections on the budding of new and the withering of old branches of that tree, partly due to the uncovering of unsuspected strata of reality and partly thanks to the development of new theoretical tools—tools that occasionally allow the unification of disciplines that earlier were regarded as independent. The development of the tree is not always caused by empirical discoveries: shifts in philosophical categorization based on purely theoretical arguments also help to explain the various shapes that the tree of knowledge has assumed in its history. Within ancient philosophy, the first insight into different types of knowledge comes with the Eleatic school's distinction between the way of opinion and the way of truth. Plato builds upon this distinction and connects it to the subdivision of the mathematical disciplines—even while pointing to a fundamental difference between philosophy and mathematics. A thinker as early as Xenocrates proposes the subdivision of philosophy into logic, physics, and ethics—a subdivision that would become canonical within Stoicism—but it is Aristotle to whom we owe the most elaborate system of knowledge of antiquity: theoretical knowledge encompasses physics, mathematics, and theology; practical knowledge, ethics and politics; and poietical knowledge, poetics and several other less important subdisciplines. Logic, however, is difficult to fit into this tripartition: in Hugh of Saint Victor's *Didascalion*, it will form a fourth part. The two main works from the Middle Ages analyzed in the essay are Bonaventure's *De reductione artium ad theologiam* and Ramon Llull's *Arbor scientiae*. Important in Bonaventure is the attempt to include the trivium of grammar, logic, and rhetoric into this system as well as the insertion of economics— that is, the discipline of the management of a family—between ethics and politics. The climax of all knowledge is a theology based on the fourfold interpretation of scripture. In early modernity, Francis Bacon proposed the most articulate and influential system of disciplines based on the three faculties of memory, imagination, and reason. However, his system is soon challenged by Descartes's radical separation of the knowledge of extended substances from that of thinking substances, which splits any science of humans in two and raises the difficult question of how we may have knowledge of other selves, since introspection is limited to oneself. In the eighteenth century, Giambattista Vico proposed the idea of a new science that addresses human culture, understood as a realm beyond those of nature and the mind. The essay then explores the subtle alterations of the Baconian system in Jean Le Rond d'Alembert's introductory "Discours" to the *Encyclopédie* and delves into Kant's epistemological challenge and his idea of a new systematization of knowledge, which was elaborated by the greatest encyclopedist among the German Idealists, namely, Hegel, who recognizes, against Bacon and d'Alembert and anticipating Frege and Husserl, the irreducibility of logic to any other discipline. Hegel's subdivision is finally contrasted with the almost simultaneous one by Auguste Comte, who had an enormous impact on the structure of nineteenth-century universities by conceptualizing the peculiar status of engineering and having his doctrine of the sciences culminate in the new discipline of sociology.

It is one of the paradoxes of our search for truth that, while knowledge has grown exponentially in the last few centuries, epistemology has not been able to answer in a satisfying way its most basic problem, which a thinker as early as Plato addressed at the end of his *Theaetetus*. Some of our knowledge is inferred from other knowledge, but this inference process cannot go on forever. But how do we grasp the ultimate premises of our inferences? Is there an immediate knowledge—is there, that is, what some have called "intuition"? But how, then, do we react to those who do not share our intuitions, which may be either conceptual or perceptual? If we try to justify our intuitions, we seem to deprive them of their immediacy and thus of their evidence, which must not depend on anything else. If, however, we refuse to do so, we seem to give up a basic demand of rationality. Therefore, coherentism has been developed as an alternative to foundationalism: there are, it holds, no basic premises from which to start, and so it is only the coherence of our whole set of beliefs at which we should aim. But does this not imply either a circular "justification" or an infinite regress? The quarrel between foundationalists and coherentists is old: Hegel may be regarded as paradigmatic coherentist, Husserl as quintessential foundationalist.

In his essay, "Intuition and Coherence in the Keystone Loop," Keith Lehrer, one of America's leading epistemologists, tries to pave a middle ground between foundationalism, which for him is symptomatically exemplified by the eighteenth-century Scottish philosopher Thomas Reid, and coherentism, as whose champion he regards the twentieth-century American thinker Wilfrid Sellars: "It may be that intuition and coherence must be joined to yield the kind of evidence required for knowledge." In fact, Lehrer tries to prove that Reid is less of a foundationalist than he seems at first glance, for he teaches the dependence of the principles of intuition on each other and on what Lehrer calls "the First First Principle," to wit, "that our faculties by which we distinguish truth from error are not fallacious." This principle, furthermore, vouches not only for the other first principles but also for itself—like light, which reveals itself as well as other objects. (Lehrer calls such principles "keystone principles.") But this means that other first principles are not by themselves maximally evident, since they are justified by the First First Principle. Sellars's rejection of the myth of the given is based on the insight that a person who has sensory states does not necessarily have a conception of them. But an intuitionist could counter that, while this is true, it does not yet show that the evidence connected with the conception has to be inferential, for "not every transition from one state to another is an inference." Still, for Sellars evidence of truth is explained by a system, while for Reid immediate convictions are "born justified." Lehrer then discusses the challenge that skepticism represents to both the foundationalist and the coherentist. He recognizes that the skeptic cannot be confuted without begging the question—but also that this does not endanger any claim to knowledge: "we can know what we suppose we know, even though we cannot prove this to the skeptic." Lehrer insists, furthermore, that the explanation of how we can know something is not a premise in the justification of that belief; therefore, we may have "an answer to the question of how the justification of all beliefs can be explained though some beliefs are noninferentially justified." Lehrer avers with Sellars that all our beliefs are subject to revision. Reflections on the difference between primitive and discursive knowledge, of which only the second may reply to objections—as well as on the nature of exemplarized exemplars, which are instances of themselves—conclude the essay.

In "What Is the Nature of Inference?" Robert Hanna, author of the standard work *Rationality and Logic*, discusses in detail the nature of the process that was the basis of the earlier epistemological investigation. He divides the issue into four separate questions regarding inference—which can be deductive, inductive, or abductive: he investigates its metaphysics, its purpose, its justification, and its mechanism before proposing as a solution what he calls "Contemporary Kantian Moralism about Inference." Concerning the first, he defends transcendental mentalism in opposition to both psychologism—which does not capture the objectivity, necessity, and apriority of inferential facts—and Platonism—which is supposed to be incompatible with the causal triggering of human knowledge. With regard to the second, he subsumes the theory of inference under the metaphysics of morals, for it deals with the summum bonum of reasoning. (He later speaks of a "special logico-practical *ought*.") Emotivism and instrumentalism (or pragmatism), on the other hand, imply that "anything goes," provided that everyone shares the same feelings and good results are produced from the standpoint of human interests respectively. Third, he deals with the old problem that the inferential principles to be justified are themselves presupposed in the process of justification. Hanna rejects noncognitivist, holist, and inferentialist strategies as unable to warrant the objectivity, necessity, and apriority of our inferential principles and defends categorically normative logical laws. (He does not investigate, however, the problem of the plurality of logics.) The mechanism of inference finally rests on the causal power of my intentional act of inference. Inference requires both consciousness and consciously free willing—an "inferential 'zombiehood'" is doomed to fail. In his conclusion, Hanna characterizes his idealism as liberal and natural, not scary. It simply states that fundamental mental properties are co-basic in nature with fundamental physical properties.

The discipline in which inference plays the most exclusive role is doubtless mathematics—excepting, of course, logic itself. Laurent Lafforgue, Fields Medalist and one of the world's leading mathematicians, honored the conference with his presence and delivered an essay, fascinating in both its content and its literary quality, titled "Speculation and Narration in Mathematics." Lafforgue starts from the fact that truth cannot simply be seen, but must be lived, for otherwise the concept of truth would be pornographic rather than nuptial. And so he offers a confession of what it means to live a mathematician's life, even if mathematics seems the most impersonal of all disciplines. But he begins his exploration with an approach, as it were, from outside: a non-mathematician who observes a department of mathematics will first notice the far higher proportion of people to equipment than in most other settings and then find out, "not perhaps without feeling a degree of terror," that they use incomprehensible words. If he then ventures to open one of their texts, he will discover that it is "as if it told a story in chronological order and . . . as if the specific story . . . were part of a general step in mathematical science and in the history of that onward march." At the same time, the mathematical text uses only the present tense and in fact refers to timeless structures of logical implication. The tension between the narrative and the speculative element is what constitutes mathematics; this tension may generate the erroneous belief that implication is a form of causality.

However, a mathematical text is not only a temporal manifestation of something eternal: if we consider the mental life of the individual mathematician, it occupies a place within the history of mathematics as well—as becomes obvious when one considers those theorems named for the mathematicians who discovered them. Lafforgue distinguishes two ways of employing the combination of speculation and narration peculiar to mathematics: one can either use old methods in new analyses or explore mathematical terrain that is entirely new. Paradoxically, Lafforgue notes, mathematicians speak of events in their mathematical texts: something "happens" in mathematics when a new vista opens through the development of a new concept or the solution of an old problem. Regarding the inner motivation of mathematicians, Lafforgue recognizes the striving for recognition and honors as a common motive. But far more important is the desire to share precious things, such as mathematical insights—even if this leads to an overproduction of texts that are ignored by almost all human beings; in fact, even the most famous mathematicians "are not sheltered from self-doubt and despair." Therefore, another motive is the desire to write to oneself: "a mathematical narrative is like a travel story in which, in fact, the journey consists of the narrative itself." The enormous effort in concentration, so Lafforgue ends his analysis, seems to go hand in hand with the experience of inspiration, and even if few mathematicians reflect on the author of these inspiring words, "they find their only joy in becoming servants to these words."

Truth can be found not only in logic and mathematics but also in the natural sciences—those that deal with the physical world, not with ideal entities. Pure thought does not suffice to get at truth in this realm; experience is indispensable. Within nature, one class of objects is of particular importance: humans. Of all the animals known to science, it is humans alone who seem to be able to grasp truth, and this is due—at least in part—to some of their biochemical and biological properties. In "A Molecular Glimpse of How Mother Nature Can Regulate Our Being," the biochemist Thomas Nowak addresses both the criteria that a scientific theory has to satisfy in order to be taken seriously in its claim to approach truth and some specific regulatory mechanisms that keep organisms alive. While a valid inference guarantees the transfer of truth—if the premises are true, then also the conclusion must be true—logic cannot answer the question of which premises should be affirmed as true. For science, it is clear what is needed in order to determine the truth of premises: observation and experimental data. Like logical positivism, Nowak sharply distinguishes between evident data (which he calls "objective truth") and its interpretation, which, though it aims at and sometimes approximates truth, remains inevitably subjective. Interpretations of data are called hypotheses or theories, and they can achieve a very high degree of plausibility: for example, "virtually all credible scientists believe in the phenomenon of evolution." Still, Nowak insists that the evolution of one species into others is only a hypothesis, not itself an immediate datum. The problem in moving from data to theories is that there are almost always many reasonable explanations of the same data. True enough, further experiments may help eliminate some of the competing explanations, for "hypotheses that are inconsistent with the data are clearly incorrect." But since the choice of experiments depends, among other things, on the technology available and the technology of one age will always be surpassed in accuracy by that of the next, absolute certainty cannot be gained. No less important than technology in devising new experiments is the imagination of the scientist using that technology. Laws of nature, according to Nowak, are nothing other than hypotheses that have withstood experimental challenge for a long time. Nowak then gives several examples where doctrines once cherished, such as Stahl's phlogiston theory, were dropped during the evolution of science: echoing Thomas S. Kuhn, Nowak speaks of paradigm shifts, such as those that led to relativity and quantum theory. He then focuses on his own research, the study of a key step in the regulation of glycolysis: "this study reflects the asymptotic process of better understanding the details of how a specific regulatory process occurs." He chooses this specific metabolic pathway because it is critical to life and virtually ubiquitous in living things. Among the regulatory mechanisms devised by nature to respond to physiological challenges, two alternative ones are paramount: an on/off process in which the catalytic reaction is active or inactive or a determination of the speed of the reaction rate by an enzyme. Light switches and rheostats are, respectively, the technological equivalents of these biological mechanisms. Modifications of the enzymes can be reversed; the secretion of metabolites and hormones may trigger a cascade of regulatory steps. Nowak then analyzes in detail the mechanism of regulation of the enzyme pyruvate kinase, discussing, among other things, the feed-forward activation, in which a metabolite formed early in the pathway activates an enzyme farther down the pathway. The relevant hypothesis was exposed to both kinetic and thermodynamic studies, and since it proved consistent with the information provided by the experiments, it continues to be held—and will be until "the results of further studies become inconsistent with the current theory."

One might voice against Nowak's reflections on the nature of science three possible objections: first, the demarcation between data and hypotheses is not easy, since, at least in modern physics, many data are gained through experiments that already presuppose theories. Second, one could try to defend certain basic principles of the natural sciences, such as conservation laws, as a priori valid because, without assuming them, experimentation itself would not be possible. Third, in the case of living things, there are certain constraints on the chemical processes that occur within a given organism that follow from the nature of that organism—specifically, from its need to survive and reproduce. Do such constraints, one might ask, allow us to exclude a priori certain possibilities that in themselves would be logically possible?

Francisco J. Ayala is one of the most famous biologists of our time, former president of the American Association for the Advancement of Science, member of many national and foreign academies, and recipient of both the National Medal of Science, in 2001, and of the Templeton Prize, in 2010. His essay, "What Light Does Biology Shed on the Social Sciences and the Humanities?," probes the question of how the disciplines that deal with that very unique species of animals, namely, humans, can benefit from the most complex natural science, biology. After discussing both the origins and the distinctive anatomical traits of humans—such as our bipedal gait, opposing thumbs, cryptic ovulation, large brains, and vocal-tract modification—he looks at our behavioral traits—such as abstract thinking, symbolic language, and toolmaking—which, together, led to a new form of evolution, cultural evolution. Within human culture, Ayala focuses on ethical behavior and investigates the issue of "whether ethical behavior was directly promoted by natural selection or has rather come about as an epigenetic manifestation of some other trait that was the target of natural selection." Ayala points to Darwin's account in the third chapter of *The Descent of Man*, whose two basic points are these: moral behavior is the result of human intelligence and thus of biology, even if it is only indirectly promoted by natural selection, but concrete moral norms are culturally determined. Ayala then touches upon post-Darwinian evolutionary ethics, such as the theories of Herbert Spencer and Julian Huxley, and rejects the idea that the evolutionary process is itself pointing toward progress: from a biological point of view, the success of bacteria is no less impressive than that of vertebrates, including humans. To return to the evolution of moral behavior (the justification of which belongs to a discipline other than biology), Ayala compares the issue at stake to language: clearly, humans have an innate capacity for symbolic language, but the particular languages are a result of culture. Analogously, the moral sense is a result of the biological capacities of anticipating the consequences of one's own actions, of passing value judgments (which presupposes the capacity to abstract), and of choosing between alternatives. (Later, empathy is added.) These conditions come about after crossing an evolutionary threshold; thus, there is a radical breach between humans and other animals, even if we can hardly know exactly when in hominid evolution morality emerged. Ayala contrasts his theory with that of Richerson and Boyd, gene-culture-coevolution, which "would rather lead to a more nearly universal system of morality." According to Ayala, the obvious differences between the moral codes of various nations are due to cultural evolution. Still, he recognizes that some concrete moral norms must have a biological basis, because they are ubiquitous and are clearly conducive to biological fitness—think of parental care—while other norms are even contrary to fitness. Finally, Ayala delves into the peculiarities of cultural evolution—peculiarities more Lamarckian than Darwinian—such as its horizontal transmission and its capacity to incorporate elements from different cultures. The norms of morality are clearly the product, then, of cultural evolution, even if civil authorities and religious institutions may reinforce them. (Of course, these institutions are themselves the products of cultural evolution.)

Zygmunt Pizlo works both in the Department of Psychological Sciences and in the School of Electrical and Computer Engineering at Purdue University and is thus doubly qualified to address the other great source of knowledge beside inference, namely, perception—even if he shows how much inference is involved in perception itself. In his essay, "What Is the Nature of Perception?" he shows, among other things, a great familiarity with the historical reflections on the problem, especially those of the nineteenth century. Pizlo defends a form of innatism—one based on strong empirical evidence. He starts by distinguishing, with Gustav Fechner, three different types of phenomena, which are causally connected: distal stimuli (physical objects or events described in the language of physics), proximal stimuli (a distribution of light, mechanical, or chemical energy on the surface of receptors), and finally percepts (i.e., mental phenomena). The problem is that sensory data are never sufficient to describe the external object, as becomes obvious when we reflect on how people construct out of a two-dimensional retinal image the corresponding three-dimensional object. While the mapping from object to image (the so-called direct problem) is many-to-one, the inverse problem, mapping from the data to the object, is one-to-many. But how, given this problem, do we succeed in having veridical perceptions—the existence of which Pizlo asserts, rightly pointing to the fact that even radical skeptics use and presuppose the functioning of their senses in experiments purported to show the unreliability of perception? But Pizlo does not follow Reid's common-sense assumption of the trustworthiness of perception: he is closer to Kant in asserting the existence of hardwired intuitions of space, time, and causality—even if Kant's concept of the synthetic a priori does not imply innate knowledge.

In order to know how other people perceive, science must start from public events—that is, phenomena that all can observe—and infer from them private perceptions. It is crucial to separate response biases from perceptions, which can be achieved by the signal detection methodology. Pizlo shows by means of the Müller-Lyer illusion that perception proper is far more independent of individual experiences, such as learning, than was earlier assumed. Our visual system does not use look-up tables influenced by experience but rather innate computational algorithms. The inverse problem can only be solved, moreover, if there are a priori constraints: otherwise, the visual system would have to try all partitions of the set of six million receptors, and there is no way this could be achieved in a time even as large as that elapsed since the Big Bang. "Were the tabula rasa anywhere near blank or clean, the task of training feature detectors in our visual system would be hopeless." However, the very computational intractability of the inverse problem can be a blessing because it points toward the constraints that we have to assume exist. Pizlo follows a tradition from Plato to the Gestalt psychologists in claiming that we perceive perfectly regular shapes not because we have encountered them in reality but because universals rather than particulars structure perception: "concrete objects are instantiations of the abstract concept of symmetry rather than symmetry being abstracted . . . from particular objects." Finally, Pizlo describes the way in which a robot constructed by his team according to such principles can deal with the inverse problem achieving results not very different from those of humans.

Osborne Wiggins is one of the best-known American philosophers working in the phenomenological tradition. That philosophical school, founded by Edmund Husserl, insists on the irreducibility of the first-person perspective to the third-person perspective, and so Wiggins's essay is in a way complementary to that of Pizlo, who, as a scientist, analyzes perception from outside—that is, from a third-person perspective. Wiggins starts with reflections on the proper object of psychology: is it mind, overt behavior, or the brain? Even if he is sympathetic to the answer that all three are legitimate, his main concern is to find out what "it is like to be a human being for the human being himself or herself." He dislikes, however, the traditional term *introspection*—which is used, for example, by William James—since it is loaded with dualistic metaphysical assumptions that Wiggins rejects; therefore, he prefers terms like *self-awareness*. Mental processes are experiences of something, of my body and the world beyond it, and the mind given through self-awareness is an embodied mind. At the same time, body and world are given as experienced. The need for a study of the latter as experienced becomes particularly obvious in psychopathology, for the spatiotemporal world the schizophrenic experiences must not be identified with space and time experienced by normal people. When I am aware of mental processes, I am thus aware of processes that are themselves aware of something. Wiggins then distinguishes two types of self-awareness. On the one hand, there is a prescientific one, which involves a direct, although indistinct, givenness of ourselves to ourselves. Connected to it is an indirect awareness of the experiences of other people, "and these intertwined and comingled experiences of the subjective teach us . . . the workings of human subjectivity as such." This first sort of self-awareness is implicit and tacit; it forms part of the field within which I focus on an object. On the other hand, the explicit self-reflection, which leads to psychology as science, draws some of its meaning from our prescientific self-awareness. The self disclosed in such reflection is embodied as well, and it is directly given to one's attention. This does not imply that its data are uninterpreted—but they are still data. The direct givenness is an epistemological advantage, since there is no need to bring in inference. Even if this direct givenness is the ultimate court of appeal, we still want claims about it to be recognized intersubjectively. And there is only one way to do this—specifically, "by inviting one's critic to try to directly see for himself." Of course, the decisive problem, which "has always constituted the Achilles' heel of a psychological science utilizing 'introspection,'" is this: how can I hold the justified belief that my own experiences exemplify general features of humans? Still, Wiggins convincingly argues that there is no way of avoiding introspection. Even in the third-person approach there is an implied appeal to the reader to "imagine" the experiences the object of the analysis is supposed to have. Only thus can we examine reflectively the properties of those experiences. Imagination has the peculiar power to create the experiences that it imagines having, and all of the social sciences presuppose this capacity. This leads to final reflections on the importance of expertise—for even direct self-reflection is a hard achievement that requires schooling.

One of the most difficult types of knowledge to understand is ethical knowledge. For a society, it seems crucially important that people know, or at least believe to know, that extorting money is wrong, and yet philosophers do not agree on the peculiar nature of this knowledge. Some philosophers, most famously Kant, have tended to assimilate it to logical or mathematical knowledge; not so the British tradition. It is in this tradition that Allan Gibbard, doubtless one of the most innovative and famous ethicists of our time, is rooted. His essay, "Could Normative Insights Be Sources of Normative Knowledge?," begins with a depiction of ethical intuitionism as it was upheld by Henry Sidgwick and George Edward Moore. Neither was an empiricist: they did not believe that moral questions can be answered by experiment and observation, even introspective observation, alone. Rather, any answer to moral questions ultimately presupposes specifically moral intuitions. Good, according to Moore, is a simple, non-natural property, and this holds also for the alternative basic concept, being warranted. Warrant is the subject of normative inquiry, of which ethics is only a part: normative epistemology is another, and thus the concept of probability is normative, too. Even denying the existence of such non-natural properties seems self-defeating, for, if we claim that we should be skeptical regarding them, we must ask, "is this 'should' itself something non-natural, and so something we should banish from our thinking?" The use of "should" seems ineludible. The grasp of fundamental normative facts, so Sidgwick concluded, occurs in intuitions. This philosophical concept must be distinguished from the psychological one, according to which intuition is a rapid and effortless type of thinking, for the latter does not imply that intuitions convey truth. Gibbard does not deny that ethical disagreements are often due to the difficulties of knowing non-normative facts. But this does not alter the outcome that all normative knowledge must rest on fundamental normative knowledge— for example, that misery is bad. This is not controversial, but other equally fundamental normative claims are: think of the question whether happiness and misery are all things that matter in themselves. Since Gibbard rejects deep analogies between ethical and mathematical knowledge but is unwilling to pay the very high price of skepticism regarding normative issues, he turns to naturalistic theories. Some of the most sophisticated are ideal response theories—the main problem with which is that Moore's objections against naturalistic definitions of *good* can be directed also against naturalistic definitions of *ideal*.

Gibbard, however, fundamentally agrees with Richard Brandt's "qualified attitude method": our affective capacities must be impartial and informed, must not stem from an abnormal state of mind, and must accord with general principles. Since this is not intended as a definition of what "morally required" means, it does not violate the prohibition against naturalistic definitions. Gibbard then deals with expressivism and criticizes Alfred Jules Ayer's version, since I can feel disapproval of something without thinking that it is really wrong. Gibbard's own version of expressivism is more complex: calling a state of mind such as approval "warranted" expresses a state of mind akin to planning how to feel. In order that the flashes of moral affect that constitute moral insights become knowledge, they have to deliver truths in a nondefective way. "For a belief to constitute knowledge . . . it must be true, it must be warranted, and the processes that eventuate in true belief must be reliable." For ethics, moral feelings are warranted if and only if they meet the standards of the qualified attitude method. Finally, Gibbard discusses one of the main objections against his theory of moral knowledge—the fact that one's moral insights may contradict those of another. This is particularly true for different cultures, even if the attitudes of both meet the standards of the qualified attitude method. But how can we speak of knowledge if my moral attitudes are determined by the happenstance of belonging to one group or another? In his answer, Gibbard points to what he calls "tempered moral realism": we are warranted in our conviction that cultures with other moral sensibilities are wrong, even if they do not manifest any epistemic defect apart from disagreeing with us. That is how ethics differs from science. Therefore, we should speak only of moral "quasi-facts" and normative "quasi-knowledge."

The humanities are probably best understood as interpretive disciplines—that is, as disciplines that try to reconstruct the intentional acts of other subjects based on the expression of these intentions in physical events or objects. They aim at mental acts, even if they are not based on a first-person approach, since they deal with other persons' expressions. But how can we access other persons' mental acts? Against the widespread skepticism that has paralyzed much of what occurs today in the humanities, Carsten Dutt, a German philosopher and literary critic who was Hans-Georg Gadamer's main intellectual interlocutor in the last decade of his life, defends in his essay, "Truth and Knowledge in Literary Interpretation," the claim that the paradigmatic hermeneutical discipline on which he focuses, namely, literary criticism, can acquire knowledge, which he explicates, with a definition going back to Plato, as justified true belief. However, literary interpretation is not only a cognitive process; it is also a creative one, for the text has "zones of indeterminacy . . . embedded in well-determined structures." This feature makes the interpretation of a text analogous to the performance of, say, a musical piece, since not every aspect of the performance is determined by the score. However, while various performances are mutually exclusive, in the case of two incompatible first-order interpretations, a second-order interpretation may be offered—averring, perhaps, that either the literary work is ambivalent or the author is undecided. According to Dutt, interpretation presupposes a non- or preinterpretive perception and then consists in a classification, such as "this text is a sonnet." It involves effort because, as Dutt understands it, interpretation deals with nonobvious states of affairs and has to be justified by giving reasons. "Felicitous interpretation adds to the knowledge we must have and make use of in order to get our interpretive business going" (italics omitted).

Dutt exemplifies the conflict of interpretation to be settled by arguments with two possible interpretations of a painting by Francesco Maffei; Erwin Panofsky finally determined its meaning by relying on the history of types. In the case of literary criticism, the interpretation may focus on single words or phrases, on larger parts of the text, on the text as a whole, or on its relation to its social and cultural context. "The web of interpretive issues in dealing with literature is chronically vast and full of repercussions: findings on the level of microinterpretation often affect our results on the level of macrointerpretation—and vice versa. A single ironic word in a seemingly full-blown happy ending novel can alter the work *as a whole.*" A literary critic must master a set of concepts; their application will at the same time lead to a refinement of the conceptual framework. Conceptual work and concrete interpretation enhance each other. Dutt grants to philosophers of interpretation such as Robert Matthews that there is a creative aspect in interpretation that follows from the (syntactical or narrative) indeterminacy of the work; nonetheless, the work has features that cannot be interpreted away—for example, linguistic content on the level of individual passages and literary content on the level of the work as a whole. Against radical anti-intentionalism, Dutt ultimately links the task of the interpreter of a text to "the intentional activity of its historically situated author," even if he grants that this does not exclude that a work of art may have more levels of complexity than its author was aware of.

While hermeneutics deals with the interpretation of products of the human mind, whether present or past, historiography studies truths about the past. According to the common understanding of the term, it aims at past events in which humans played a role, but this is not a necessary component of the concept of historical research, since this also forms an aspect in the natural sciences: think of paleontology. Aviezer Tucker, a well-known scholar of the methodology of historiography, counters in his essay, "Historical Truth," the objection that there are no universally recognized classics of historiography that enjoy the paradigmatic status that, say, Newton and Einstein do in physics and that could be the starting point of normative conclusions about what constitutes good historiography: Tucker points to figures like Jacob Burckhardt and his theory of the Renaissance. He recognizes, however, that most of the methodology of historians is implicit in their practice and that there is today even a certain animus against any explicit theory of historiography: "Collective tacit knowledge is acquired through social embedding. Explicit knowledge, by contrast, may be transmitted via intermediaries." All disciplines that generate historical truth "use different information theories about the transmission of information in time via different media." The nature of the information transmitted varies—just think of the differences among documents, languages, and DNA—but "the stages of inference are identical: they first attempt to prove that the evidence is more likely given some common source of its shared preserved information than given separate sources by finding dysfunctional homologies that are unlikely given separate sources." These dysfunctional homologies may be biological rudiments or infelicities in texts. Tucker confutes the naive realistic assumption that we can "see" the past. In fact, we can only infer it, and thus "epistemology is built into the historiographic enterprise, unavoidable and inevitable." Where we refuse epistemology, skeptical consequences force themselves upon us. Tucker wants to defend both the specific evidential basis for historiographic claims and the probabilistic inference from the evidence to the fact.

The difference between most natural sciences and historiography is that the former are interested in replicable types of events, the latter in individual tokens such as the French Revolution. When a natural science aims at an individual event such as the Big Bang, according to Tucker, it becomes itself historiographical and is no longer a theoretical science. Needless to say, historical sciences, too, "are theory laden in the sense that they are founded on information transmission theories." Tucker points to the difference between repeated visits of the same archival sources and replicated experiments—only in the second case are different tokens studied—and fights the theory according to which historiography is always built on communal narratives with a "unity of story, storyteller, audience, and protagonist," since this is only one of the origins of historiography. He rejects also the doctrine according to which historiography simply embellishes aesthetically the facts: all such facts are the result of inferences, which therefore have to be justified. Tucker furthermore argues against Michael Dummett's subjunctive justificationism and insists that certain facts may be inferred today even if they could not have been observed at the relevant time. "So, while the tendency in cosmic time is for information to decay, the tendency in the much shorter modern era of historical science has been to discover more of the past by developing new methods for extracting existing nested information." Against all skepticism with regard to the truth claims of historiography, Tucker points to uncoerced consensus regarding many historical facts and the stability of basic historical theories, a consensus that cannot be explained merely sociologically since historians as a group are more heterogeneous than natural scientists. Next, he distinguishes cases in which the temporal evolution of the studied systems is identical with the transmission of information and where this does not hold. Finally, he discusses situations in which historical truth is over- or underdetermined by the evidence. In the latter case, it depends on the context and the concrete consequences whether we are willing to speak of historical truth. "It is one thing to infer from a document that somebody was a spy for the Habsburg monarchy in the nineteenth century; it is quite another to prove that a living person was an informer for the Communist regime a few decades ago on a comparable evidential basis."

The volumes on beauty and goodness included Asian perspectives (an Indian one on aesthetics, a Chinese one on ethics and politics); this third volume contains an analysis of a Chinese approach to a form of knowledge particularly important for a nation that gained statehood earlier and has maintained its political unity for longer than any other human culture. Nicola Di Cosmo belongs to the permanent faculty of the Princeton Institute for Advanced Study and is a world-renowned expert in both Chinese and Mongol-Manchu history. In his essay, "Truth and Unity in Chinese Traditional Historiography," he gives a rich overview of the questions with which Chinese historians struggled. Despite enormous changes, the various strands of Chinese historiography "produced what is arguably the foundation of China as a unified cultural entity." He distinguishes two basic types in the structuring of the historical material: while the annalist proceeds diachronically year after year, the historian tries to group his material thematically. For the latter, history is not simply a series of events, but, for example, the evolution of certain institutions. Sima Qian's *Shiji*, written around 100 BC, is praised as the first truly comprehensive account of Chinese history, "the largest repository of historical knowledge in human civilization," well corresponding in its unity to that of the empire itself and even dealing with foreign peoples. The high political and intellectual stakes of the historians' work explain why, under the Tang dynasty, a History Office was created: the state regarded it as both its duty and its prerogative to write the history of the preceding dynasty. From this time on, the tension between private and public historiography forms one of the basic dichotomies of this tradition; others deal with the contrast between philosophical foundations and the need for objective records, with that between the dynastic and the comprehensive models, that between the annalistic procedure and the procedure of more elaborate narration, and that between the separation and the inclusion of the Confucian classics from and in the realm of historiography respectively. Regarding truth, the reliability of sources is a major concern for Chinese historians. But one may doubt that they ever aimed at a slavish report of the facts; instead, their model was that of a "ritual reality" in which only that was regarded as recordable that corresponded to established codes of conduct.

Early on, there was an awareness that, due to "appropriate concealment," certain events may have vanished from historical accounts even if they did in fact occur. This presupposes the implicit imperative to be "true" to events, even those that were impalatable. Clearly, different rules hold when the historian is not simply the interpreter of ancient sources, but is himself witness to the facts that he reports. In opposition to the highly bureaucratized official historiography, a systematic critique of historical writing emerges; Liu Zhiji insists on rectitude and passion as remedies against the alteration of truth. At the same time, the official historiography, while often unduly influenced by those in power, had the advantage of access to more documents. The aim of reliability does not mean that the historiographer is not animated by a moral purpose. The great problem of Western theories of historiography, the relation between general laws of the social world and individual facts, is not alien to Chinese historians, who wanted to penetrate the universal moral essence of events. But the neo-Confucian orthodoxy that began in the Song dynasty was increasingly challenged by the philological turn that characterizes the scholarship of the last, the Qing dynasty. Characteristic of the work of Zhang Xuecheng is the combination of notions of cyclicality and evolution. While the traditional subdivision of knowledge in China had separated the Classics as eternally valid from history, he subsumes them under history because he recognizes their historical origin and context. One is tempted to think of radical European historicism that, in the nineteenth century, also threatened to absorb the traditional systematic disciplines of the Western tradition into history.

Since the first conference on beauty did not include architecture among the arts with which it dealt, an architect was invited to the third conference on truth to explain in which sense architecture contributes to the unity of knowledge. Michael Lykoudis is dean of the University of Notre Dame School of Architecture, which is committed to classical and sustainable architecture. Lykoudis begins his essay, "The Architecture School within the University," with the argument that architecture combines, perhaps more than any other art, almost all forms of knowledge. For the architect needs a basic understanding of mathematics, engineering, physics, chemistry, and biology—he must know, for example, which chemical interactions might contribute to or threaten the durability of a building. He needs, furthermore, knowledge of psychology, law, and business. But, of course, "most important, architecture is an art." Lykoudis returns to the old comparison of architecture and music, famously expressed in Friedrich Schlegel's aphorism about architecture as frozen music: in these two arts, formal structures play a far more important role than any mimetic relation to reality. Lykoudis interprets architecture as mirroring the fact that the visible universe consists of solids and voids and explains why the voids are as important as the solids. "The pattern of the openings or voids in a wall creates rhythms that make up the composition. The changing size of these openings adds to the grammar and syntax of architectural compositions, much like notes on a piece of music. . . . The rhythm of the building can be seen in the regular cadence of openings and the melody in the punctuating changes in size and proportion of the openings." Colonnades are said to be as much about the space between the columns as about the columns themselves. Regarding the different types of buildings, Lykoudis grounds his typology in the double nature of humans as both private and social creatures. The first aspect leads to private residences and commercial centers, the second to town halls, libraries, and other public buildings. He adds a third category by considering sacred buildings. All these buildings must fit together, and so urbanism is added as a third scale to construction—the assembly of the elements of a building—and architecture—the design of an individual building as a whole. Buildings have openings toward one another, and toward the surrounding environment, that vary in size from the small windows of a kitchen to the huge ones of a library—not to mention arcades, which one might interpret as porous walls.

Lykoudis does not at all deny cultural variations between the various architectures of the world, but he believes in architectural universals that have their ultimate justification in anthropological facts: for example, "there is a clear distinction between public, private, and sacred buildings irrespective of time." The reason that Lykoudis favors classical architecture over modern architecture is that classical architecture is committed to the principle of equilibrium: "balance and durability are harmonized." He pleads for a combination of traditional aesthetic principles with the demand for sustainability, which will impose itself upon us with the increasing depletion of fossil fuels. His traditionalism is open to improvements: after all, tradition is "the projection of society's highest aspirations into the future." Good architecture has to adapt to the natural world that surrounds it, as does the cavea of the Epidaurus theater to the valley in which it sits, while at the same time alluding to myths, which elevate mere craft to architecture. The essay ends with a list of the requirements that individual buildings as well as cities will have to satisfy in an age of energy limits. This return to simplicity, paradoxically, will help us to regain beauty—for, even if humankind has built more buildings since 1950 than in its entire history beforehand, modern cities are much uglier than those of the past.

Celia Deane-Drummond is particularly qualified to answer the question "How Is Theology Inspired by the Sciences?" as she received a PhD in plant physiology before she became a theologian. She begins by pointing to the different philosophical traditions behind theology and the natural sciences: theology is "committed to metaphysical theism as a starting point, while science generally eschews theism in favor of methodological naturalism." At the same time, Aquinas's concept of theology may convince us that theology may benefit from the sciences—and even perform its specific task better as a result of its engagement with them. Deane-Drummond supports "a self-conscious search and aspiration for unity of knowledge rather than the bolder claim that such unity can easily be achieved." Shared practical concerns can mediate the search for such unity, and she chooses the issue of sustainability as an area the investigation of which must be multidisciplinary: both science and ethics, for example, are relevant to issues of sustainability. Deane-Drummond distinguishes such fruitful cooperation from the reductionist absorptions of one field by the other. Though the situation was once quite the opposite, today it is biology that threatens to absorb theology: Deane-Drummond discusses several "explanations" of religion that are couched in evolutionary terms. Since it is not easy to point to its selective advantages, one may interpret religion either as an exaptation (something which is beneficial now but was not when it arose) or a spandrel (something lacking selective advantage both today and in the past). Referring to the distinction between proximate and ultimate causes introduced by the great biologist Ernst Mayr, Deane-Drummond insists with Bonhoeffer that all scientific explanations are by nature penultimate rather than ultimate, since the latter are about God. She does not deny that evolutionary biology may successfully explain particular traits of religion. But even outside of the theological framework, there are many other sciences, from cognitive psychology to linguistics to anthropology, that can shed light on other features of religion. Theological "God language," finally, is about second-order metaphysical claims that cannot be tested empirically. According to Karl Rahner, "theology has a better chance than another branch of science of acting as mediator between disciplines."

What remains common to natural science and theology is their sense of wonder in the face of nature's beauty and complexity. Deane-Drummond has an ambivalent stance toward the tradition of natural theology, so powerful in Christian theology until it was destroyed by Charles Darwin. Her two main objections relate to the following problems: how can humans be in relation with a God who manifests himself in mathematical laws, and how is a good God compatible "with the apparently cruel and wasteful processes found in the natural world"? The second question particularly vexes biologists, "which may be one reason that theism is less common among prominent contemporary biologists compared to physicists." Clearly, natural theology cannot prove the existence of God: it can only try to find God in nature based on the independent conviction of his existence. In the context of ecological praxis—which she distinguishes from the science of ecology—normative questions inevitably enter. Despite the rejection of teleology by modern biology, sustainability is directed toward future generations, and this introduces a form of teleology of which theology may help to make sense. Even if we want to repristinate an ecosystem and biology is able to tell us how it was before the advance of industrialization, biology as such is never in the position "to adjudicate which historical period is the one that should be aimed at today." For that, prudence is necessary. She ends with a plea for wisdom, "that classical sense of rediscovering the relationship between fields of study and . . . inclusive of a relationship with God," for only wisdom can rightly prioritize some fields of research above others.

This volume could not address the concept of truth in every discipline—much less its articulation in the context of every major culture. Some disciplines are painfully missing—such as physics and sociology; but the reflections of the chemist and of the psychologist respectively shed some light on them, too. Some disciplines are implicitly covered—even if Dutt focuses on literary interpretation, he uses examples from the visual arts, and his theory of interpretation can easily be generalized over all humanities. Even if much work remains to be done, the volume gives an overview of how practitioners of the various sciences and humanities understand the methodological challenges they have to face in order to achieve, or at least approach, truth in their own work. Even if the methods they use and the problems they address are very different, their commitment to truth is the same, and perhaps this book can strengthen the conviction that the variety of methods does not endanger the ultimate unity of knowledge, without which an institution such as the university would hardly make sense. Though the branches of the disciplines vary from one another considerably, they stretch from one stem—and the differences between logical inference, the observation of external phenomena, introspection, and interpretation correspond to the inner articulation of the one world and the principle that ultimately explains it. Perhaps the epistemological dilemma between intuitionism and coherentism can be addressed more in depth by considering the inner architecture of knowledge. This, at least, was Hegel's central conviction, and there is much to be learned from it.

I cannot end this introduction without thanking Don Stelluto, associate director of the Notre Dame Institute for Advanced Study; Carolyn Sherman, its programs administrator; and Grant Osborn, its operations coordinator, for their excellent work in the organization of this conference and their indefatigable help in support of this volume. Without their dedication, efficiency, and kindness, the Institute would not have quickly become a place where scholars, so to speak, learn to look and sometimes even to climb from one branch of knowledge to another.

PART I

The Historical Development of
the Tree of Knowledge

CHAPTER ONE

How Did the Western Culture Subdivide Its Various Forms of Knowledge and Justify Them?

*Historical Reflections on the Metamorphoses
of the Tree of Knowledge*

───────

Vittorio Hösle

Even more amazing than the sheer amount of knowledge that human-kind has acquired in the last millennia is the heterogeneity of its nature and its sources. Aesthetic values, moral obligations, logical inferences, regular polygons, laws of nature, events, states, and processes connected with atoms and molecules, stars, organisms, mental states, technical ar-tifacts, social institutions as diverse as the family and war, signs, lan-guages, and artworks are some of the objects we may know something about, and as their ontological features are strikingly different, it is reasonable to presume that at least some of the cognitive operations connected with them vary, too. On the one hand, the increase of knowl-edge over time suggests the possibility that perhaps already in the near future completely different types of objects and corresponding sciences may be added to the list that we accept today and alter it in an unpre-dictable way. On the other hand, reductionist programs betray the desire

to subsume all this variety under some simple concept, "natural selection" being a relatively recent and plausible candidate, for it can indeed be applied both to the evolution of organisms and cultures.[1] The
pulls of expansion of research and unification of principles drive the
cosmos of knowledge in opposite directions and reshuffle it in every
generation, and the organizational changes that the social institution
that tries to capture this cosmos, the university, has experienced and
still experiences in its history clearly reflect these pulls. Probably most
convincing is an intermediate position that recognizes an irreducible
plurality of cognitive operations and disciplines but is committed to
trying to understand why the universe of disciplines is structured as it
is. The old metaphor of the tree of knowledge, which is still used when
a discipline tries to determine its own position in the system of knowledge,[2] suggests that, while new branches may always grow, there are
certain constraints in such a system. For all trees have certain parts in
common, such as roots and trunks, and thus the plausibility of the
metaphor rests on the assumption that there are some constraints in
the ordering of disciplines.

In this essay, I want to pursue the question of how the subdivision
of knowledge was conceived at certain crucial moments in Western intellectual history. Even before we look at the most salient subdivisions
and try to find the causes and reasons that stand behind the major
changes, it is plausible to hazard the hypothesis that two major factors
determine the way a culture organizes its knowledge. First, there is the
rise of certain disciplines in given historical epochs. The scientific revolution of the seventeenth century or the historicist turn of the nineteenth, for example, brought forth a wealth of new disciplines, and even
if some of the objects studied by them were already known to antiquity and the Middle Ages, there are good reasons to speak of the creation of a new discipline when new principles and methods are used in
relation to the same objects. For what constitutes a discipline are the
logical links between its various tenets, and when the amount of these
links increases dramatically, we should speak of a new discipline even
if its object has been thought about by humans from age immemorial.
Edmund Husserl's famous distinction, in § 64 of the "Prolegomena"
to the *Logical Investigations*, between abstract, or theoretical, and con-

crete, or ontological, sciences points to what I have in mind: Geography, and natural history in general, are concrete sciences, because their unity is constituted by the common object they address, often with completely different methods (think of the distinction between physical geography and anthropogeography), while theoretical sciences, such as theoretical physics, are grounded in homogeneous principles of explanation.[3]

The rise of a new discipline has to do with various causes, among which two can be easily distinguished. First, there is the discovery of new strata of reality, be it due to journeys of exploration to parts of the earth, or the cosmos, still unknown, be it due to new instruments of observation, such as microscopes or telescopes. Anthropology was triggered by the conquest of the new world,[4] microbiology by the development of microscopes in the seventeenth century.[5] Second, there is the development of new theoretical tools, often mathematical ones, that allow us to unify certain sets of assumptions and thus to grant theoretical status to a discipline: Modern physics would not have succeeded without calculus, which permitted, among many other things, determining instantaneous velocities; the social sciences originated in the nineteenth century thanks to the application of statistics to social data by the mathematician Adolphe Quetelet in his *Sur l'homme et le développement des ses facultés, ou Essai de physique sociale* (Treatise on Man) of 1835.

But the study of the scientific revolution shows us that even before the great discoveries by physicists such as Newton, philosophers such as Bacon and Descartes had developed the program of the new science partly on epistemological, partly on moral and political grounds. Thus, it is not simply scientific discoveries that determine the various shapes that an epoch gives to the tree of knowledge. There are, second, philosophical ideas that motivate the intellectuals of a certain time to look out for, or even to found, a new discipline. Conceptual reasons generate the feeling that there is a gap in the tree of knowledge where, with the help of some philosophical pruning, a new discipline may blossom. Its absence up to now may have at least three different causes: people may have ignored the objects theorized by such a discipline (think of subatomic particles), they may have wrongly identified them with the proper topic of another discipline (the study of religions was for a long time a province of theology), or they may have recognized their distinct existence but not have regarded their study worth their time. Long before Richard von Krafft-Ebing's *Psychopathia sexualis* (Sexual Psychopathy) of 1886, people knew about the vast variety of human sexual behavior, but they avoided the trouble of systematizing and even exploring it in detail, perhaps with the exception of poets such as Ovid. In the following historical overview, dealing in four sections with antiquity, the Middle Ages, early modernity, and the nineteenth century, I will move back and forth between philosophical arguments in favor of a certain structure of knowledge and the emergence of new disciplines as an empirical phenomenon. I do not deny at all that there are external causes, linked to power interests, behind the rise of certain sciences: The development of economics, for example, was obviously fostered by the successes of a capitalist economy, and it is well known that the study of Oriental cultures was deeply linked to French and British imperialism.[6] Still, genesis and validity belong to two different orders, and it remains an indispensable task for philosophy to find a place for new disciplines within the whole of knowledge. Sometimes this attempt leads to revolutions in the architecture of epistemology that, although triggered by external factors, usher in a conceptually more satisfying structuring of epistemic operations.

I

The first comprehensive attempt to systematize human knowledge occurred in the Academy and the Peripatos. The prehistory of art and religion demonstrates that early on humankind must have grasped the peculiar nature of at least animals and stars; for their depiction and divinization was a recognition that they have a special place in the universe. The artistic and religious focus on such objects goes beyond the prescientific knowledge about many objects that humankind must have gathered from its beginnings in order to survive (I name only plants and the human body), and most probably out of religious cults civilizations such as Mesopotamia developed the first science of humankind.

I have in mind astronomy, which must have already begun with the Sumerians and which achieved the level of precise observations in the Old and particularly the Neo-Babylonian epochs.[7] But it was the Greeks who first proposed a systematization of knowledge with a differentiation not achieved by any other culture. This is due to the fact that the fifth century saw the rise of a discipline of so peculiar a status that it soon triggered complex ontological and epistemological reflections. I mean, of course, pure mathematics. The discovery of incommensurable magnitudes by a rigorous indirect proof, no later than 450 BC, lifted mathematics from a useful tool helping to solve practical problems, known also to other cultures, to the level of an autonomous science, which at the same time was used for understanding features of the physical world. Already at the end of the fifth century, the subdivision of what was later called *quadrivium* into arithmetic, geometry, music, and astronomy had become standard.[8] It is not clear whether Parmenides's epistemological and ontological revolution had anything to do with mathematics (it is only his pupil Zeno who obviously struggles with the problem of the continuum and the issue of applying mathematics to the empirical world); but there is little doubt that Parmenides discovered that a metaphysical principle connected with the law of noncontradiction has a different epistemic status than the explanation of nature, which is categorized as δόξα or opinion. It is not at all necessary to interpret this opinion as fallacious,[9] but it clearly is epistemically inferior to what Parmenides calls the way of truth, and it deals with a distinct ontological realm.

The peculiar epistemic status of mathematics as well as the ontological status of its objects are two of the problems that motivate Plato's philosophy. The subdivision of ontological realms and epistemological faculties in the analogy of the line in the *Republic* first distinguishes between the visible and the intelligible, each of which two sections is then itself bisected. While belief (πίστις) and imagination (εἰκασία) deal with physical objects and their images, understanding (νόησις) and thought (διάνοια) deal with the intelligible realm. What are the differences between the last two faculties, which underlie dialectic, the core of philosophy, on the one hand, and concrete disciplines (τέχναι), such as geometry, on the other? According to Plato's elusive comments they consist of two facts: First, thought accepts its starting points as unquestioned first principles while understanding tries to ascend to the unhypothetical first principle. Second, thought, for example in geometry, is obliged to use images, even if mathematicians do deal with squares and diagonals themselves, not the ones they draw.[10] What Plato means by "dialectic" is notoriously difficult to grasp, but two things are obvious from the *Charmides* as well as the *Euthydemus* where it is called "the kingly art." Dialectic is the highest metadiscipline that determines the status of the other sciences, including itself (for it is a reflective science);[11] the epistemological considerations of the *Republic* are themselves an example of this function of dialectic. And dialectic is also knowledge of good and evil. For even if someone had all factual knowledge, including of all future events, but lacked ethical knowledge, he could not become happy.[12] A knowledge is needed that combines making (ποῖειν) and knowing how to use the things made in the appropriate manner.[13] The distinction between theoretical and practical philosophy is alien to Plato, not because he could not imagine, but because he deliberately rejects it. Ethics and political philosophy, so the *Republic* tells us, can succeed only due to an epistemological and metaphysical turn, and theoretical philosophy has its center in the grasping of the Form of the Good.

Within the mathematical disciplines, Plato, deviating from the order that Euclid presents in the *Elements*, but followed by Nicomachus of Gerasa in his *Introduction to Arithmetic* from the first or second century AD, begins with arithmetic, continues with geometry, and then introduces stereometry, to which astronomy and harmonics are finally added. For Plato, these disciplines increase in concreteness: Geometry deals with two dimensions, stereometry deals with three, while astronomy and harmonics, which are considered closely akin, add movement.[14] But Plato does not seem to acknowledge that there is a radical epistemological difference between arithmetic and geometry (including stereometry), on the one hand, and astronomy and harmonics, on the other; he seems to regard all these disciplines as equally nonempirical. Still, Plato comes much closer than Aristotle to the modern program of a mathematical description of nature, even if he clearly underrates the necessity of experiments; his dualistic epistemology seems to make it impossible to have a true science of the world that we perceive.[15] The deliberate connection between the *Timaeus* and the *Critias* points to the fact that Plato somehow wants to situate humans, their political institutions and their historical development, within nature. But his answer is complex, since, first, humans consist of an immortal soul that is connected with material parts, and, second, the most divine human organs, head, sight, and hearing, are directly shaped by the gods, while the other parts of the body are a result of both divine reason and the workings of necessity.[16] Plato has no doubt that the human capacity to grasp reasons is something that transcends any naturalistic explanation of humans.[17] At the same time, he sees in the movement of the planets and the fixed stars the most divine feature of nature, something which in its sublimity far outstrips humans in their folly and vices.

We know that Plato's second successor in the Academy, Xenocrates, subdivided philosophy—and that means for his time knowledge in general—in a way that remained canonical for the Hellenistic age into physical, ethical, and logical philosophy.[18] In this division, physical philosophy probably was not limited to natural philosophy but also included metaphysics.[19] Since the same subdivision can be found in an early work of Aristotle,[20] it is not implausible that it goes back to discussions in which Plato himself participated. Logic must have contained much more than the syllogistic that Aristotle by the time of the *Topics* had not yet developed, namely, analyses of the relations between fundamental concepts, thus being not very distant from the discipline that Plato called "dialectic" (while Aristotle will devaluate this term). But far more elaborate than this subdivision is an alternative, which is also incidentally mentioned in the *Topics* and then presented in chapters E 1 and K 7 of the *Metaphysics*.[21] Here Aristotle tries to determine the place of "physics," that is, of natural science in general, in the whole of knowledge. He states that every thought is either theoretical, or practical, or poietical (productive). While the distinction between theoretical and practical disciplines is still used today (but note that Aristotle's concept of "practical" has nothing to do with "applied"), the difference between poiesis and praxis is peculiar to Aristotle: Praxis, action, is an end-in-itself and linked to moral choice, while poiesis aims at producing an external object.[22] Crafts are by nature poietical, but there is only one craft with enough philosophical dignity that Aristotle studies it in depth: poetry and its products, namely, poems.[23] Practical philosophy does not aim at knowing the world, as theoretical philosophy does, but at actions and acquisitions.[24] Since humans are by nature the most political animals, whose moral actions can only succeed in the context of a city-state, practical philosophy is also called political philosophy in the broader sense of the term.[25] In the narrower sense, however, politics is distinguished from ethics.[26] Several disciplines are subordinate to politics, such as strategy, economics (which is still the doctrine of administering a household), and rhetoric.[27] Of these three, Aristotle has dedicated a separate work only to rhetoric, which he qualifies as "an offshoot of dialectic and also of ethical studies," which may also be called "political."[28] That rhetoric is a counterpart of dialectic is claimed in the first sentence of the book; the trait common to both disciplines is that neither deals with a definite topic but can be applied to all subjects.[29] While dialectic is the doctrine of debating, rhetoric deals with continuous speeches. It does, however, not seem possible to give the logical works of Aristotle a clear place in the triadic system of knowledge that he himself has set forth.[30] This explains why they were later called *Organon*, that is, instrument for the real sciences.[31] With logic and rhetoric Aristotle already had two of the three sciences of the later so-called *trivium*, and when grammar was added from the third century BC on, the seven *artes liberales* were ready to determine for fifteen centuries the structure of European education.[32]

The theoretical sciences stand higher than the other sciences, for contemplation is the ultimate source of happiness.[33] In *Metaphysics* E 1 and K 7, Aristotle mentions three theoretical disciplines: physics, mathematics, and First Philosophy, or theology. While Aristotle acknowledges that mathematics considers some of its objects as immovable and separable from matter, he does not want to commit himself to an independent existence of mathematical objects and in fact denies it. Physics, on the other hand, deals with objects that both exist separately and are movable. First Philosophy, finally, studies objects that exist separately and are immovable. It is also called theology, since only such objects can truly be called divine. And since the value of a science depends on the value of its object, this will be the noblest science. I cannot discuss here how the various tasks that Aristotle ascribes to First Philosophy—from theology to science of being qua being—can, according to him, indeed be contained in one science.[34]

Aristotle's peculiar connection between astronomy and theology, so obvious in *Metaphysics* Λ 7–9, is based on a radical separation between the sublunar and supralunar world. The regularity of the movement of the stars and their presumed immutability is contrasted with the generation and corruption of the sublunar world. Still, Aristotle is the founder of zoology as a science, and he goes out of his way to justify the value of this subdiscipline of physics. True enough, only astronomy deals with eternal objects, but we can know much less about them than about plants and animals. Besides its greater certitude and completeness, biology trumps astronomy also thanks to its greater nearness to us humans. As the true object of architecture is not bricks but the house, so natural philosophy must look not at the material elements but at their composition, that is, at the formal and final causes that shape them; and thus biology is the highest science of sublunar nature.[35] Psychology, too, is grounded in biology, for the soul is the principle of animal life, and so Aristotle can claim that it belongs to physics. The greatest part, if not all, of the affects refer to the complex of body and soul, and thus both physicist and dialectician can approach a phenomenon like anger. The human intellect, however, does not belong to the province of natural science.[36]

For those who became familiar with it, the Aristotelian systematization of knowledge remained more or less convincing up to the seventeenth century. The simpler tripartition of Xenocrates, however, became authoritative in Stoicism and retained its plausibility much longer: Kant still appreciates it at the beginning of the Preface to his *Groundwork of the Metaphysics of Morals*. Both Zeno[37] and Chrysippus make use of it. The latter teaches that one has to begin with logic, then proceed with ethics, and finally conclude with physics. For logic strengthens the mind and secures it; ethics can improve one's manners only if it can rely on logic, and physics is the most divine discipline and in need of deeper foundations. It is crucial to mention that for Chrysippus physics contains as its final part theology, the teaching of which is compared to an initiation; this follows from Stoic pantheism and corporalism.[38] Since the Neoplatonists reject this corporalism and the integration of theology into physics, they insist that even in the classification of the Platonic dialogues a fourth group has to be added: While the *Timaeus* can be described as a physical dialogue, the *Parmenides* has to be called a theological one.[39] As in Aristotle, theology must not be subsumed under physics.

II

Christian medieval philosophy is dominated by the subordination of all knowledge to theology, to be precise: a theology that is not simply based on reason, such as the rational theology of ancient philosophy, but accepts scripture as its ultimate basis. Of the various encyclopedias of the Middle Ages,[40] the most influential was doubtless the *Speculum Maius* (The Great Mirror) by Vincent of Beauvais in three parts (*Speculum Naturale, Doctrinale, Historiale/ Mirror of Nature, Mirror of Doctrine, Mirror of History*; the *Speculum Morale/Mirror of Morals* was added later). But I want to focus on two more philosophical works that deliberately structure the cosmos of knowledge of their time according to abstract philosophical principles. The first is *De reductione artium ad theologiam* (The Reduction of the Arts to Theology) by Bonaventure, the second the *Arbor scientiae* (Tree of Science) by Ramon Llull. In his short treatise,[41] Bonaventure distinguishes between mechanical arts (chap. 2), sensual cognition (chap. 3), philosophical cognition (chap. 4), and the light of grace and Holy Scripture (chap. 5) as the four main steps of knowledge. The first deal with artificial figure, the second with natural form, the third with intellectual truth, and the last with salvific truth. Regarding the mechanical arts, Bonaventure follows Hugh of Saint Victor, who in his *Didascalicon* (I 5, I 11) had added them to theoretical philosophy, practical philosophy, and logic, a fourth part still missing in Aristotle's tripartition, while the mechanical arts somehow continue his poietic disciplines but clearly enjoy a greater attention and respect.[42] The seven mechanical arts are quite heterogeneous: spinning and weaving, forging, agriculture, hunting, navigation, medicine, and the theatrical arts. Bonaventure tries to reduce them to the satisfaction of basic human needs and acknowledges the unique position of the theatrical arts, which will later join the fine arts; the theatrical arts are pleasing, while the others are useful, relating to the needs of covering, feeding, or supporting oneself. In the chapter on sensual cognition, Bonaventure connects in an arbitrary way the five senses with the five elements; and it is in general difficult to understand why the senses can be intermingled with the arts. Philosophical cognition has three parts, each of which is itself tripartite. Rational philosophy deals with the truth of speeches, natural philosophy with the truth of things, and moral philosophy with the truth of behavior. Rational philosophy covers the *trivium*, that is, grammar, logic, and rhetoric, which are understood as the disciplines of expressing, teaching, and motivating. Bonaventure does not see that the traditional order conflates disciplines of different structure: he has mainly logic in mind when he claims that rational philosophy deals with the *rationes intelligendi*, the reasons for grasping something, and he clearly refers to grammar and rhetoric when he claims that the first part of philosophy governs interpretation. Only the vague concept of teaching allows him to correlate logic with the other disciplines, but it is obvious that all disciplines want to teach, and that there is only one discipline *of* teaching, namely, pedagogy, but certainly not logic. Natural philosophy is subdivided like Aristotle's theoretical sciences into physics proper, mathematics, and metaphysics; they are supposed to correspond to matter, the soul, and divine wisdom. Practical philosophy finally obtains its third part by including between individual ethics (*moralis philosophia monastica*) and political philosophy economics, which, as in Aristotle's remarks in the *Politics* and in most of the heterogeneous work of the Corpus Aristotelicum with the title *Oikonomika* (Economics), deals with the institution of the family, not with the object of the modern discipline. Fourth, Bonaventure discusses scripture and its literal, allegorical, moral, and anagogical interpretation.

That this is the ultimate end of knowledge becomes even more manifest in the second part of the treatise where the reduction of the arts to theology announced in the title occurs. Bonaventure begins by counting the three steps of philosophical cognition as of equal ranking with the mechanical arts, sensual cognition, and the light of Holy Scripture; thus, he can move from a fourfold to a sixfold subdivision. And why is this desirable? Because it allows him to parallelize the steps of knowledge with the hexaemeron, that is, the six days of the creation story of the Genesis, the knowledge to be achieved in the eschatological glory corresponding to God's sanctification of the seventh day (chaps. 6 and 7). The last nineteen chapters try to detect in the cognitions of the senses, the operations of the mechanical arts, and the three parts of philosophy a reflection of the same Trinitarian structure, sometimes immanent, sometimes economic. The wisdom of God is hidden in all cognition and all nature; and in each thing that is sensed and known God himself is internally present. Therefore all cognitions serve theology: "omnes cognitiones famulantur theologiae" (chap. 26). Bonaventure's interest in these cognitions independently of their pointing to the fundamental principles of Christian theology is limited.

It is controversial whether Ramon Llull's *Arbor scientiae* of 1296/97 was first written in Latin or in Catalan.[43] Although alluding to the tree of Genesis 3:17 and influenced by the dichotomic subdivision of reality in the famous *arbor porphyriana*, it is, as far as I can see, the first attempt to use the tree metaphor for encyclopedic purposes. However, Llull does not really present, as later authors will do, a tree branching out into various disciplines. On the contrary, despite the two singulars in the title, Llull's book in reality deals with a small forest, namely, sixteen trees, fourteen of which stand for different objects and the corresponding sciences. Only the last two books, the longest ones that make up half of the work, dedicated as they are to the *arbor exemplificalis* and the *arbor quaestionalis*, the tree of examples and the tree of question, are of a different nature; they partly exemplify the doctrines of the work in a literary manner, partly give hints on how to answer questions connected with the contents that were exposed. But the first fourteen sciences are conceived as capturing different strata of reality, an extension of the nine subjects of his famous Art.[44] The *arbor elementalis, vegetalis, sensualis, imaginalis, humanalis, moralis, imperialis, apostolicalis, caelestialis, angelicalis, aeviternalis, maternalis, divinalis et humanalis*, and *divinalis* are dedicated to the elements, the plants, organisms with sense perception, organisms with the capacity of imagination, human nature, virtues and vices, political structures, ecclesiastical hierarchies, the heavenly bodies, the angels, paradise and hell, Maria, Jesus Christ, and God. Llull unfolds the great chain of being,[45] which has to be grasped by the corresponding sciences and which extends from inorganic nature through different types of organisms to humans, their moral, political, and ecclesiastical organization, up to the heavens. Also for him the supralunar bodies have a higher dignity than humans, for they are connected with the angels. The last five realms belong to theology proper, even if Llull is one of few medieval thinkers to embrace a radical rationalism, that is, to insist that all articles of faith have to be proven rationally. It is noteworthy that in this classification the distinction between theoretical and practical sciences has disappeared; moral philosophy is integrated into the continuum of the traditional theoretical disciplines. Furthermore, mathematics is missing, as are the disciplines of the trivium, even if Llull wrote texts on geometry, logic, and rhetoric. One explanation may be that Llull had difficulties integrating the formal nature of logic and mathematics into his ontological scheme. Less surprising, despite Vincent of Beauvais, is the absence of history, which was not regarded as a science.

The tree metaphor, however, is applied to each single tree, which consists of seven parts: radices, truncus, brancae, rami, folia, flores, fructus, that is, roots, trunk, branches, twigs, leaves, flowers, fruits. In the case of the first tree, to give only one example, the roots are identified with the principles, the trunk with undifferentiated corporality, the branches with the powers, the twigs with the operations, the leaves with the accidents, the flowers with the instruments, and the fruits with the bodies consisting of the various elements. Llull both insists on the fundamental isomorphism between the various trees and renders justice to the fact that the later trees presuppose the earlier ones. So he writes that the *arbor vegetalis* has each of its roots duplicated, since it has both an elemental and a vegetable nature. Analogously, the sensitive nature is grafted upon the vegetable and the latter upon the elementative—here metaphors relating to the cultivation of trees are indeed used to clarify the relation between the various sciences.[46]

III

The most impressive attempt at systematizing knowledge in early modernity is due to Francis Bacon, who published *Of the Proficience and Advancement of Learning, Divine and Human* in 1605.[47] Until the middle of the eighteenth century it remained authoritative: d'Alembert's famous "Discours préliminaire de l'encyclopédie" (Preliminary Discourse to the Encyclopedia) of 1751 discusses it thoroughly. Still, the seventeenth and eighteenth centuries are among the most important epochs in the budding of new branches in the tree of knowledge; thus, a comparison between Bacon and the *Encyclopédie* promises fruitful insights into the way in which the rise of new disciplines obliges philosophy to adapt to a new reality while trying to keep as much as possible of the basic structures that have been developed so far.

The peculiar charm of Bacon's system of knowledge results from his intermediate position between Renaissance erudition and the scientific revolution of the seventeenth century, which he anticipates with his methodological ideas, even if he hardly contributed to its contents.[48] While the first book of the *Advancement* defends the excellence of learning and the merit in its augmentation against theological and political objections as well as "the errors and imperfections of learned men themselves" (4), the second book offers "a small globe of the intellectual world" (221). Inspired by the crossing of the Atlantic Ocean (61), Bacon does not want to limit himself to "sciences already extant and invented" but also tries to explore "parts of learning not sufficiently laboured and prosecuted" (63). He does not simply exhibit "a great muster-roll of sciences," but looks for "some seed of proficience" (140).[49] I will ignore his institutional demands, such as investing in "fundamental knowledges," appropriate salaries for lecturers, funding of experiments, continuous control of academic institutions, and international collaboration between the European universities, and focus on his subdivision of knowledge. Since he is committed to the "continuance and entireness of knowledge," he presents his partitions "rather for lines and veins than for sections and separations" (105); but he claims that they follow nature and not simply use (152 f.). Bacon, this means, is after natural kinds, and he also avers that no area of being is left out in his scheme, "that nothing be in the globe of matter, which should not be likewise in the globe of crystal, or form" (188). The first cut is between human and divine learning, and while the latter is, as in the Middle Ages, still the "sabbath of all man's contemplations" (90, 209), thus examined at the conclusion of the book, it is striking that far less space is dedicated to it than to human learning. Both learnings are initially divided according to the three parts of human understanding, memory, imagination, and reason, into history, poetry, and philosophy (69), even if the final chapter dedicated to divinity replaces this tripartition by a dichotomy dedicated to the nature of revelation and the matters revealed, the latter being subdivided into faith, manners, liturgy, and ecclesiastical government (213, 219), that is, what today we would call dogmatics, moral theology, liturgical science, and canonical law.

Bacon's correlation between disciplines and faculties has the problematic consequence that different realms of being appear twice, both in history and in philosophy. This is true not only for what we today call humanities but also for the knowledge of nature; for Bacon subdivides history into natural, civil, ecclesiastical, and literary. "Knowledges are as pyramids, whereof history is the basis. So of natural philosophy, the basis is natural history" (95).[50] While Bacon in my eyes is right in avoiding Wilhelm Windelband's famous characterization of the natural sciences as nomothetical sciences and the humanities as ideographical sciences (after all, the geology of the Great Lakes deals with particulars and general linguistics with universal features of languages), it is easy to object to Bacon that also historiography presupposes inferences and the other sciences memory. It is furthermore unsatisfying that in the cosmos of learning only poetry has its place, not, however, its theoretical analysis. And even more puzzling for our taste is the separation of poetry from the other fine arts, which are mentioned only in the Latin version, and there in connection with the sensual arts relating to the human body.[51] In the subdivision of history, Bacon's demand for a literary history is his most original contribution: "For no man hath propounded to himself the general state of learning to be described and represented from age to age . . . ; without which the history of the world seemeth to me to be as the statua of Polyphemus with his eye out; that part being wanting which doth most show the spirit and life of the person" (69). Only familiarity with the history of learning "will make learned men wise in the use and administration of learning" (70). Bacon subdivides natural history into history of nature in course, nature erring, and nature altered—"that is, *history of creatures, history of marvels*, and *history of arts*" (70; original emphasis). The distinction between the first two twigs presupposes a metaphysics of nature that is still more Aristotelian than Spinozian: Bacon does not believe that all natural events have to be explained by appealing to general laws and antecedent events, even if he encourages rejection of fables. (Montaigne, who lacks a metaphysics of the laws of nature, at least recognized that even monsters, such as conjoined twins, belong to nature and cannot occur against it: *Essais* II 30.) Very important is the place that he grants to the still largely deficient mechanical arts, which "shall be operative to the endowment and benefit of man's life" (72). They are supposed to be an offshoot of the marvels of nature: There is still no idea that the engineering sciences are best built upon the natural sciences proper. The divide in the Aristotelian Corpus between *Physics* and *The Mechanical Problems*, that is, the treatise, probably not by Aristotle himself, on what happens "contrary to nature, done through art for the advantage of humanity" (847a10ff.), continues in Bacon (see, however, *Novum Organum* II 28) and up to d'Alembert.[52]

Bacon's subdivision of civil history into memorials, antiquity, and perfect history has to do with different steps of approaching the same material, not with different areas of history. What he calls "ruminated history," such as Machiavelli's *Discourses on Livy*, "I think more fit to place amongst books of policy . . . than amongst books of history" (79). Here history appears to be a preparatory stage for what we call today the social sciences. Natural and civil history are then combined together with mathematics into cosmography. Ecclesiastical history finally consists of history of the church, of prophecy, and of providence. Poetry, defined as feigned history, is subdivided into narrative, representative, and allusive (or parabolical). While the first two categories go back to Plato,[53] the third category clearly does not belong to the same type; for one could have allusive narrations or dramas, and Bacon hardly wants his terms to overlap. It remains surprising how long it took for lyrics to appear as a separate subgenre of poetry. But Bacon points to the revolution occurring in the reevaluation of poetry at the end of the eighteenth century when he recognizes that poetry for wit and eloquence is not much inferior to orators (85), even if rhetoric belongs to a completely different branch.

Philosophy proper is then subdivided into divine philosophy, natural philosophy, and human philosophy (85, 105). But all three branch out from a common stem, "which hath a dimension and quantity of entireness and continuance, before it come to discontinue and break itself into arms and boughs." This common science is First Philosophy, which, unlike in Aristotle, is separated from theology (92). It treats principles that apply to all special parts of philosophy. It may surprise that Bacon mentions divine philosophy, since we already saw that divine learning comes at the end of the book. But what Bacon has now in mind is a very different discipline, namely, natural theology, based not on revelation, but on "the contemplation of His creatures" (88), with angelology as a legitimate appendix, even if often treated in a "fantastical" way. Natural philosophy is composed of natural science and natural prudence, which organizes experiments. Bacon arranges the first into physics and metaphysics (the latter no longer identical with First Philosophy), the former dealing with material and efficient, the second with formal and final causes of nature. Herein similar to Leibniz, Bacon does not at all reject a teleological interpretation of nature but only as long as this does not replace the search for the efficient causes (97 f.). The connection of metaphysics with formal causes explains why Bacon regards mathematics as a branch of metaphysics, not, as Aristotle, as a third discipline added to physics and metaphysics, and he articulates it in pure and mixed mathematics: geometry and arithmetic belong to the first, perspective, music, astronomy, and others to the second group, the further increase of which he predicts. But the problem remains that, since metaphysics belongs to natural philosophy, an application of mathematics to the sciences of humans is excluded by this categorization. Even less does Bacon grasp the autonomy of mathematics as a science.

Biology, so important in Aristotle's conception of science, is widely absent in Bacon, certainly due to the Christian gap between humans and the other animals. His human philosophy investigates humans first "segregate," then "congregate," that is, as individuals and in society. Humans as individuals consist of body and mind, and so we have a doctrine of the "sympathies and concordances" between the two (106), a study of the body's health, beauty, strength, and (in a pre-Cartesian way) pleasure by medicine, cosmetic, athletic, and "art Voluptuary," and, finally, a knowledge of the mind, both its substance and its functions. Appendices to the first deal with what we today call parapsychological phenomena, such as extrasensory perception and telekinesis. Far more detailed are the discussions of intellectual and volitive functions, the objects of rational and moral philosophy. In rational philosophy the sources of knowledge, with which Bacon started, become themselves objects of knowledge (121); their study is called "the art of arts" (122). Bacon distinguishes four arts: of invention, of judgment, of memory, and of elocution. The first is further subdivided into invention of sciences—a knowledge that "should purchase all the rest" (122)—and invention, or rather preparation and suggestion, of arguments, that is, topics. The doctrine of judgment is made up of analytics and elenches, which fulfill the functions of direction and caution respectively.[54] The custody of knowledge occurs either through writing or through memory, the latter being directed by prenotions and emblems. Regarding the transferring of knowledge to others, Bacon distinguishes the organ, the method, and the illustration of tradition, which roughly correspond to the three disciplines of the *trivium*. While Bacon acknowledges that method "hath been placed, and that not amiss, in Logic," he focuses on the tradition of knowledge, which is material to its progress, since knowledge is an intersubjective venture (140). Two appendices deal with critical and "pedantical," that is, pedagogical, issues. Moral philosophy ought to deal both with the nature of the good and moral culture. The moral good may concern the individual as such or in his social functions; and the private good is divided into active and passive good, which itself can be distinguished into conservative and perfective, while the doctrine of duties addresses both general duties as member of a state and special professional duties, trying to solve possible conflicts between the various duties. The chapter on moral culture asks for what we today would call moral psychology and insists on a doctrine of characters and affections; without it, morality may "make men too precise, arrogant, incompatible" (175). Civil knowledge is finally subdivided into doc-trine of conversation, negotiation, and government, the last of which in-cludes jurisprudence. The major objection against this categorization is that Bacon fails to grasp the difference between psychology of thinking and logic as well as between psychology of volition and morals. There is no place in his empiricist framework for a radical division between Is and Ought.

Before we look at the changes that occur in the articulation of the *Encyclopédie* compared with Bacon's text, I have to mention the two most far-reaching mutations in the outlook of the tree of sciences that happen in the meantime. Clearly, the Cartesian revolt is the first one. Descartes himself continues to use the metaphor of the tree of sciences: in the preface to the French edition of *Les Principes de la Philosophie* (Principles of Philosophy), he speaks of philosophy as a tree, whose roots are made up by metaphysics, the trunk by physics, and the main branches, from which alone fruits can be reaped, by mechanics, medi-cine, and morals (the perfect one, not the provisional one he himself sketches).[55] But this simile hides more than it captures his own intel-lectual revolution, as long as one does not realize the originality of his concept of metaphysics. Its subjects are only God and the soul. The Aristotelian and medieval vision of the cosmos, in which the supralu-nar world mediated between the sublunar realm, in which we live, and God, is completely replaced by a view that in the course of the seven-teenth century, most impressively with the Newtonian synthesis of Galilei's terrestrial physics and Kepler's astronomy, tears down all pre-sumed differences between the two realms, as it does the ancient bar-rier between physics and mechanics. There is no peculiar ontological status of the stars, the concept of the scale of nature thus losing at least its traditional structure that extended beyond humans into the uni-verse, and our machines are as natural as the other events in the world. Matter is extension; mathematical quantities, not qualities, consti-tute its essence. While this invites human technological activities on a large scale, the price to be paid is a feeling of loss: The eternal silence of these infinite spaces scared Pascal.[56] The subjective center that forms the basis of Descartes's project, the soul with its *cogito*, is no longer part of nature but is accessible in a completely different way from the rest of the world—through introspection, which is limited to oneself. Neither Descartes nor his successors embrace solipsism, but the sharp distinction between first- and third-person access threatens the traditional idea that different intellectual operations apply to different ontological realms. Epistemologically, introspection refers only to me, while ontologically I do not seem to be different from other persons who access themselves in the first person, too, even if this access is ruled out for anyone else, including me. While the Aristotelian subdivision drew a horizontal separation line between those mental activities that we share with animals and the human intellect, for Descartes the basic divide is, so to speak, a vertical line between *all* our mental acts and the physical states with which they interact. Since Descartes denies subjectivity to any other organism except humans, this vertical divide appears at a place in nature that coincides with one of the great cuts in the traditional scale of nature. Yet for his successors, who were more generous to the animal realm and did not want to become pan-psychists either, the situation grew more complicated.

While the Cartesian revolution suggests a subdivision of knowledge into theology, natural science, and a psychology based on introspection, already the early eighteenth century felt the need to integrate what Bacon called "congregate" human philosophy into a post-Cartesian theory of sciences. The most original work in this direction is Giambattista Vico's *Principj di scienza nuova* (Principles of a New Science) of 1725 (with the definitive third edition in 1744). It presents a new science of the "world of nations," which is conceived as a third ontological realm beside the world of God and mind and that of nature.[57] (The conflation of the world of God and that of mind probably originates in Vico's sympathy for occasionalism.) While it is wrong to interpret Vico's philosophy of human culture, which encompasses both the humanities and the social sciences, primarily as a philosophy of history, Vico raises the intellectual level of historiography by claiming to have found an ideal eternal history: Being connected with a universal structure, history can itself become a science. The millennia-old distinction between history and science thus begins to fade. Vico furthermore reflects on the fact that the humanities had to develop later than the natural sciences—like the eye needs a mirror before it can see itself.[58] The

largest second book of his main work is explicitly articulated according
to the tree of sciences: The stem is made up of metaphysics, one branch
of logic, morality, economics, politics (to which reflections on history
are added), the other of physics, its daughters, cosmography and astronomy, and the latter's daughters, chronology and geography.[59] While
Vico probably believes that this is the right way of systematizing knowledge also for his own enlightened age,[60] the second book does not give
an account of the knowledge of Vico's time. It deals with poetical wisdom, and all the disciplines just mentioned are qualified as "poetical."
What does this mean? Vico is interested in reconstructing the metaphysics, logic, moral values, family structure, political order, and vision
of nature peculiar to the archaic time; so he engages in a hermeneutical
effort even while dealing with the second branch of his tree. In the
New Science, Vico does not deal with natural philosophy; thus, he is
no longer an encyclopedist thinker. But he aims at understanding the
encyclopedic vision earlier cultures had of the world; and in this absorption of the idea of the tree of sciences by what in the earlier archi-
tectonics had been only one discipline of it, Vico points, albeit still from
afar, to the hermeneutic imperialism of the twentieth century, which is
based on the fallacy that since every theory is a product of culture the
theory of culture encompasses everything.

The greatest project of French Enlightenment, the *Encyclopédie
ou dictionnaire raisonné des sciences, des arts et des métiers* (Encyclopedia, or a Systematic Dictionary of the Sciences, Arts, and Crafts),
mediates already in its title between the idea of a systematic unfolding
of all disciplines for a general public (this is the original meaning of
ἐγκύκλιος παιδεία and particularly its humanist adaptation) and the
agglomeration of knowledge by alphabetically ordered entries on all
possible topics.[61] Jean Le Rond d'Alembert's introductory "Discours"
has often been considered the most eloquent manifesto of French Enlightenment.[62] In its third and last part it integrates Denis Diderot's
"Prospectus" of 1750; it is followed by Diderot's "Explication détaillée
du systeme des connoissances humaines" (Detailed Explanation of
the System of Human Knowledge), accompanied by a chart, and by an
analysis of the "Systeme général de la connoissance humaine suivant le
chancelier Bacon" (General System of Human Knowledge according

to Chancellor Bacon), before the single entries begin.[63] I cannot discuss here its many ideas, such as its sensualist epistemology influenced by Locke and Condillac, which rejects innate ideas but preserves the distinction between sensation and reflection and on the basis of the latter claims to get to the ideas of God and natural law (6 ff./72 ff.); its analysis of the origin of the various sciences that start from basic needs but lead to concepts more and more abstract (14 ff./77 ff.); its opposition of systematic spirit, which is affirmed, and spirit of system, which is condemned (22 f./83, 94 f./135 f.), although d'Alembert at the same time hopes for a monist explanation of the universe as "one great truth" (29/88); its passionate defense of the dignity and superior usefulness of the mechanical arts (40 ff./96 ff., 122 ff./153 ff.), to which so many of the plates of the encyclopedia are dedicated; and the profound reflections on the price to be paid for the loss of Latin as a common scientific language (92 f./134). I will focus on the "genealogical or encyclopedic tree which will gather the various branches of knowledge together under a single point of view and will serve to indicate their origin and their relationships to one another" (45 f./99). Two aspects are crucial. First, d'Alembert is much more aware than his predecessors that his subdivision is only one among many possible alternatives. Since for him only individual objects are real, there are many equally legitimate ways of abstracting common properties, and the tree should not divert attention from the study of the particulars (48 f./101 f.; 58 f./109 f.). D'Alembert does not have a theory of natural kinds; thus, he cannot answer to his own or the reader's satisfaction why some subdivisions are more plausible than others. Second, d'Alembert nevertheless deliberately rejects a classification based on the historical development of the sciences. For this development is discontinuous and disorderly; in it, a foundational discipline such as logic appears historically relatively late (30/89; 46 f./100). And he wants to offer with his tree "a kind of world map," "une espece de Mappemonde," while the articles would be individual maps of the countries (47 f./101).

It is in this context that d'Alembert refers to Bacon (50/102), the inaugural figure in the series of those geniuses who are later celebrated as the creators of modernity (74 ff./120 ff.; 87 f./130 f.). But despite his desire to follow "the immortal Chancellor of England," d'Alembert's tree of knowledge is more different from Bacon's than he is making explicit in the "Discours," for, as Diderot says at the end, "it would take too long to explain" all the reasons in detail why he deviated from his model (159/183), reasons that only philosophers can judge (164/ 187 f.). Let me try to name the main differences between the two trees. First, in d'Alembert there is no version of divine learning equivalent to human learning. This has to do with the eighteenth century's increasing doubts both with regard to the contents of revelation and with the phenomenon of revelation as such, doubts partly due to historical-biblical criticism. There is a submissive allusion to revealed religion (26/85 f.), but its importance is, as we shall see, drastically reduced. Second, while d'Alembert accepts Bacon's subdivision of the arts and sciences into those based on memory, imagination, and reason, he inverts the order of the last two. Imagination is declared to bring together memory and reason, and reason in its most abstract operations, metaphysics and geometry, to become imaginative itself (51 f./103 f.). Third, while in Bacon only poetry correlates with imagination, in d'Alembert it has been supplemented by the other fine arts (51/103; 55/106). This is the result of a long process, starting in the sixteenth century and completed in the eighteenth, which finally led to the separation of architecture, sculpture, painting and engraving, music and poetry from both the mechanical arts and the sciences and their collection into a separate group (156 f./181).[64] Narrative and dramatic poetry are further subdivided (144); the opera was not yet known to Bacon, and the novel had just begun its rise. Fourth, regarding the subdivision of history and philosophy, d'Alembert upholds the great chain of being and therefore is irritated that in Bacon's subdivision of philosophy natural philosophy mediates between divine and human. He inverts the order that we find in Llull and begins with God, under whom revelation teaches the existence of spiritual beings (the sentence makes it clear that d'Alembert does not really believe in angels), then deals with man, composed of soul and body, and finally nature.[65] He thus begins with sacred history, which, as based on revelation, is distinguished from ecclesiastical history, as relying on tradition.[66] Literary history is furthermore subsumed, with civil history proper, under civil history in a broader sense, which covers "the great nations and the great geniuses" (53/104). Natural history is, as in Bacon, subdivided into uniformity of nature, deviations of nature, and arts, trades, and manufactures as uses of nature, which, as in Bacon, are still connected with the errors and deviations of nature (146/172). The third part is, fifth, far more extended; the chart at the end does not even list all trades but ends with "etc.," because there are supposed to exist more than 250 (144; 147 f./173). The first two parts deal with history celestial, of meteors, of the earth and sea, of minerals, of vegetables, of animals, and—oddly—of elements at the end. It is worth mentioning that celestial history (in the section on uniformity of nature) is typographically separated from the rest; perhaps only because in the French original the other qualifications all begin with "des," perhaps because d'Alembert, not unlike the Greeks, has a particular veneration for the magnificent spectacle that astronomy offers us (21/82). His order seems in any case to presuppose that stars are higher in the scale of nature than organisms, even if man, who is higher than nature, is itself an organism.

Rational philosophy has four parts: a general, namely, ontology or metaphysics, which includes the science of possibility (149/174), and three particular ones, theology,[67] the science of man, and that of nature. Note that d'Alembert, sixth, has a concept of metaphysics much closer to Aristotle than Bacon (who subordinates that discipline to the philosophy of nature) but that, unlike Aristotle, he does not identify it with theology. D'Alembert recognizes, probably only de forma, both natural and revealed theology and interprets revealed theology as reason applied to the facts delivered by sacred history. His criticism of Bacon that "to separate Theology from Philosophy would be to cut the offshoot from the trunk to which it is united by its very nature" (54/105) is weak, for in his own system of knowledge philosophy is one of three branches, not the trunk. The chart at the end mentions only in this specific case an abuse, namely, "superstition" (144, 149/175). Since in d'Alembert's system man comes before nature, his body is not mentioned under the science of man; concerning this issue, d'Alembert proves to be a true heir of Descartes, while Bacon comes closer to Aristotle. Regarding the mind, d'Alembert follows Bacon by recognizing a science of the soul (pneumatology) as well as a science of its operations, subdivided into logic and ethics. Logic has only three parts, because the art of invention has disappeared. The art of thinking includes apprehension of ideas, judgment of propositions, reasoning, and method; the art of remembering is not very different from Bacon's; the art of transmitting wisely no longer contains logic but only grammar and rhetoric, with philology, criticism, and pedagogy as parts of grammar. Ethics falls into a general and a particular part, the latter being the science of law or jurisprudence, which is further divided into natural, economic, and political. It is fascinating how "economic" is now acquiring a second meaning. First d'Alembert tells us that it is the "science of the duties of a man as a member of a family," but since societies should be no less virtuous than individuals, he mentions also interior and exterior commerce by land and sea (151/176). Here economics is no longer the doctrine of the household, as it still is in Vico, but the discipline taught today as a social science, even if Adam Smith's synthesis *The Wealth of Nations* appeared only in 1776. The rise of economics as science presupposed that people understood that there are laws of the social world that are irreducible to individual intentions and sometimes even run against them, an insight to which Vico contributed considerably. But only in the nineteenth century will this lead to an emancipation of the social sciences from ethics, to which they still belong in d'Alembert's tree. The science of nature begins with a general part, subdivided into a metaphysics of bodies, dealing with properties such as impenetrability, and their measurement by mathematics, which encompasses pure, mixed, and physicomathematics, quantity being considered either alone or in real beings or in their effects. As far Bacon, and so differently from Plato, mathematics is not an autonomous science but a subdiscipline of the science of nature. Needless to say, d'Alembert increases the number of mathematical disciplines (77/122) by adding algebra and infinitesimal calculus (152 f./177 f.), but even military architecture and tactics are listed under pure mathematics (145). Mixed mathematics contains mechanics, geometric astronomy, optics, acoustics, pneumatics, and the analysis of games of chance. Particular physics finally is structured not according to the features of the objects studied but according to the subjective criterion of what "is worthwhile for us to know" (55/106). In the chart, zoology, under which medicine is subsumed, comes first and is separated from botany by physical astronomy, meteorology, and cosmology, with mineralogy and chemistry following at the end. In the "Detailed explanation," however, zoology and medicine come after astronomy, meteorology, cosmology (which includes, among other things, geology and hydrology), mineralogy, and botany, of which agriculture and gardening are branches. Chemistry, however, even in his ordering, follows suit because it is "the imitator and rival of nature" (155/180).

IV

As far as I can see, the two last great endeavors to furnish an encyclopedic overview of all the sciences stem from two very different philosophers, Georg Wilhelm Friedrich Hegel and Auguste Comte. Their philosophical positions are at variance on most points: Hegel develops an alternative to concept empiricism, whereas Comte's positivism is committed to experience as ultimate criterion. Still, they share not simply an encyclopedic ambition but also a rejection of Bacon's and d'Alembert's attempt to found the subdivision of sciences on human faculties.[68] Instead, they want to coordinate the various sciences with different orders of phenomena, and they want to move from the simpler to the more complex ones, which presuppose the earlier ones without being presupposed by them. Hegel inherits his encyclopedic interests from Immanuel Kant's philosophical revolution. True enough, Kant's interests were more foundational than encyclopedic, he thoroughly destroyed the subdivision of knowledge used in the Leibniz-Wolff school, and he himself corrected his vision of how philosophy had to be subdivided in the decade from 1781 to 1790 (after all, he did not yet dream of the *Third Critique* when he published the *First*). Still, the encyclopedic interests of German idealism are anticipated in the chapter "The Architectonic of Pure Reason" at the end of the *First Critique*.[69] The intellectual changes due to Kant are fundamentally two: Against the empiricism of the British tradition, Kant insists on synthetic a priori features of our knowledge, and he particularly claims that ethics must have an autonomous foundation in a formal law and cannot be reduced to a prudential doctrine of how to become happy. It is his desire to separate sharply a priori and a posteriori elements in human knowledge that distinguishes his classification of sciences most obviously from those of Bacon and d'Alembert. Metaphysics, according to Kant, has been wrongly understood as a science of the first principles. This is misleading, not only because this definition does not give us any criterion by which to separate the first and second principles, but also because the proper definiens of metaphysics must be its a priori origin, not the extent of its objects.[70] The third chapter within the "Transcendental Doctrine of Method" of the *Critique of Pure Reason* defines architectonic as the art of constructing a system. A system is opposed to an aggregate and compared with an organism. While it can grow, the proportions must remain the same; the lack of a single limb will be immediately felt, and the addition of a new one will be rejected. Kant distinguishes furthermore between technical and architectonic unity; the former delivers a merely empirical and thus accidental scheme, the second is grounded in an idea.[71] The founder of a science need not have a conscious understanding of this idea, even if in fact he is gravitating around it. But not only is each individual science aiming at a systematic form, all the sciences together form a system, too, that is, unfold an underlying idea. Kant is only interested in the system of pure reason, that is, of one of the two stems originating from the root of knowledge.[72] He then distinguishes, quite similarly to Bacon, between historical and rational knowledge. But for Kant this distinction has only to do with the form of subjective appropriation: Whoever learns a philosophical system by rote and can even repeat, like a parrot, its proofs, possesses only historical knowledge of it. The next subdivision is between philosophy and mathematics; the first dealing with concepts, the second with their construction. Philosophy itself is differentiated according to its scholastic and its cosmic concept. Philosophy in the latter sense has the task to relate all knowledge to the essential aims of human reason, whose legislator it becomes—a task reminiscent of the kingly art of Plato's *Euthydemus*. Among the essential aims there is only one final end, namely, the destination of man; and the philosophy dedicated to it is moral philosophy. It deals with what ought to be and is opposed to the philosophy of nature, which deals with what is, even if both belong to a single philosophical system. Still, the separation of normative and descriptive disciplines, as we could call them, is something new and very characteristic of Kant.

Orthogonal to this division is the distinction between pure and empirical philosophy. Kant is interested in the former, which he further subdivides into propaedeutic, the work of the *Critiques*, and metaphysics proper, which is then divided into metaphysics of nature and metaphysics of ethics, which must not presuppose anthropology, since the latter belongs to empirical philosophy. Metaphysics of nature has four parts, of which, however, only the first two offer true knowledge; but insofar as illusory knowledge is a necessary offshoot of reason, Kant wants to include it in his tree of knowledge; he is in this respect quite uncommon.[73] The last two branches deal with the illegitimate transcendent use of reason and lead to rational cosmology and rational theology, the first looking at an internal connection of the objects of experience, the second at an external connection. The two legitimate branches are ontology, dealing with objects in general, and rational physiology, dealing with given objects. It is split into rational physics and rational psychology: The object of the first is accessed by the external senses, the object of the second by the internal sense.

It is not difficult to trace the Hegelian system, as exposed in the *Encyclopedia of the Philosophical Sciences* in its three editions of 1817, 1827, and 1830, back to this last subdivision. Hegel's main work does not offer a classification of all sciences in general but only of the philosophical sciences, that is, subdisciplines. But since each philosophical science grounds the principles of a science and there is no legitimate science that lacks such a philosophical foundation, the difference can be neglected for our purposes. Similarly to Kant, Hegel's science of logic deals, among other things, with properties of objects in general, the philosophy of nature with nature, and the philosophy of spirit with spirit. At the same time, the differences are so far-reaching that the analogy between Kant and Hegel can easily be overlooked. First, Hegel does not have anything comparable to Kant's propaedeutic part, for he regards the attempt to study knowledge beforehand, that is, before committing oneself to knowledge, as self-contradictory.[74] Second, Hegel uses trichotomic subdivisions, while Kant prefers dichotomic ones. As is well known, in Hegel's dialectic the object corresponding to the third category is supposed to return from the alienation represented by the second one to the unity of the first one, and spirit's peculiar role within being is exactly this: to grasp the ideal structures that underlie nature (§ 18). This structure allows Hegel to understand humans as very special organisms. In his ordering of sciences, he is closer to Aristotle and Bacon than to d'Alembert, whom we saw treating the humanities before the natural sciences. Even if Hegel does not have any theory of evolution, it is therefore not difficult to integrate it into his system. But at the same time, Hegel is committed to a recognition of the special role of spirit: humans have the capacity to rise to the level of normativity, which means that they can explicitly connect themselves with the logical realm. Hegel's tripartition has some affinity to Gottlob Frege's distinction of thoughts, external objects, and ideas in his essay *The Thought*.

Third, Hegel's science of logic combines several quite different functions. It pretends to analyze, like the Aristotelian *Metaphysics*, determinations of being as such, before the latter is differentiated into nature and spirit, but it also contains a formal logic. Indeed, Hegel can claim to offer one of the first alternatives to the theory of psychologism developed, under this name, only in the second half of the nineteenth century but in fact characterizing the placement of logic both in Bacon and d'Alembert. (In Aristotle, as we have seen, its position remained unclear.) Like Husserl in the *Logical Investigations*, Hegel rejects the idea that logic is a subdiscipline of psychology: Inferences, for example, refer to being as such and must therefore be united with metaphysics. At the same time, concept, judgment, and syllogism are not only categories of the science of logic (§§ 163 ff.), but reappear in the philosophy of spirit, now, however, as the intellectual faculties and acts grasping those structures (§ 467). The science of logic has two further functions. It is a theory about the conditions of possibility of all theories, including itself; thus it is a reflexive transcendental work. And it claims to be a doctrine of the attributes of the absolute (§ 86), thus a form of rational theology. (Since Hegel is a panentheist, all his disciplines are somehow dealing with God. Therefore he writes that the science of logic deals with God's essence before creation.)[75]

It may surprise that Hegel combines these four different tasks in a single discipline, and indeed one must harbor doubts that the Hegelian science of logic is a viable discipline. But Hegel has both good reasons and illustrious predecessors for his approach. Like d'Alembert and Kant, he has no place for revealed theology; we will see, however, that he has a philosophy of religion, which, among other things, deals with belief in revelation. But this philosophy of religion belongs to the philosophy of spirit and is sharply distinguished from philosophical theology. While Bacon and d'Alembert distinguish between First Philosophy and metaphysics respectively, on the one hand, and natural theology, on the other, Hegel returns to the Aristotelian fusion of metaphysics and theology, which was based on the idea that God is being in its highest form. Hegel goes further, since for him it is misleading to believe that God is one particular object beside others. God is the reason that manifests itself in reality. Logic and transcendental theory have to be merged with theology, too, since they are necessary presuppositions for thinking in general and thinking God in particular; and these presuppositions cannot be something external to God but must constitute part of his essence.

Despite the basic trichotomic division, Hegel has also a dichotomic subdivision of his system of philosophical sciences, namely, into logic and the so-called *Realphilosophie*. For the philosophy of nature and the philosophy of spirit agree in dealing with real objects that are all temporal (the natural ones also spatial), while the logic deals with ideal structures without spatial or temporal properties. In recognizing such an ideal realm, Hegel is closer to Plato than to Bacon and d'Alembert, even if at the same time he rejects the radical separation of Is and Ought characteristic of Kant, since he believes that the ideal structures permeate the real world. His philosophy of nature is subdivided into mechanics, physics, and organic physics. Interestingly, in the first edition of the *Encyclopedia*, Hegel calls the first part not "mechanics'" but "mathematics," probably in order to cover this discipline, too, in his encyclopedia. The change of title has probably to do with the insight that it is rather arithmetic and calculus, which are dealt with in the science of logic, that are parts of mathematics, while geometry, which according to Hegel presupposes space and thus the first category of nature, is not pure mathematics. Hegel does not yet grasp the distinction between mathematical and physical geometry, but his connecting arithmetic, and not geometry, with logic can be considered a distant precursor of Frege's attitude.[76] In the second and third edition, "mechanics" starts with space, time, movement, inertia, and gravitation and ends with "absolute mechanics," the basis of astronomy. Physics deals with more concrete phenomena, such as light, sound, electricity, chemical processes—no doubt the most heterogeneous and least convincing part of the *Encyclopedia*, also because the corresponding scientific theories were still very much in the making. The strongest part of the philosophy of nature is the organic physics. Hegel recognizes, following Aristotle and the Kant of the *Critique of Judgment*, the peculiar dignity of organisms, which he ranks much higher than the stars.[77] Not only botany and zoology, but surprisingly also geology, has its place in Hegel's organic physics.[78]

It would not be correct to identify the mental realm with the object of Hegel's philosophy of spirit. For, on the one hand, Hegel does not deprive animals of mentality (§ 351), though he denies that they have spirit, and, on the other hand, his philosophy of spirit includes social institutions: While unfamiliar with Vico's *New Science*, Hegel, a great admirer of Montesquieu, wants to integrate the disciplines of the social world, which began to emerge in the eighteenth century, into his encyclopedia. Hegel subdivides his philosophy of spirit into three parts: subjective, objective, and absolute spirit. The disciplines dealing with the first are called anthropology, phenomenology, and psychology; they move from the soul to spirit proper, which is able to know and to will. Hegel locates language within psychology; striking in this context is the absence of rhetoric, whose decline began in the late eighteenth century, largely connected with the ascent of poetry, which from Aristotle on had been regarded as inferior to rhetoric. Spirit proper is subdivided into theoretical and practical spirit (only in the third edition does Hegel add a third part, called "the free spirit," to maintain his general trichotomical procedure); and the social institutions generated by the practical (or free) will form the objective spirit. Hegel's doctrine of the objective spirit tries to cover several disciplines: It is a normative theory of natural law, it has elements of a theory of moral behavior, even if at the same time it criticizes the emancipation of Kantian morality from ethical institutions, and it offers a doctrine of the main social institutions, family, civil society, and state. Particularly important is the recognition of political economics as a new discipline and of economy as a driving force of civil society (§§ 524 ff.; see *Philosophy of Right* § 189). The intermediate status between a normative theory and a descriptive theory of the social world is doubtless the main problem of this part of the *Encyclopedia*. It ends with a doctrine of the absolute spirit. This is not at all an otherworldly God: absolute spirit for Hegel are the activities in which humans try to make sense of the meaning of the universe, that is, art, religion, and philosophy. Hegel thus covers the modern humanities, which study the different arts from architecture to poetry, the various religions, and philosophy in its historical development and to which the German culture in the late eighteenth century had been particularly dedicated: I only mention Johann Joachim Winckelmann, Johann Gottfried Herder, and the brothers August Wilhelm and Friedrich Schlegel. While the width of these intellectual interests overcame the parochial narrowness of traditional Christianity, what distinguishes Hegel's approach from the value-free modern humanities is, however, that the absolute spirit has its grounding in the logical structures developed in the science of logic. On this basis, Hegel claims that Christianity is the highest religion, even if the form of religion is itself inferior to that of philosophy. History is for Hegel not an independent discipline, since it only deals with the temporal unfolding of entities that have to be grasped from a systematic point of view before their evolution can be studied. While the *Encyclopedia* locates world history at the end of the objective spirit, Hegel's lectures discuss in detail also the historical development of art, religion, and philosophy. Hegel's familiarity with non-European cultures, which began to be studied from the sixteenth century on, is impressive, even if he has no place in his system for the foundational discipline of hermeneutics, which was raised to a new level by his colleague Friedrich Daniel Ernst Schleiermacher. He also lacked a specific interest in linguistics, which, thanks to another colleague, Franz Bopp, became able to reconstruct features of the verbal system of the Proto-Indo-European language and with Wilhelm von Humboldt developed a powerful categorization of all human languages.

In the same year in which Hegel published the last edition of his *Encyclopedia*, the first volume of Comte's *Cours de philosophie positive*

(Course on Positive Philosophy) appeared, which included a "tableau synoptique," a synoptical table detailing the lectures planned for the following volumes as well as the underlying system of sciences. In the first lecture, Comte develops his famous law of the three stages, according to which the positive stage, characterized by the scientific method and the belief in invariable laws, follows the theological and the metaphysical stage, both in the individual and the social development. But, alas, this development does not occur with the same speed in all disciplines, and while the rise of the positive method has been irresistible in the natural sciences since the seventeenth century, the social sciences are still in the grip of the metaphysical or even the theological stage. The ultimate aim of Comte's *Course* is to offer a scientific social physics, but in order to get there, we must understand its place in the tree of knowledge (the metaphors of stem and branch are used often: 61, 65, 67, 77, 85). Only by understanding philosophically the nature of the other sciences, do we have a chance to develop a truly scientific "sociology"— this is the term that Comte coins for the new discipline (50).[79] Comte recognizes that the division of labor, so necessary for the progress of sciences, has had adverse effects, and he wants to counter them by introducing the generalist positivist philosopher as a new specialist (69). His overview of the results and methods of the various sciences is the only way to discover the logical laws of the human mind, which have to be founded on observation, and on observation only by the external sense, since Comte rejects introspection, favored by Pierre Maine de Biran, as an invalid method. For observation of one's own thinking is impossible, because subject and object would coincide, and observation of one's passions is impeded by the passions themselves (71 ff.). Comte wants to restructure the system of education (75 ff.), hopes that the new generalists will foster the development of the single sciences (77 ff.), and, from bringing all sciences into line with one another, expects greater social stability (80 ff.). But how does he order, in the second lesson, the various sciences, whose peak is sociology? The first division is between theoretical and practical endeavors, sciences and arts (89 ff.). Note that "practical" here has a very different meaning from that in Aristotle; it is closer to his "poietical" and the later mechanical arts. Comte insists that the existence of human technology does not challenge the invariability of natural laws, as Bacon and somehow even d'Alembert had suggested. While defending the utility of non–applied research, Comte recognizes as a characteristic of his time the emergence of an intermediary class between theoretical scientists and applied artists, namely, engineers. Within the sciences, Comte distinguishes between general theories aiming at laws and descriptions of individual objects, somehow continuing the old contrast between science and history. General physiology on the one hand, zoology and botany, on the other, are his examples (94 ff.). The subject of the *Course* is only the general sciences. But how should they be ordered? While recognizing that each classification is partly artificial (77, 98), Comte suggests as a criterion for the ordering of their mutual dependence. Such dogmatic classification, so Comte in agreement with d'Alembert, is not the same as a historical one, which follows the factual rise of the various disciplines, even if there are some parallelisms between the two approaches (98 ff.). The dogmatic classification must start with those phenomena that are simpler, more general, and more abstract—an idea that already underlay the ordering of the *quadrivium* (or, better, *quinquivium*) in Plato's *Republic*. For Comte, the first basic subdivision in reality is the one between dead matter and organisms; but the doctrine of the first is itself subdivided into astronomy, as the more general discipline, and terrestrial physics, which itself consists of physics proper and chemistry. The doctrine of organisms is then split into physiology and behavior relating to conspecifics; and this second part, social physics, is particularly important for humans. Comte ascribes four advantages to his own classification: It corresponds to the factual subdivision of the sciences; it matches with their historical rise as rigorous disciplines; it explains why the earlier sciences, which depend less on others than the succeeding ones, are more precise; and it is a canon for an appropriate education. Only at the end does Comte reveal the greatest lacuna of his classification: He deliberately omitted mathematics, which is not part but the basis of natural philosophy (120). So mathematics, astronomy, physics, chemistry, physiology, and sociology constitute his encyclopedic formula. In each of them, the positivist method is modified but within the same fundamental science (117).

It is not difficult to detect the main limits of Comte's sketch. First, he does not really explain the peculiar difference between mathematics and the natural sciences; and even less does he have a place in his system for logic or his own reflection on science. Second, putting astronomy before physics and chemistry may still have had a certain plausibility in the early nineteenth century but is untenable after science discovered the chemical processes occurring in stars. Clearly, astronomy is less general than physics and chemistry, as geology is less general than astronomy. Most glaring is, third, the absence of psychology. We have seen that it is connected to the difficult methodological status of introspection; the experimental psychology that was created at the end of the nineteenth century by thinkers such as Wilhelm Wundt and William James would probably have passed Comte's test and happily be integrated into his system, as long as it remained bound to physiology (71). His claim that the social behavior of humans is only a particular case of animal sociality has been triumphantly verified by sociobiology; and doubtless Comte would have welcomed the Darwinian revolution with the same enthusiasm as Herbert Spencer, had he not already died in 1857. Fourth, Comte does not have an equivalent of Hegel's absolute spirit, and his generic commitment to the positivist method does not allow him to grasp the peculiarities of the hermeneutical method without which the humanities cannot operate, as Wilhelm Dilthey well understood in his polemic against positivism. True enough, Comte's concept of sociology encompasses also the sociology of art and particularly of religion and philosophy; but it is reductionist and does not render justice to the specific categorical novelties that appear in this realm. The later sociology, particularly of Max Weber, explains much more of this realm, now relegated from absolute spirit to culture; but the price of this transformation has been that now the social sciences are detached from both ethics and a view of the world that still has a place for the validity of one's own reflection.[80]

   This essay is intended only to offer a story of our predicament, not a solution to our quandaries. Comte's and Hegel's systematizations of our knowledge remain the most advanced efforts by encyclopedic philosophers to make sense of the cosmos of disciplines, and while Comte's approach is certainly simpler and less fraught with metaphysical assumptions than Hegel's, in my eyes we can learn more from Hegel if we want to inject normativity back into the tree of knowledge. For an approach such as Comte's is fundamentally unable to explain where normativity comes from (even if he later added his ridiculous religion of humanity to solve this problem). No arborist, however, should forget that all work of grafting is deeply flawed that deprives the final tree of a recognizable connection to the tree of the knowledge of good and evil, an interaction that, once upon a time, triggered the process of humanization.

Notes

1. See, on a very high intellectual level, Edward O. Wilson, *Consilience: The Unity of Knowledge* (New York: Knopf, 1998).

2. See, e.g., Gregg Henriques, "The Tree of Knowledge System and the Theoretical Unification of Psychology," *Review of General Psychology* 7 (2003): 150–82.

3. *Logische Untersuchungen. Erster Band: Prolegomena zur reinen Logik* (Hamburg: Felix Meiner, 1992), 235 ff.

4. Cf. Margaret T. Hodgen, *Early Anthropology in the Sixteenth and Seventeenth Centuries* (Philadelphia: University of Pennsylvania Press, 1998).

5. See Edward G. Ruestow, *The Microscope in the Dutch Republic: The Shaping of Discovery* (Cambridge: Cambridge University Press, 1996).

6. See Edward Said, *Orientalism* (New York: Vintage, 1978).

7. On the star catalog MUL. APIN, see Rita Watson and Wayne Horowitz, *Writing Science before the Greeks* (Leiden: Brill, 2011).

8. See Plato, *Protagoras*, 318e.

9. See the interpretation in the long introductory essay by Luigi Ruggiu to Parmenide, *Poema sulla natura: I frammenti e le testimonianze indirette* (Milan: Rusconi, 1991).

10. *Republic* 509d ff. Cf. 533b.

11. *Charmides* 166c, 168a. I cannot justify here why I think that Plato indeed believes in the existence of the reflective science hypothetically discussed in the dialogue. See my analysis in *Wahrheit und Geschichte: Studien zur Struktur der Philosophiegeschichte unter paradigmatischer Analyse der Entwicklung von Parmenides bis Platon* (Stuttgart–Bad Cannstatt: Frommann-Holzboog, 1984), 424 ff.

12. *Charmides* 174a ff.

13. *Euthydemus* 289b.

14. *Republic* 528a f., 530c f.

15. See Alfred E. Taylor, *A Commentary on Plato's Timaeus* (Oxford: Clarendon Press, 1928), still the most impressive work of scholarship on

Plato's dialogue due to its familiarity with both ancient science and Aristotle's philosophy.

16. *Timaeus* 42d ff., 69c ff.

17. See the criticism of Anaxagoras in *Phaedo* 97b ff.

18. Sextus Empiricus, *Adversus logicos* I 16 = Xenocrates, frg. 1 Heinze = Xenocrates frg. 82 Isnardi Parente.

19. See Senocrate Ermodoro, *Frammenti*, ed. Margherita Isnardi Parente (Naples: Bibliopolis, 1982), 310. She mentions several Platonic passages where φύσις includes the world of ideas but overlooks the most important one: *Laws* 892c.

20. *Topics* 105b20 f. See also Cicero, *Academica* 1,4,19.

21. *Topics* 145a15 f.; *Metaphysics* 1025b25, 1063b35 ff.

22. See *Nicomachean Ethics* 1140b6 f. See also *Politics* 1254a1 ff. on tools as instruments of production and slaves as tools of action.

23. Even if the Greeks did not have a specific term for the fine arts, Aristotle is aware of the fact that poetry is only one of several mimetic arts (*Poetics* 1447a18 ff.).

24. *Eudemian Ethics* 1214a11.

25. *Nicomachean Ethics* 1094b11.

26. The latter term is used, for example, in *Politics* 1261a31 to refer to the *Nicomachean Ethics*.

27. *Nicomachean Ethics* 1094b3.

28. *Rhetoric* 1356a25 ff.

29. *Rhetoric* 1354a1 ff., 1359b2 ff.

30. Within reasoning, Aristotle distinguishes between demonstrative, dialectical, and contentious (*Topics* 100a25 ff.). The difference between the first two has to do with the nature of the premises, not of the inference.

31. See Diogenes Laertius V 28.

32. While Varro's *Disciplinae* encompassed nine books, touching also upon medicine and architecture, the latter are excluded as mechanical arts from the celestial ones in Martianus Capella's *De nuptiis Philologiae et Mercurii*; at the allegorical wedding they are silent guests. Rome's greatest contribution to the universe of knowledge is jurisprudence. While almost all human cultures know law, i.e., enforceable social norms, only the Romans developed a science of law.

33. Already in the *Protrepticus* (frg. 6), Aristotle argues that theory is higher than *poiesis*, since the latter can never be an end in itself.

34. Cf. Giovanni Reale, *Il concetto di "filosofia prima" e l'unità della Metafisica di Aristotele* (Milan: Bompiani, 2008).

35. *On the Parts of Animals* 644b22 ff.

36. *On the Soul* 402a4 f., 403a3–b19, *On the Parts of Animals* 641a22 ff.

37. See *Stoicorum veterum fragmenta*, ed. I ab Arnim (Leipzig: Teubner, 1903–5), I 45 f.

38. Ibid., II 42 ff.

39. See Anonymous, *Prolegomena to Platonic Philosophy*, ed. L. G. Westerink (Amsterdam: North-Holland Publishing, 1962), 47, referring to a lost work by Iamblichus.

40. On this genre, see the two essay collections by Bernard Ribémont, *De Natura Rerum: Études sur les encyclopédies médiévales* (Orléans: Paradigme, 1995); *Littérature et encyclopédies du Moyen Âge* (Orléans: Paradigme, 2002).

41. I use the following bilingual edition: St. Bonaventure, *On the Reduction of the Arts to Theology*, ed. Z. Hayes (St. Bonaventure, NY: St. Bonaventure University, 1996). I ignore here Gundassalinus's *De divisione philosophiae*.

42. See Franz Schupp, *Geschichte der Philosophie im Überblick*, 3 vols. (Hamburg: Meiner, 2003), II 212 ff.

43. Pere Villalba Varneda, the recent editor of the work in the Corpus Christianorum Continuatio Mediaevalis (Raimundi Lulli *Opera latina 65. Arbor Scientiae*, 3 vols. [Turnhout: Brepols, 2000]) argues in his long "Introductio generalis" (I 5*–188*) for a Latin original. Lola Badia, however, thinks that the Catalan text predates the Latin ("The *Arbor Scientiae*: A 'New' Encyclopedia in the Thirteenth-Century Occitan-Catalan Cultural Context," in *Arbor Scientiae: Der Baum des Wissens von Ramon Lull*, ed. F. Domínguez Reboiras, P. Villalba Varneda, and P. Walter [Turnhout: Brepols, 2002], 1–18, 2).

44. On the complex numerology of the *Arbor Scientiae*, see Robert Pring-Mill, "The Role of Numbers in the Structure of the *Arbor Scientiae*," in *Arbor Scientiae: Der Baum des Wissens von Ramon Lull*, 35–63.

45. On the history of this concept, see the classical study by Arthur A. Lovejoy, *The Great Chain of Being: A Study of the History of an Idea* (Cambridge, MA: Harvard University Press, 1936).

46. I 117 and 131. See the excellent clarifications in Anthony Bonner, "The Structure of the *Arbor Scientiae*," in *Arbor Scientiae: Der Baum des Wissens von Ramon Lull*, 21–34.

47. I will focus on the English original, not the expanded Latin translation integrated into the *Instauratio magna*, which Bacon planned to have six parts, again in correspondence with the six works of creation. For the English text, I use the following edition: Francis Bacon, *The Advancement of Learning*, ed. G. W. Kitchin (London: J. M. Dent & Sons, 1973). Only occasionally, I point to the Latin version.

48. On predecessors of Bacon's classification, such as Petrus Ramus, see Stephen Gaukroger, *Francis Bacon and the Transformation of Early-Modern*

Philosophy (Cambridge: Cambridge University Press, 2001), 18 ff. On some encyclopedists from the sixteenth century on, see T. Frängsmyr, ed., *The Structure of Knowledge: Classifications of Science and Learning since the Renaissance* (Berkeley: University of California Press, 2001).

49. Cf. Sachiko Kusukawa, "Bacon's Classification of Knowledge," in *The Cambridge Companion to Bacon*, ed. Markku Peltonen (Cambridge: Cambridge University Press, 1996), 46–74, 70: "Bacon's was a unique journey through the intellectual globe, leading to unknown territories, not a metaphysician's guide to a spiritual Jerusalem, or a humanist's guide to the ideal of classical learning."

50. See Aristotle, *Prior Analytics* 46a26, on the use of ἱστορία in the sense of a prescientific collection of facts regarding nature.

51. Francis Bacon, *The Works of Francis Bacon*, ed. J. Spedding, R. L. Ellis, and D. D. Heath, 7 vols. (Boston and Cambridge: Houghton Mifflin/ Riverside, 1857–59), II 343, where Bacon mentions that the arts concerning sight and hearing, more than the other sensual arts, have been considered liberal: "Atque artes, quae ad visum aut auditum spectant, prae aliis praecipue liberales habitae sunt." In the English text, architecture is mentioned as a branch of mixed mathematics (99) and once in a simile (163).

52. A philosophy of technology, as based on the deliberate use of rare antecedent conditions but presupposing the same universal laws of nature, can be found in Dieter Wandschneider, *Technikphilosophie* (Bamberg: Buchner, 2004).

53. *Republic* 392c ff.

54. Bacon does not follow the interpretation of the Aristotelian *Organon*, according to which the *Topics* mediate between the *Analytics* and *On Sophistical Refutations*, an interpretation suggested by the ordering of the works in the Andronicus edition and sometimes upheld in the Middle Ages. It was definitively rejected when Christian Brandis showed in 1833 that the *Topics* is older than the *Analytics*.

55. *Œuvres de Descartes*, ed. C. Adam and P. Tannery, 13 vols. (Paris: L. Cerf, 1897–1913), IX 2, 14 f.

56. "Le silence éternel de ces espaces infinis m'effraie" (*Les Pensées de Pascal*, ed. F. Kaplan [Paris: Les Éditions du Cerf, 1982], 152 = Nr. 130).

57. See *Opere di Giambattista Vico*, ed. F. Nicolini, 8 vols. (Bari: Laterza, 1911–41), IV 1, 5 f. and 34. (I give also the canonical paragraph numbering of Nicolini: 2, 42.)

58. IV 1 95, 118 (= par. 236, 331).

59. IV 1 140 (= par. 367).

60. IV 1 217 (= par. 502).

61. On the basic changes to the classifications of the *Encyclopédie* with regard to Bacon and Ephraim Chambers (who was not a philosophical mind), see Robert Darnton, *The Great Cat Massacre and Other Episodes in French Cultural History* (New York: Basic Books, 2009 [1984]), 191–213: "Philosophers Trim the Tree of Knowledge: The Epistemological Strategy of the *Encyclopédie*." I particularly appreciate Darnton's cautionary remarks that the eclectic (or, as he says, even inconsistent) epistemological statements of d'Alembert should not be interpreted as a sign that d'Alembert wanted to discredit what he was saying (203 f.). I miss, however, in this brilliant essay a discussion of the remarkable philosophical differences between Diderot and d'Alembert, even if they became more evident later in their lives, and I do not consider the comparison between Bacon's and d'Alembert's systems of knowledge sufficiently detailed.

62. The French text can be found in the beginning of the first volume of the reprint of *Encyclopédie ou dictionnaire raisonné des sciences, des arts et des métiers* (New York: Readex, 1969) but is more easily accessible in Jean d'Alembert, *Discours préliminaire des éditeurs de 1751 et articles de l'*Encyclopédie, ed. M. Groult (Paris: Honoré Champion, 1999), which, however, does not contain the chart. An excellent annotated English translation is Jean Le Rond d'Alembert, *Preliminary Discourse to the Encyclopedia of Diderot*, ed. R. Schwab (Chicago: University of Chicago Press, 1995). (I have corrected one error on p. 148; the chart on p. 144 furthermore dropped "architecture.") I will give first the translation's page numbers and add afterward the page number of the Groult edition. When I give only one number, I am referring to the chart.

63. In the English version, pp. 143–64 contain Diderot's text; in Groult's edition, pp. 171–88.

64. Cf. Paul O. Kristeller, "The Modern System of the Arts: A Study in the History of Aesthetics," *Journal of the History of Ideas* 12 (1951): 496–527; 13 (1952): 17–46. Note that "practical" architecture and sculpture are still listed under the arts, trades, and manufactures (145; 148/173).

65. The inversion, however, is not complete, because vegetables and animals as well as humans and stars hold the same order in both trees.

66. In the chart at the end, the two seem to hold equal rank to civil and natural history; but in the "Detailed explanation" they are subsumed under sacred history in a broad sense (143/171).

67. In the "Detailed explanation" theology belongs, together with the doctrine of angels and of demons and the science of the soul, to pneumatology (149/174 f.). It is curious that the chart, even if by Diderot, too, is closer to the text of the "Discours" proper. Did he draw the chart before writing his own text?

68. Comte calls these attempts "par cela seul radicalement vicieuses," "for this reason alone radically faulty" (Auguste Comte, *Philosophie des sciences*, ed. J. Grange [Paris: Gallimard, 1996], 86). This edition contains only the first two lectures of the *Cours de philosophie positive*, but they are the only ones that interest me in this context. While Comte rejects a priori classifications (88), he sees his own subdivision as an alternative to a purely empirical one (112).

69. See also the beginning of § 79 of the *Critique of Judgment* (B 364).

70. *Critique of Pure Reason* B 870 ff./A 842 ff.

71. B 861/A 833. On the opposition between technical and architectonic, cf. B 875/A 847 and *Critique of Judgment* B 305.

72. *Critique of Pure Reason* B 863/A 835. On the stem metaphor, see B 29.

73. Cf. B 869/A 841.

74. *Encyclopedia* § 10 Remark. If not otherwise noted, I refer to the last edition of 1830.

75. Introduction to the *Science of Logic* (Georg Wilhelm Friedrich Hegel, *Werke in zwanzig Bänden*, ed. E. Moldenhauer and K. M. Michel [Frankfurt: Suhrkamp, 1969–71], 5:44). On the tasks of Hegel's logic, see Vittorio Hösle, *Hegels System* (Hamburg: Felix Meiner, 1987), 61 ff.

76. I refer to § 14 of *The Foundations of Arithmetic* (*Die Grundlagen der Arithmetik*, ed. C. Thiel [Hamburg: Felix Meiner, 1988], 28 f.).

77. See the oral additions to § 268 and § 341.

78. On Hegel's philosophy of biology, see the excellent book by Christian Spahn, *Lebendiger Begriff, begriffenes Leben: Zur Grundlegung der Philosophie des Organischen bei G. W. F. Hegel* (Würzburg: Königshausen & Neumann, 2007).

79. We know today that the word had already been used half a century before in an unpublished manuscript by Emmanuel Joseph Sieyès (Jacques Guilhaumou, "Sieyès et le non-dit de la *sociologie*: du mot à la chose," *Revue d'histoire des sciences humaines* 15 [2006]: 117–34).

80. On the development of the value-free social sciences, see my essay "Zur Philosophie der Geschichte der Sozialwissenschaften," now in Vittorio Hösle, *Die Philosophie und die Wissenschaften* (Munich: Beck, 1999), 125–65 and 230–33.

PART II

Epistemology, Logic, and Mathematics

CHAPTER TWO

Intuition and Coherence in the Keystone Loop

KEITH LEHRER

There is a traditional controversy about the role of intuition and co-herence in justification and knowledge. Some have thought that intu-ition is itself a source of evidence. The character of intuition and co-herence stand in need of clarification. I shall state my own conception of intuition and coherence without arguing these are superior to oth-ers. One must start somewhere in philosophical discussion, making some assumptions, and, therefore, from the perspective of some oppo-nents the starting point begs important questions. Perhaps the best one can hope to do is to beg some important philosophical question in adopting a starting point, thereby focusing attention on it. I make, in short, no claim for starting where I do. So what about the alleged role of intuition and coherence in epistemology? The minimal answer is that intuition is a source of evidence for what one accepts that is im-mediate and does not depend on other things one accepts, while co-herence is a source of evidence for what one accepts that is mediated by and depends on other things that one accepts. Put in this way, it seems that intuition implies that not all evidence depends on coher-ence, and the claim that all evidence results from coherence implies that intuition is not a source of evidence. However, the matter stated in this way leaves open the possibility that the kind of evidence required for knowledge is a combination of intuition and coherence. It may be that intuition and coherence must be joined to yield the kind of evidence required for knowledge.

There is another way to put the matter in terms of the metaphors of the foundation and coherence theories of knowledge. Intuition as a source of evidence can be the basis of a foundation of knowledge because the foundation is based on intuition, a source of evidence that does not depend on other things one accepts. A coherence theory, by contrast, affirms that evidence for what one accepts always depends on other things one accepts. The standard objection to a foundation theory is that evidence, since it does not depend on anything else one accepts, cannot be explained in terms of what one accepts, and leaves us with an explanatory surd. The standard objection to the coherence theory is that it leaves us with a regress or circle of the evidence because the acceptance of something always depends on something else.

It is interesting to note historically that one famous foundationalist, Thomas Reid (1785), affirmed the role of intuition very avidly while at the same time affirming the dependence of the principles of intuition, which he called first principles, on each other and, notably, on one special first principle which he says has a priority in the order of evidence over the others. Leaving aside a good deal of detail, he affirms the intuitive character of principles of our faculties, which he says are original capacities of the mind, to yield truth and knowledge, which include convictions concerning consciousness, perception, memory, and others. In each case, he says that the principles yield convictions about things that really do or did exist. So the principles appear to simply affirm the connection between conviction and reality without saying anything about evidence. But he holds that such principles are principles of evidence, for he affirms that evidence is the ground of belief, and first principles are the grounds of belief. What is more interesting is that he anticipates the objection to his first principles as a source of evidence, namely, that we are deceived and they are fallacious. His reply, a natural one, is principle 7 in his first principles, which I call the First First Principle (Lehrer 1998, 2010) though listed after others, which affirms that it is a first principle that our faculties by which we distinguish truth from error are not fallacious. He remarks that this principle is a principle of evidence that has priority over the others, noting, of course, that our faculties must not be fallacious or else the claims on behalf of the other first principles of our faculties fall victim to the fallaciousness of our faculties. He compares the evidence of principle 7 to light that reveals itself as it reveals the illuminated object. The First First Principle is a first principle of our faculties and, therefore, vouches for itself as it vouches for the other first principles of our faculties.

I think that this is more than a historical oddity in the philosophy of Reid. He is candid in noting that a foundationalist, someone who holds that intuition is a source of evidence, is assuming, whether or not he or she makes it explicit, that some convictions have immediate evidence. Without that assumption how can one defend the claims of intuition and the foundational character of evidence? Putting it another way, the foundationalist is assuming that some convictions have the evidence of intuition, and others do not. What is the source of the evidence of that assumption? Those defending intuition and foundation theories will usually claim that evidence of intuition does not depend on general assumptions in order to avoid the conclusion that the evidence of the foundation depends on such assumptions. They seek to avoid the claim that the evidence of intuition depends on any general assumption about which convictions have that evidence. But this is as if the intuitionist, having specified in general terms which convictions have the status of intuition, says, "Shh, we won't mention this."

Reid was more candid. However, he left us with a puzzle about the nature of evidence that is as simple to state as it is puzzling to solve. Reid argued that first principles, and particular instances of them as well, both have immediate evidence and do not obtain their evidence from reasoning. Even more strongly, he argued that reasoning could add nothing to the evidence of them. The evidence is immediate and neither requires nor admits of appeal to reasoning for their evidence. Now this leaves us with a puzzle concerning the First First Principle. It is simply that the evidence of intuition, the evidence of first principles of our faculties, seems to depend on the First First Principle, or, if that is too strong, to admit reasoning in favor of such by appeal to that special principle. Reid suggests that it has a priority, that it vouches for the other principles, and, in so doing, appears to provide a premise for reasoning in favor of the evidence of other principles from the First First Principle. Indeed, it seems, as Reid's analogy to light suggests, that the First First Principle explains the evidence of the other principles, to wit, that they are evidence because they are first principles of our faculties and, given the evidence of the First First Principle, those faculties by which we distinguish truth from error are not fallacious.

Reid offers one answer to the question of why the first principles do not admit of reasoning in their favor, namely, that first principles have all the evidence they admit of, all that they can have, and, therefore, do not admit of an increase in their evidence as the result of reasoning. They come into the mind evident, as he puts it in another place: their evidence is their birthright. But why can't we add to that evidence? His answer is that they have all the evidence they admit of. What he means becomes clear when he remarks that the evidence they have is equal to that of an axiom of Euclid. The point is that there is a maximum degree of evidence that any conviction can have, and the first principles, as well as their particular instances, come into existence with that degree of evidence. You cannot add evidence to something that is maximally evident to begin with. So reasoning from the First First Principle could not increase the evidence of first principles and their instances because they are maximally evident prior to such reasoning. However, an objection remains. The First First Principle appears to explain why the other first principles are evident and, thereby, explains why intuition is a source of evidence. The illuminated object would not be visible without light, after all, and the illumination of light reveals why it is visible. Evidence admits of explanation by reasoning from the First First Principle.

Oddly, a famous coherence theorist, Wilfrid Sellars (1963), who defended a coherence theory of knowledge, was equally candid in affirming that there were some beliefs whose evidence was noninferential. Sellars was famous for his rejection of the myth of the given, which sounds like a rejection of intuition. He argued that the mere existence of some sensory state could not entail knowledge of the existence of it. His argument was that language was required for a person to have any conception of the sensory state and, therefore, for a belief that the state exists. The conclusion that the entailment did not hold was the simple consequence of the premise that the existence of a sensory state did not entail the existence of language. Not everyone is willing to grant the view that conception of something required the existence of language. However, the argument has a cogency that does not depend on that assumption about language being required for conception. The argument against the given requires only the premise that the existence of sensory state, a pain as a salient example, does not entail that the person who has the state has a conception of it. Sensory stimuli are one thing, a conception of them another, and the first does not logically entail the second. Sometimes the argument is formulated in terms of representation rather than conception. It would use the premise that knowledge requires some representation of the state that is not logically entailed by the existence of the state.

The reply of a Reidian intuitionist to this argument may grant that the evidence of intuition may presuppose conception and conviction, as Sellars avows. He may grant that the mere existence of the sensory state does not entail any conception or representation of the state. But he argues that the conception and conviction that accompanies the sensory state, though not entailed by it, has evidence that is noninferential. Reid and Sellars differed concerning the source of the explanation but agreed that it was noninferential. Reid was a nativist who argued that conception and belief arose, in the case of first principles, from the exercise of an original faculty, by which I suggested he meant an inborn capacity, whereas Sellars was a behaviorist who argued that conception and belief arose from stimulus-response (S-R) conditioning. However, a conception and belief that arises from response to a stimulus, whether as the result of an innate faculty of response or S-R conditioning, could, in either case, be a response that was not inferred from anything else. It is tempting to think that any background principle, whether an innate principle or a conditioned principle, that explains the response is, therefore, a premise from which one reasons to arrive at the response of conception and conviction. That is a mistake. Moreover, neither the foundationalist Reid nor the coherentist Sellars made that mistake. They understood that inference from a principle is a causal process of a special sort, a kind of transition from one representational state to another, while other responses are transitions from states that are nonrepresentational, input states in contemporary vocabulary, to ones that are representational output states. Noninferential conception and belief is of the second variety. Not every transition from one state to another is an inference.

Sellars was, however, adamant that the evidence of even noninferential conception and conviction depended on a background system. Though the noninferential conviction was not generated by inference from premises of the system, the evidence of the conviction, or as he would put it, the justification for the conviction, depended on the background system. Here is the basis of disagreement. Sellars thought that the background system served the goal of maximizing explanation, and it played a crucial role in what he called the justification game of evidence. Thus, the belief that arises noninferentially is justified because of the role it plays in the background system that explains why it should be accepted. So there is an initial contrast between Reid and Sellars that is characteristic of the contrast between intuitionist foundation theories and coherence theories concerning evidence of noninferential or immediate conviction. Reid thought it was the way in which they originated that accounts for their evidence, the evidence of intuition, without appeal to a background system. He says they are born justified; their justification is their birthright of intuition. Sellars, by contrast, though he might admit that how they came into existence enters into their justification, held that is only because of a systematic explanation of why beliefs that come into existence in that way turn out to be true. For Reid, evidence of their truth is a birthright. For Sellars, evidence of their truth is explained by a system.

So who is right? Notice that Reid like Sellars holds that the first principles constitute a system. Reid says that they are joined like links in a chain and that you cannot have the links without the chain. His meaning is disputed, but I believe that it is the First First Principle that contains the answer to what he means. It tells us that all the first principles by which we distinguish truth from error are not fallacious. So if a person like Hume, Reid's target of criticism, accepts a first principle of consciousness but rejects a first principle of perception, he undermines his evidence for one by rejecting the second, for they are equally first principles of our faculties. By the First First Principle they stand or fall together. Moreover, Reid says that no one will note his conviction of first principles, including the First First Principle, until they are challenged. So Reid like Sellars appears committed to the view that the First First Principle plays a systematic role in the justification game, that is, in answering challenges to evidence of truth, including intuition for our noninferential convictions.

We have reached an issue that is not merely a historical curiosity in the study of Reid and Sellars. Any foundationalist insisting on the role of intuition, whether Reid or his splendid twentieth-century follower, Chisholm (1966), confronts a question about the claim that some convictions have intuitive evidence of truth. Why do those beliefs and not others have this status? If you answer the question by appeal to some principle, how do you avoid the problem that Reid faces in our account of him? Why is the principle that accounts for the intuitive evidence of the belief not a principle of evidence itself? And if it is a principle of evidence itself, why is it not a premise from which the evidence of the foundational belief is inferred? Harman (1973) suggested that all justification, all evidence, is inference to the best explanation. But even Sellars, to whom Harman is indebted, conceded that there are noninferentially justified beliefs. How can justification of all beliefs be explained when some beliefs are noninferentially justified?

The nature of the problem can be further illuminated when the intuitionist and the coherence theorist confront a skeptic about justification of the justified beliefs. How is either to answer the skeptic's challenge that we are not justified? If he appeals to something he accepts to justify the convictions, for example, Reid's First First Principle, or any other principle, he begs the question against the skeptic. Reid says that when confronting the total skeptic he puts his hand over his mouth in silence. Yet the First First Principle is a principle of evidence, he says, though he cannot prove this to the skeptic without begging the question. Reid does not take the path of his follower, Moore (1939), who simply insisted that he had a proof he did know what the skeptic denied he knew. That would beg the question. So can we prove that the skeptic is wrong? If to prove he is wrong is to offer an argument such that he ought to accept the conclusion, we cannot prove that he is wrong. Must we concede, therefore, that the skeptic is right and we are ignorant? No. We may know that the skeptic is wrong; we can know what we suppose we know, even though we cannot prove this to the skeptic.

Moreover, the explanation for why we find ourselves in a situation in which we know something we cannot prove will provide us with an answer to the question of how the justification of all beliefs can be explained though some beliefs are noninferentially justified. The point, which is already implicit in what has been said above, is that what is justified by proof or inference must be distinguished from the explanation of why the belief is justified. A noninferential belief may be justified, as Reid avowed, because it is the First First Principle of a faculty, or as Sellars says, because of the role it plays in what we might call the Explanatory System, without appeal to the principle being a premise in reasoning or inference by which we come to have the belief. The First First Principle, for example, is not a premise in the justification of beliefs that are first principles. Appeal to the First First Principle or the Explanatory System in defense of the beliefs only arises when the beliefs are called into question. Moreover, when they are called into question, the explanation for why they are noninferentially justified may be supplied. A foundationalist like Reid and a coherence theorist like Sellars may agree that beliefs of this kind that arise from clear and distinct perceptions of an object or quality, for example, have a security from error in the way they come into existence that provides evidence of their truth. Once we distinguish proof and inference from explanation and defense, we may, without claiming to prove that a challenged belief is true, explain why some beliefs come to exist in a way that makes their truth evident. Proof and explanation separate to account for how we know the total skeptic is wrong and how we know some things without proof or inference from anything else.

There is an upshot and a remaining problem. Explanation requires truth. If we offer an explanation from a false premise, we have explained nothing. Thus, the system that explains evidence and justification, even intuitive evidence of noninferential beliefs, must provide us with an explanation for why the evident beliefs are true. Moreover, the explanation must include a defense of those beliefs against objections, for objections against the beliefs call into doubt either the truth of the beliefs or our reasons for thinking they are true.

Quine (1969) argued the overall system must contain a subsystem, a truth system, telling us when our beliefs are true, at least those we accept when we aim at obtaining truth and avoiding error in a trustworthy way. As I have argued elsewhere (2012), if we aim at maximizing explanation, then the truth system, while it explains why other beliefs we accept are true, must explain why it itself is true. Notice that the First First Principle, which explains why other first principles are not fallacious, explains at the same time why it is not fallacious, that is, why it itself is true. I have called such principles that both explain the truth of other principles and the truth of themselves keystone principles. For such principles that explain the truth of other principles, and thereby support the explanatory system, also require the support of the truth of the other beliefs, or the system will collapse. I have argued against the metaphors of a foundation and a bootstrap in favor of the keystone. The truth system, or some principle thereof, loops back onto itself, which may suggest a bootstrap or a foundation, but those metaphors are misleading. Take the First First Principle as an example, or my formulation of a principle of trustworthiness that we are trustworthy in what we accept to distinguish truth from error. Such a principle cannot pull itself up to the level of justification alone, nor can it serve as a foundation for the justification of itself and all the rest. For the principle itself depends on our trustworthiness in distinguishing truth from error in the other things we accept, in Reid's terms, on the first principles not being fallacious, or in Sellars's terms on the structure of systematic explanation, and with it the truth system. Otherwise, if we follow Reid's formulation, the First First Principle will collapse in the rubble of error. A false truth system in a system of explanation is a snare and delusion. It explains nothing.

Now it might seem as though the connection between truth and the Explanatory System has become so tenuous that no one should trust it. All justification, including the evidence of intuitive truth, depends on a background system whose truth system loops back onto itself. So how can we ensure for ourselves that our truth system is connected with experience and is not just a fanciful delusion? The first step is to distinguish the kind of knowledge that I have so far discussed, which I (Lehrer 2000) have called *discursive knowledge*, from another, simpler kind of knowledge. This simpler knowledge may be possessed by young children, in whom neither the capacity to distinguish truth from error nor the capacity to reply to objections to explain arriving at truth is present. I call (Lehrer 2000) this kind of knowledge *primitive knowledge.*

Sosa (2007) later distinguished animal knowledge from reflective knowledge, but that is a different distinction. Reflective knowledge is a kind that engages reflection, and, though discursive knowledge may presuppose a *capacity* to reflect, in the activity of the justification game, for example, it does not presuppose the *engagement* of the activity of reflection. Reid introduces principle 7, the First First Principle, after other principles of consciousness, perception, and memory without any mention of truth or falsity. I think the reason, though this is specu-lation, is that Reid thought that young children were helplessly gullible to the reports of their faculties and to the testimony of others because they lacked the distinction between truth and error. So principle 7 may find its place in the order of the principles because conception and con-viction may exist in a person, in young children, perhaps in animals, who lack an understanding of the conception of truth and the ability to evaluate the truth of what they believe in the light of evidence. They have primitive knowledge but lack discursive knowledge and the ca-pacity to evaluate and play the justification game, even within oneself.

The question is, what is primitive knowledge? I would like to sug-gest that it is based on a positive attitude, perhaps belief p, or perhaps having the impression that p. The attitude is not inferentially articu-late, though it may imitate inference by association of the attitude to-ward p with other contents and ideas. Basically, I think that primitive knowledge is an automatic response to stimuli in the form of output of representation, perhaps encapsulated as Fodor (1983) suggested, per-haps not, but not an attitude amenable to reflection on the distinction between truth and error. Resilient illusions of sense, the bent stick in water, the puddle of water on the sunbaked highway, are good examples. They are the conversion of sense to representation. Neither entailment nor logical necessity is involved in the conversion, for it is only the con-version of input by an innate internal program or principle to represen-tation. Will this serve as an anchor to connect conception with truth in a way that ensures that the truth system is anchored in experience?

It is inadequate. The innate response system may be the result of processes, evolutionary tales of survival, that protect us from danger by overstating the danger we confront. Survival selection is not likely to lead us to a truth-refined response system. It may be better to think a beast is bigger and faster than he is to avoid getting eaten.

We need another way to get truth into the game of justification and even intuitive evidence to take us to truth. I have proposed an idea, one that Reid should have held but seems not to have adopted, though what he says leads in that direction. For Reid (1785) noted that sometimes our conception of a sensation, a sensory experience, may be a capital part of our conception of some external quality, for example, in the case of smell. A conception of sensation, an odor, may lead us to a conception of a quality in the object that gives rise to the sensation, and, initially, that may be all there is to our conception of the quality. We have a conception of a quality in the object, a stink, for example, that occasions the sensation in us. This is his view of our initial conception of secondary qualities. However, since the conception of the quality is based on our conception of a sensation, the account implies that we have a conception of a sensation. How? According to Reid, from our consciousness of the sensation that occasions a conception of it. So the sensation gives rise to a conception of it, and Reid says the sensation itself is a capital part of the conception. Now this hypothesis reminds us of the view of Hume (1739) according to which the particular sensation becomes general by being used to stand for a class of sensations. That takes us to the proposal of Goodman (1968) according to which a particular, a sample, may be used to refer to a property that exemplifies it, a color patch of paint, for example.

I have incorporated the view suggested by remarks of Reid, Hume, and Goodman about the use of an individual experience and the individual qualities thereof into a notion of exemplar representation (Lehrer 2012). The experience is used as an exemplar to exhibit what it is like as well as the plurality of things, perhaps just experiences, perhaps something beyond experiences, that the exemplar represents by exhibiting what the represented objects are like. Now an advantage of the account, not noticed by the other authors it seems, is that exemplar representation gives us a minimal truth security as the exemplar, which represents a plurality of objects by showing us what the represented objects are like, loops back onto itself as one of the objects represented. We may think of the exemplar as a term of representation, a sensation of pain representing pains of the kind it exhibits, for example, and thus true of sensations it is used to represent. But it is one of the sensations it represents exhibiting what it is like as well as what they are like, and, therefore, the sensation true of other sensations is true of itself. The representational loop gives us some truth connection and security. Perhaps that is why we speak of *knowing* what the sensation is like, what kind of thing it is, as a result of simply experiencing it. We say, after all, that we experience the sensation and, therefore, *know* what it is like. Exemplarizing the sensation gives rise to a conception, a representation of the sensation, as well as other things being used to exhibit what it represents. It is true of what it represents, including, of course, itself. True representation is not enough for discursive knowledge, for a person may lack the capacity to defend the representation, but it may suffice for primitive knowledge when affirmed by the mind.

A question for Sellars scholars is whether this argument is a rejection of Sellars's argument against the myth of the given. Have we converted the sensation into a representation of the sensation in such a way that having the sensation *entails* knowledge of what the sensation is like? The connection is not entailment. When one uses an exemplar in exemplarization to represent a class, one adds, as a contingent matter of fact, a mental operation to the sensation. Some, Kriegel (2004), for example, hold that consciousness involves a representational loop of the sensation back onto itself as constitutive of the conscious sensation, which may lead to the myth of the given. That view, though tempting, seems wrong. In an initial state of waking and other disordered forms of consciousness, the cognitive operations have not reacted yet, in spite of the presence of the sensation. Exemplarizing, however automatic in some cases, adds a mental operation to a sensation, to a conscious experience. Exemplarization explains why having the sensation adds a representation of the state that is not available before the experience of it. You have to have a sensation in order to exemplarize it, in order to engage in *exemplar* representation using it as a token of representation, but having the sensation does not entail that you exemplarize it or represent it in any other way. So exemplarization is consistent with Sellars's attack on the myth of the given. It allows us to explain how sensory experience can give rise to representation without entailing the existence of the representation. My conclusion is that a secure truth connection can result from a contingent operation on a sensation creating a truth loop of the sensation back onto itself yielding primitive knowledge. This is the simplest form of exemplarization, ostensive exemplar representation.

We are now in a position to understand how the keystone principles of the truth system are connected to experience. Exemplarization draws a truth loop into the truth system. There is a similarity in the way in which the exemplar loops back onto itself and disquotation in sentences like the following:

RT. "Red is a color" is true in English if and only if red is a color.
RM. "Red is a color" means in English that red is a color.

They quote a sentence that is used to formulate a truth condition or a meaning condition. Sellars noted that the sentences use the unquoted second occurrence of "red is a color" to exhibit the role or meaning played by the quoted use in the sentences, in other words to exhibit what sort of semantic roles they have. However, these sentences involve two tokens, different particulars, to exhibit the truth condition and the meaning condition. The relation affirmed between the two particulars is subject to the hazard of error that can arise in the formulation of any relation between two particulars. The exemplarization of a state avoids that hazard as it exhibits what the state itself is like; it is the particular state itself and not another particular that represents itself and is true of itself. To achieve this security, exemplarization is required, which differs from exemplification which brings in another entity, whether a property or a predicate that introduces all the possibilities of error that result from relating one thing, a property or predicate, to another thing, an instance of it. In the case of exemplarization, as Ismael (2007) noted followed by Tolliver and myself (Lehrer and Tolliver 2011; Lehrer 2011), the exemplarized exemplar is an instance of itself reflexively.

It is of some historical interest that both Sellars and Reid seem to have held views close to exemplarization but did not embrace it, while Hume did so. Sellars held the interesting view that in discursive thought our description of mental states is best understood as a theory to explain the behavior of others in terms of postulated inner episodes. These descriptors then acquire a reporting role as the terms of the theory are applied in the first person. As Stern and I (Lehrer and Stern 2000) have argued, it appears that Sellars, when pressed in correspondence by Hector-Neri Castaneda to explain the reporting role, argued that there were physical states of a special kind, *sensa*, which we learn to use like elements in the disquoted sentences to exhibit what the inner episodes are like. His model, if we have understood him correctly, is that certain internal physical states have a special feature that allows us to use them by disquoting them to exhibit what kind of state they are. Papineau (2002) later held this view concerning conscious states much more explicitly. Reid failed to embrace the view that the sensations are representations of themselves, though he says that they occasion conceptions of themselves in consciousness. When I ask why he did not hold the view that sensations are exemplarized and, therefore, a reflexive sign of themselves, I can only conjecture that he thought a sign must signify something other than itself, or as he puts it otherwise, a sign must suggest the existence of something else.

Forgive me this historical diversion, but it may help to explain the special way that I am arguing that our truth system can incorporate experience into the stones of the keystone arch of truth and knowledge rather than leave us with a mystery of how experience is related to representation. If experience is itself representational and represents itself as well as other things, we obtain the truth connection within the truth system of representation without the need to explain how the representations of the system are related to what they represent. The exemplars *are* what they represent. Exemplarization closes the truth gap between representation and what is represented, at least in the reflexive case. Moreover, as we know what the sensation is like as we exemplarize it, so we know what the relation of representation is like in that instance. The knowledge of what it is like may be in the first instance primitive. I am seeking in this essay and elsewhere to make it discursive.

I end with a caveat and qualification. I am not claiming that exemplarization is the historical or genetic starting point of our conception of the world. Actually, I am inclined to agree with Fodor (1983) that the starting point of representation is a form of representation that is automatic, perhaps encapsulated or at least protected from reflection, where we obtain a representation of the world, the output of an input system, without knowing what the stimulus, the input, is like. Originally, at a very young age, the response to stimuli may be remotely analogous to the response of my computer to compression of the keys. However, we acquire the ability to reverse the direction of attention from what is represented to the input state evoking the representation. We thereby become aware of such states and gain the capacity to exemplarize them. Once we have a representation of the input of our sensory experience from exemplarization, we have made a great cognitive leap. We are now in a position to evaluate the output of the input system, the representational meaning of the output, and revise it. Most simply, we can decide that the appearance of the bent stick in water, a representation of the output system, is erroneous and should be reinterpreted, re-represented. But that requires that we know what the appearance is like. We cannot reinterpret a term without knowing what it is like, even if we can unconsciously change how we react. So, exemplarization is an ingredient in our cognitive autonomy. It gives us plasticity to change how we represent our world, ourselves, ourselves in our world, and our world in ourselves. The ongoing dynamic of semantic change, of revising our systematic view of the world, including our system of truth and evidence, aggregates vectors of exemplarized experience.

I could say more. I could tell you how the background system is used to meet objections to how we represent the world in terms of our exemplarized experience of it and how this converts primitive knowledge of what representation is like into discursive knowledge. But that is what I have already attempted to do in this essay. I conclude by drawing the account of this essay into the keystone loop of discursive knowledge. It is an account of the loop of intuitive evidence because exemplarization is immediate, truth-reflexive, and discursive. It explains how experience loops back into the truth system of the theory. Saying more would only widen the keystone loop that maximizes explanation. Welcome to the power of the loop.

References

Chisholm, R. M. 1966. *A Theory of Knowledge*. Englewood Cliffs, NJ: Prentice-Hall.

Fodor, J. A. 1983. *The Modularity of Mind*. Cambridge, MA: MIT Press.

Goodman, N. 1968. *Languages of Art: An Approach to a Theory of Symbols*. Indianapolis: Bobbs-Merrill.

Harman, G. 1973. *Thought*. Princeton: Princeton University Press.

Hume, D. 1739. *A Treatise of Human Nature*. London: John Noon.

Ismael, J. 2007. *The Situated Self*. Oxford: Oxford University Press.

Kriegel, U. 2004. "Moore's Paradox and the Structure of Conscious Belief." *Erkenntnis* 61: 99–121.

Lehrer, K. 1998. "Reid, Hume and Common Sense." *Reid Studies* 2 (1): 15–26.

———. 2000. "Discursive Knowledge." *Philosophy and Phenomenological Research* 60 (3): 637–54.

———. 2010. "Reid, the Moral Faculty and First Principles." In *Reid on Ethics*, ed. S. Roeser, 25–44. London: Blackwell.

———. 2011. "What Intentionality Is Like." *Acta Analytica* 26 (1): 3–14.

———. 2012. *Art, Self and Knowledge*. Oxford: Oxford University Press.

Lehrer, K., and D. G. Stern. 2000. "The 'Denoument' of 'Empiricism and the Philosophy of Mind.'" *History of Philosophy Quarterly* 17 (2): 201–16.

Lehrer, K., and J. Tolliver. 2011. "Truth and Tropes." In *Philosophical Papers Dedicated to Kevin Mulligan*, ed. A. Reboul. www.philosophie.ch/kevin/festschrift.

Moore, G. E. 1939. "Proof of an External World." *Proceedings of the British Academy* 25: 273–300.

Papineau, D. 2002. *Thinking about Consciousness*. Oxford: Oxford University Press.

Quine, W. V. O. 1969. "Epistemology Naturalized." In *Ontological Relativity and Other Essays*. New York: Columbia University Press.

Reid, T. 1785. *Essays on the Intellectual Powers of Man*. Edinburgh.

Sellars, W. S. 1963. "Empiricism and the Philosophy of Mind." In *Science, Perception, and Reality*. New York: Humanities Press.

Sosa, E. 2007. *A Virtue Epistemology: Apt Belief and Reflective Knowledge*. Vol. 1. Oxford: Oxford University Press.

CHAPTER THREE

What Is the Nature of Inference?

ROBERT HANNA

A **general** but **pure** logic . . . has to do with strictly *a priori* principles, and is a **canon of the understanding** and reason, but only with regard to what is formal in their use, be the content what it may (empirical or transcendental). A **general logic**, however, is then called **applied** if it is directed to the rule of the use of the understanding under the subjective empirical conditions that psychology teaches us. . . . [G]eneral and pure logic is related to [applied logic] as pure morality, which contains merely the necessary moral laws of a free will in general, is related to the doctrine of virtue proper, which assesses these laws under the hindrances of the feelings, inclinations, and passions to which human beings are more or less subject, and which can never yield a true and proven science, since it requires empirical and psychological principles just as much as that applied logic does.

—I. Kant, *Critique of Pure Reason*

What is the nature of inference? In order to answer that question, we must first have in front of us a commonsensical or intuitive, more or less theoretically neutral, working definition of what it is we are talking about. By "inference," then, I mean a cognitive process leading from the mental representation of the premises of a deductive, inductive, or abductive (abduction = inference-to-the-best-explanation) argument[1] to the mental representation of the conclusion of that argument, where the cognitive transition from the representation of the premises to the representation of the conclusion is governed by some rule-based standards of cogency, such that if all the premises are believed by a cognizer or cognizers and if the cognitive transition from representing the premises to representing the conclusion is also believed by that cognizer or those cognizers to be cogent, then, other things being equal,[2] the conclusion will also be believed by that cognizer or those cognizers.

I am also assuming that an inference can have many *further* important properties, but I am also thinking that this will suffice as an intuitive working definition of inference in a *minimal* sense.

The apparently univocal philosophical question, What is the nature of inference?, however, is in fact four distinct yet intimately related philosophical questions all rolled up into one:

(1) what are the metaphysics of inference?
(2) what is the goal or purpose of inference?
(3) what justifies an inference?
(4) what is the mechanism of inference?

In order to answer these questions, I will propose what I call "Contemporary Kantian Moralism about Inference," or CKMI. In a nutshell, according to CKMI, inference is essentially *an act of cognitive free agency*. By this, I do not mean that rational human cognizers can choose to regard any inference whatsoever as cogent (inferential *voluntarism*): on the contrary, what I mean is that rational human cognizers can freely choose to make the inferences they rationally *ought* to make; they can also freely fall short of inferring as they rationally ought to, and thereby freely commit inferential *errors*; and in either case, they are cognitively *responsible* for their inferences.

CKMI differs substantially from other theories of inference currently on offer, first, in its being robustly *mentalistic* about the metaphysics of inference, and neither platonistic nor psychologistic; second, in its being robustly *reasons-internalist* about the rational normativity of inference, and neither emotivist nor instrumentalist; third, in its being robustly *practical* about the justification of inference, although *non-*

voluntaristically practical, and neither noncognitivist nor holist nor inferentialist; and fourth, in its being robustly *cognitivist* and *phenomenological* about the mechanism of inference, and neither functionalist nor separatist.

The Metaphysics of Inference: Transcendental Mentalism, and Neither Psychologism nor Platonism

As I noted at the beginning, an inference in the minimal sense is a cognitive process of a certain kind. More precisely, however, the cognitive process of inference is an *intentional* or representationally *object-directed* or *propositional-directed* process, with intrinsic "aboutness." The metaphysics of inference is therefore a subspecies of the metaphysics of intentionality.

Psychologism about the metaphysics of inference says that inferential facts and inferential laws are fully *explicable* by the natural sciences together with the formal sciences, including mathematics, and therefore explanatorily *reducible* to physical, chemical, or biological facts, plus their mathematical properties.[3]

The basic problems with Psychologism about the metaphysics of inference are that Psychologism cannot account for (i) the manifest objectivity, (ii) the manifest necessity, and (iii) the manifest apriority of inferential facts. One could try to defend Psychologism by trying to reject *the very ideas* of the objectivity, necessity, and apriority of logic, but it is hard to see how one could do so without relying on deductive, inductive, and abductive principles that are themselves tacitly assumed to be objective, necessary, and a priori, without self-stultification.

Platonism about the metaphysics of inference says that inferential facts and inferential laws are *non-natural* in the strong sense of being abstract, non-spatiotemporal, nonexperiential, and noncontingent.[4]

The basic problems with Platonism about the metaphysics of inference are (i) that the non-spatiotemporality and causal inertness of Platonic facts and objects are clearly incompatible with the causal triggering of all human knowledge (a.k.a. "Benacerraf's Dilemma"),[5] and (ii) Platonism cannot explain how the truth-making connection between its non-spatiotemporal, acausal truth makers and the truth of inferential propositions and inferential beliefs is anything other than a massive coincidence (this is what I will call "the Problem of Cognitive-Semantic Luck").[6]

By sharp contrast to Psychologism and Platonism alike about the metaphysics of inference, according to CKMI, the mentalistic metaphysics of inference are those of what I call "weak or counterfactual transcendental idealism," or WCTI. Now, in a nutshell, WCTI about the metaphysics of inference says that, first, necessarily, inferential facts are also facts about rational animal minds whose cognition necessarily begins in causally triggered sensory experience but without either its content or its form being either reducible to or strictly determined by causally triggered experience; second, necessarily, inferential facts in the manifest natural world structurally conform to the nonempirical or a priori forms of those mentalistic facts but without being identical to those forms of mentalistic facts; and third, necessarily, if inferential facts exist, then if there were to be rational human minds, they would be able to cognize those worldly inferential facts directly, at least to some extent.[7]

It follows from these three theses that, according to CKMI, an inference is a naturalistically irreducible cognitive process in rational animal agents or persons, whose cognition always begins in causally triggered sensory experience *but is strictly underdetermined by that or any other actual or possible causal sensory triggering*, such that there is necessarily a nonaccidental or intrinsic truth-making relation between the inferential facts in the manifest world, on the one hand, and the truth of inferential propositions and inferential beliefs cognized by those rational animals agents or persons, on the other. This view both neatly avoids Benacerraf's Dilemma and also solves the Problem of Cognitive-Semantic Luck.

THE RATIONAL NORMATIVITY OF INFERENCE: SELF-TRANSCENDING SECOND-ORDER CARING FOR THE SAKE OF THE SUMMUM BONUM OF REASONING, AND NEITHER EMOTIVISM NOR INSTRUMENTALISM

Issues concerning the goal or purpose of inference are issues about the *normativity* of inference. Normativity, in turn, has specifically to do with motivation and action guidance, and with the ideals, standards, rules, principles, and laws governing intentional choices, actions, procedures, and practices.

Emotivism about the normativity of inference says that the evaluative content of inferences is not itself truth-apt, or truth-evaluable, and consists instead exclusively in our pro attitudes and contra attitudes toward inferences, and is strictly determined by those attitudes.

The basic problem with Emotivism about the normativity of inference is that it posits pro attitudes or contra attitudes that are essentially unconstrained by rational norms of consistency, truth, logical consequence, or soundness: in effect, *anything goes*, provided that everyone shares the same feelings. So the problem is antirational arbitrariness. A particularly pointed and reflexive version of the problem of antirational arbitrariness arises when one applies Emotivism to one's *own* inferential practices from the outside in: Do I *really* think that the cogency of my *own* inferences should be held hostage to arbitrary pro attitudes or contra attitudes?

Instrumentalism (a.k.a. "pragmatism") about the normativity of inference says that the evaluative content of inferences consists exclusively in and is strictly determined by the good or bad results, from the standpoint of human interests in either a narrowly self-oriented or a larger social sense, that are produced by inferences.

The basic problem with Instrumentalism about the normativity of inference is that it allows for the partial or total sacrifice of consistency, truth, logical consequence, and soundness if good consequences will ensue or bad consequences are avoided: in effect, *anything goes*, provided that good results are produced and bad consequences avoided from the standpoint of human interests in either a narrowly self-oriented or larger social sense. So, again, the problem is antirational arbitrariness. As with Emotivism, a particularly pointed and reflexive version of the problem of antirational arbitrariness arises when one applies Instrumentalism to one's *own* inferential practices from the outside in: Do I *really* think that the cogency of my *own* inferences should be held hostage to the mere production of good or bad results?

By sharp contrast to Emotivism and Instrumentalism alike about the normativity of inference, according to CKMI, an inference is aimed at the classical soundness of an argument (soundness = true premises and semantic consequence or validity, thereby guaranteeing the truth of the conclusion) together with authentic knowledge (authentic knowledge = justified true belief, such that there is an intrinsic connection between the evidence that justifies belief and the truth maker of the propositional content of that belief) of its conclusion, as the highest or supreme good (summum bonum) of reasoning, but is also strictly constrained by minimal consistency (minimal consistency = not every proposition or statement is both true and false), in such a way that it is underdetermined by any instrumental reasons that may also support it.

Now *Internalism* about reasons grounds motivation and action guidance on desire-based conation and evaluation.[8] In this way, according to CKMI, the normativity of inference involves a specifically *Kantian* version of reasons-internalism that posits an innate conative capacity to desire self-transcendence, and in particular an innate capacity for having second-order desires to be moved by effective first-order desires that are nonegoistic, nonselfish, nonhedonistic, and non-consequentialist, according to and for the sake of the summum bonum of reasoning in particular and the summum bonum of morality in general.[9] In short, the theory of inference properly falls under what Kant calls *the metaphysics of morals*.

The Justification of Inference: Categorical Legitimation, and Neither Non-Cognitivism, nor Holism, nor Inferentialism

The justification of belief, choice, or action is appealing to (what purport to be) sufficient reasons for holding some belief, for heeding or following some principle, for making some choice, or for carrying out some action.

A fundamental problem for any attempt to justify inference is that some or all of the specific deductive, inductive, or abductive inferential principles that are being justified must also be presupposed and used in the justification of those very principles. So, it seems, either the inferential principles are unjustified or else the purported justification fails because it is viciously circular.

One way out of this "logocentric predicament"[10] with respect to inference is to hold that the inferential principles have what Hartry Field calls "default reasonableness," in that we are *rationally entitled* to presuppose and use them in the absence of any sufficient reason not to.[11] So the inferential principles do not *need* to be justified.

The entirely reasonable question then arises, What is *the ground or source* of this nonjustificatory rational entitlement?

Field himself holds that the nonjustificatory default-reasonable entitlement to inferential principles does not require a further ground or source, that there is no deeper fact of the matter, and that the entitlement merely reflects our strong pro attitudes toward the inferential practices we are already engaged in. That is the *noncognitivist* (a.k.a. "nonfactualist") strategy.

Others hold that we are default-reasonably entitled to the presupposition and use of these inferential principles by the smooth fit or "reflective equilibrium" that gradually emerges over time between our own inferences insofar as they are guided by these principles, our intersubjective agreement about them, and other judgments about the world made by ourselves and others.[12] That is the *holist* strategy.

And still others hold that the concepts actually deployed in the inferences guided by these principles themselves give rise to a priori truths essentially involving these concepts, hence we are semantically and default-reasonably entitled to the presupposition and use of these principles.[13] That is the *inferentialist* strategy.

The main problem with all three strategies is that there seems to be no essential connection between *rational entitlement* and either pro attitudes, or coherence, or inferentialist semantics. For there could clearly be pro attitudes, coherence, and inferentialist semantics in the *absence* of the objectivity, necessity, and apriority of these inferential principles.

By sharp contrast to Non-Cognitivism, Holism, and Inferentialism alike about the justification of inference, according to CKMI, an inference is inherently governed by categorically normative logical laws of deduction, induction, or abduction. The justification of these specific inferential principles then flows directly from rational obligations: Because you are a rational human animal, you categorically *ought* to reason according to these principles. Hence you have an overriding practical reason for carrying out that inference according to that inferential principle. The ground or source of obligation, in turn, is rational human nature and its absolute nondenumerable intrinsic value (a.k.a. "dignity") and, correspondingly, the *specific constitution* of our nature, namely, our innate capacities for practical and theoretical reason. Furthermore, if WCTI is also true, then the objectivity, necessity, and apriority of the specific inferential principles is necessarily reflected in the manifest world itself.

Given its robustly practical approach to the justification of inference, the CKMI account of the justification of deductive, inductive, and abductive inference is quite similar to, and very much in the same spirit as, what David Enoch and Joshua Schechter somewhat misleadingly call "the pragmatic account" of justification—because it involves a direct appeal to the overriding value of the ends and principles of human rationality, over and above any merely instrumental motivation—according to which

(i)   there are certain projects that are rationally required for thinkers like us and thereby *rationally obligatory* for thinkers like us, and
(ii) we are epistemically justified in employing a basic belief-forming method that is indispensable for successfully engaging in one or another of these rationally obligatory projects.[14]

The basic and important difference between the CKMI account and the so-called pragmatic account, however, is that the CKMI account is explicitly grounded in a Kantian "metaphysics of morals," and also fully committed to WCTI, as well as to transcendental mentalism and—as I argue in the next section—cognitive phenomenology. So the CKMI account, in effect, *includes* the so-called pragmatic account and situates it within a much broader and deeper epistemological and metaphysical framework.

THE MECHANISM OF INFERENCE: COGNITIVE PHENOMENOLOGY WITHOUT FUNCTIONALISM OR SEPARATISM

An inference in the minimal sense, as I spelled it out in the opening discussion, is a certain kind of cognitive process. But what is the *mecha-*

nism of the cognitive process of inference: that is, how does inference *actually happen*? A "mechanism" in the sense I mean here is simply an ordered spatiotemporal process with causal efficacy, perhaps goal-directed or teleological, or perhaps not. Consequently, I do not mean to imply that this ordered causally efficacious spatiotemporal process has to be *mechanical* or *mechanistic* or in some narrower, non-teleological sense of the notion of a mechanism—for example, Turing computability—although that narrower sense is not ruled out by my use of this notion either.

Is the mechanism of inference *naturalizable*, in the sense that it is fully explicable by the natural sciences together with mathematics, in the way that a digital computer (hardware) and its program (software) are both fully explicable by the natural sciences together with mathematics? Let us call the thesis that the mechanism of inference is naturalizable in essentially the same way that computers are naturalizable *Functionalism* about the mechanism of inference. The main problems with Functionalism about the mechanism of inference are that either

(i)   it is *reductively* naturalist and a version of Psychologism, and thereby subject to the basic problems of Psychologism, or else

(ii) it is *nonreductively naturalist*, but then inference has no causal powers of its own to produce beliefs or intentional actions because this production power is causally and explanatorily *excluded* by the causal powers of its physical underpinnings,[15] hence inference is *epiphenomenal*, which seems clearly false.

For example, I believe that if *P* then *Q*, & *P*; so I believe that *Q*. It seems to me clear that nothing other than *my intentional act of inference itself* causally produced that belief,[16] for otherwise I would not have been the agential source of *that inference*, and consequently I could not have been the agential source of *that belief*. On the contrary, something or someone else would have been the causal source of that inference and that belief instead, so it would have been out of my hands and *not up-to-me*, and thus not truly either *my* inference or *my* belief.[17]

And is the mechanism of inference intentional or representational without necessarily being phenomenally conscious? Let us call the thesis that the mechanism of inference is intentional or representational without necessarily being phenomenally conscious *Separatism* about the mechanism of inference.[18] More specifically, according to Separatism about the mechanism of inference, the intentional or representational content of inference is logically and metaphysically distinct from, and also independently variable in its specific character with respect to, any phenomenal content that is associated with inference. Therefore, not only can the intentional or representational content of inference vary unrestrictedly its specific character with respect to the phenomenal content of inference, but also the intentional or representational content of inference can even occur altogether without *any* phenomenal content, as in "nonconscious inference" or inferential "zombiehood."

The main problem with Separatism about inference mechanisms is that the normativity of inference clearly *requires* both consciousness and consciously free willing—otherwise it cannot be "in the space of reasons" and is merely in the space of causes and brute valueless facts. Randomly variable specific characters simply cannot be normative specific characters, because normativity is a certain special kind of regularity; and zombies do not have norms, because, by hypothesis, zombies cannot *care* about anything, and also because they are naturally determined either by a distal or local causal source of choice and action in such a way that they cannot be agential sources and so cannot be free. So if Separatism with respect to inference mechanisms is true, then the normativity of inference, and especially the *categorical* normativity of inference, but also even the *instrumental* normativity of inference, cannot be explained.

According to CKMI, an inference is an intentional process that is internally and/or externally consciously represented linguistically, with more or less clear and distinct inferential phenomenology, and is carried out by means of a prereflectively conscious or self-conscious free choice of the will, under categorically normative metalogical laws and specific inferential principles, for the sake of classical soundness and minimal consistency. So the mechanism of inference is freely willed conscious linguistic cognition, inherently constrained by a special logico-practical *ought*. Or in other words, as I put it right at the beginning of this essay, inference is essentially *an act of cognitive free agency*. As I also mentioned, this view does not imply voluntarism about inference but also adequately explains our cognitive responsibility for the inferences we make.

CONCLUSION

If I am correct, then Contemporary Kantian Moralism about Inference, or CKMI, outperforms all the relevant competing theories of the nature of inference along all the basic dimensions of that problem. So I conclude, by abduction, that CKMI is true.

That CKMI requires a weak form of transcendental idealism should not be regarded as cause for philosophical alarm. For weak or counterfactual transcendental idealism, or WCTI, is not *scary* idealism—that is, it is not either *subjective* or Berkeleyan idealism, according to which only individual minds and the contents of such minds exist, or absolute or Hegelian idealism, according to which reality is just ideal rationality, both of which seem highly implausible. All WCTI says, at bottom, is that fundamental mental properties—for example, those instantiated in your conscious understanding of this essay—are essentially co-basic in nature with fundamental physical properties. Nature is not only essentially physical; it is also essentially *alive, purposive, and mental.* This is *not* to say that *every* part of nature is *actually* alive, purposive, conscious, caring, desiring, thinking, or rational but rather only to say *some* parts of nature are *actually* alive, purposive, conscious, caring, desiring, thinking, and rational (i.e., *we* are), and therefore that, necessarily, nature as a whole always inherently included within itself, from the Big Bang forward, the metaphysical ground of the *potentiality* of the actual existence of living, purposive, conscious, caring, desiring, thinking, and/or rational animals. Call that thesis *liberal naturalism.*[19] This is *natural* idealism, not scary idealism.

NOTES

1. For the purposes of this essay, I won't attempt to define deduction, induction, or abduction. See, e.g., S. Shapiro, "Classical Logic," in *The Stanford Encyclopedia of Philosophy (Winter 2009 Edition),* ed. E. N. Zalta, available at http://plato.stanford.edu/archives/win2009/entries/logic-classical/;

J. Hawthorne, "Inductive Logic," in *The Stanford Encyclopedia of Philosophy (Winter 2011 Edition)*, http://plato.stanford.edu/archives/win2009/entries /logic-inductive/; and I. Douven, "Abduction," in *The Stanford Encyclopedia of Philosophy (Spring 2011 Edition)*, ed. E. N. Zalta, available at http://plato .stanford.edu/archives/spr2011/entries/abduction/.

2. As always, the devil is in the "other things being equal" (a.k.a. ceteris paribus) clause. I won't attempt to spell it out here, but certainly special allowances would have to be made for the distinction between monotonic (= adding premises cannot reduce the set of logical consequences of the original set of premises) and nonmonotonic (= adding premises can reduce the set of logical consequences of the original set) reasoning, etc.

3. See R. Hanna, *Rationality and Logic* (Cambridge, MA: MIT Press, 2006), chap. 1.

4. For a modern version of Platonism, see B. Russell, *The Problems of Philosophy* (Oxford: Oxford University Press, [1912] 1980), esp. chaps. 7–11.

5. See P. Benacerraf, "Mathematical Truth," *Journal of Philosophy* 70 (1973): 661–79; Hanna, *Rationality and Logic*, chap. 6; and R. Hanna, *Cognition, Content, and the A Priori* (Oxford: Oxford University Press, forthcoming), chaps. 6–8.

6. The explicit recognition of this problem goes back to Kant—see, e.g., Kant's famous letter to Marcus Herz of 21 February 1771; and also the *Critique of Pure Reason* Bxv–xviii and B166–68. But it has also been recently rediscovered by Hartry Field, in connection with the Benacerraf Dilemma, in "Recent Debates about the A Priori," in *Oxford Studies in Epistemology*, ed. T. Szábo Gendler and J. Hawthorne (Oxford: Oxford University Press, 2005), 69–88.

7. For a more explicit formulation and defense of WCTI, see Hanna, *Cognition, Content, and the A Priori*, sec. 7.3.

8. See, e.g., B. Williams, "Internal and External Reasons," in *Moral Luck* (Cambridge: Cambridge University Press, 1981), 101–13.

9. See also Hanna, *Rationality and Logic*, chap.7; R. Hanna and M. Maiese, *Embodied Minds in Action* (Oxford: Oxford University Press, 2009), sec. 3.4; and Hanna, *Cognition, Content, and the A Priori*, chap. 5.

10. See Hanna, *Rationality and Logic*, chap. 3.

11. H. Field, "Apriority as an Evaluative Notion," in *New Essays on the A Priori*, ed. P. Boghossian and C. Peacocke (Oxford: Clarendon Press, 2000), 117–49.

12. See, e.g., N. Goodman, "The New Riddle of Induction," in *Fact, Forecast, and Fiction*, 4th ed. (Cambridge, MA: Harvard University Press, 1983), 59–83; and J. Rawls, *A Theory of Justice* (Cambridge, MA: Harvard University Press, 1971).

13. See, e.g., P. Boghossian, "Knowledge of Logic," in Boghossian and Peacocke, *New Essays on the A Priori*, 229–54; and C. Peacocke, "Explaining the A Priori: The Programme of Moderate Rationalism," in Boghossian and Peacocke, *New Essays on the A Priori*, 255–85.

14. See, e.g., D. Enoch and J. Shechter, "Meaning and Justification: The Case of Modus Ponens," *Noûs* 40 (2006): 687–715; and D. Enoch and J. Schechter, "How Are Basic Belief-Forming Methods Justified?," *Philosophy and Phenomenological Research* 76 (2008): 547–79.

15. See J. Kim, *Supervenience and Mind* (Cambridge: Cambridge University Press, 1993), esp. chaps. 13, 14, and 17; J. Kim, *Physicalism, or Something Near Enough* (Princeton: Princeton University Press, 2005), esp. chaps. 1 and 2; and also J. Kim, *Philosophy of Mind*, 3rd ed. (Boulder, CO: Westview Press, 2011), chap. 7.

16. See also R. Wedgwood, "The Normative Force of Reasoning," *Noûs* 40 (2006): 660–86. Wedgwood's nonreductive physicalist causal theory of inferential basic intentional action is, as regards its intentional-action-oriented and robustly normative approach to reasoning, similar to the CKMI account. But Wedgwood's theory also falls short of CKMI in two other important respects: first, classical causal theories of action, no matter how sophisticated, cannot ultimately solve the deviant causal chains problem; and second, nonreductive physicalism, no matter how sophisticated, cannot ultimately avoid the causal-explanatory exclusion problem and epiphenomenalism. See Hanna and Maiese, *Embodied Minds in Action*, esp. chaps. 3, 4, 6, and 7.

17. The argument strategy I have just used is a version of what, in the contemporary debate about free will, is known as "source incompatibilism."

18. On Separatism vs. Anti-Separatism, see T. Horgan and J. Tienson, "The Intentionality of Phenomenology and the Phenomenology of Intentionality," in *Philosophy of Mind: Classical and Contemporary Readings*, ed. D. Chalmers (Oxford: Oxford University Press, 2002), 520–33.

19. See, e.g., G. Rosenberg, *A Place for Consciousness* (Oxford: Oxford University Press, 2005); Hanna and Maise, *Embodied Minds in Action*, esp. 11 and 312–13; R. Hanna, *Kant, Science, and Human Nature* (Oxford: Clarendon Press, 2005), esp. 16–17, 310–11; T. Nagel, *Mind and Cosmos* (Oxford: Oxford University Press, 2012); and R. Hanna, "Nagel & Me: Beyond the Scientific Conception of the World" (unpublished MS), available at http://academia.edu/3769311/Nagel_and_Me_Beyond_the_Scientific_Conception_of_the_World.

CHAPTER FOUR

Speculation and Narration in Mathematics

———

LAURENT LAFFORGUE

The inspiration for the topic of this essay came from two pages by the young French philosopher Fabrice Hadjadj, published in a recent book of interviews, *L'Héritage et la promesse* (Legacy and Promise).[1] Asked about the key question on the articulation between theology and sciences, Hadjadj replied:

> If science seems to us so far removed from faith, it is not so much because of the supposedly insurmountable obstacle between experiment and faith, as the fact that 'truth', as most often represented by sciences, blanks out the proper noun, rejects actual existence, ignores the relationship. Truth tends to be thought of as seeing, and not living. Knowing truth is understood as being in the position of a spectator dominating his object. In that sense, contemporary technology, television, the virtual world, would all appear to emanate from this concept of truth, where seeing takes over from living. You could say that this is a concept of truth that is not nuptial but pornographic: we want to see love made, possibly make love, but not live it. For truth to be nuptial, it needs to resemble an embrace: I must give up being an invulnerable spectator to enter into a relationship with someone.

Christ's extraordinary words to Thomas, "I am the way, the truth and the life" (John 14:6), do indeed reveal the fact that "truth will not be found in general terms, in what could be called anonymous clauses; no, Truth is a person, with his uniqueness, with a proper Name of which Peter says: 'there is no other name under heaven given to mankind by which we must be saved'" (Acts 4:12).

Which is why, says Hadjadj, "in theology, exploring truth always requires both a speculative and a narrative approach, it has elements of both science and biography. Yet, for us, biography and science have been separated, speculation and narration have been perceived as opposites."

The intuition we have of the existence of truth and of its unity therefore prompts us to think of sciences from the point of view offered by Hadjadj: are they purely speculative and in accordance with the way we currently represent them, or are they also narrative and therefore closer than is usually acknowledged to the model of the Revelation? Are they purely theoretical—that is, etymologically, visual—or are they also life experiences? Are they completely impersonal, or do they also include at least in part relationships with people?

It seems perfectly natural to consider mathematics, as it is in the first analysis seemingly the most speculative among the sciences, the most theoretical and the most impersonal of all, as well as one that provides the models for modern physics and, to a lesser extent, to other sciences. The mathematician that I am therefore believes it quite justifiable for me to speak in front of philosophers and representatives from other fields of learning and—because that is the crux of the matter—address the link between this unique science and truth.

Let us first ask ourselves what thoughts would go through the mind of a person who was a complete stranger to mathematics and who, for the first time in his life, was invited to visit a university department or research center dedicated to this discipline.

The first thought to take hold of his mind after this visit would surely be that, in a mathematics center, there is "nothing to see": in other words, there is no spectacular experimentation equipment, no out of the ordinary object that might spark some curiosity or interest, just corridors, offices, rooms, and amphitheaters furnished only with chairs, tables and seats, chalkboards or sometimes wipe boards, the sort of computers and keyboards that you see everywhere nowadays, books stacked in shelves, a few printers and photocopiers, some printed and some blank paper, and pens.

Thinking about it a little more, the visitor might also reflect that, as well as being very common and uninteresting, the objects seen are few. In comparison with places of social activity—shops, transportation hubs, industry, construction, craft, hospitals, police stations, the military—places of mathematics would seem to comprise an unusually far higher proportion of people to material objects. Only teaching places—schools and high schools—and those other places of abstract and speculative activity—banks and insurance companies—seem to offer a similar appearance: everyday objects, few of them in fact, and proportionally many people.

It is not just the case that places of mathematics *look like* teaching places: they *are*, mostly. Our visitor could attend lectures, and if he did, would first and foremost be struck by the fact that he understood nothing, that all the sentences were woven with words the meaning of which escapes him, or more intriguingly still, words that are familiar in the common language but that become incomprehensible in the context of the sentences spoken or written on the board. He could also attend seminars, that is, sessions similar to lectures, but where, as he could see, mathematicians would be teaching other mathematicians, and not students, another cause for surprise and questions.

If, for want of anything interesting to look at, the visitor tried to catch the people who inhabit places of mathematics in all their activities, he could also overhear informal conversations among mathematicians—and find then, not perhaps without feeling a degree of terror, that it seems natural for these people to speak in a casual way with words no less obscure than those used in lectures and seminar presentations. He could also observe many people in offices busy reading—reading books as well as printed texts or texts bound into what these people quaintly call journal fascicules (in French, the same word is used for a journal as for a newspaper)—or busy writing on a keyboard or with a pen. In the last instance, he could catch a few people apparently lost in thoughts more mysterious than everything else.

In short, the visitor would conclude that places of mathematics are inhabited mainly by people who are busy talking and listening in large and small groups, or reading, writing, and thinking alone.

So, are mathematicians related to writers, journalists, orators, or activists, who commit to the cause presented in the talks they hear, or to friends putting the world to rights, chatting over a café counter?

To attempt a reply to these questions, there is no other way than to explore the contents of mathematicians' lectures, presentations, conversations, journals, and books. What are they in fact talking about in their prolific speech and writing, what are they expressing to one another, and what are they expressing to themselves when they think?

For this reason, our visitor would need to venture into opening articles and books written and read by mathematicians. Even if not one word made sense, he would be struck by the extremely structured and organized appearance the texts display: they are broken down into parts, chapters, paragraphs, and subparagraphs, each with a title or at the very least a sequencing and identification number. In addition, they comprise clearly identified and themselves numbered statements, with names such as "definition," "lemma," "proposition," "theorem," together with well-framed expositions introduced with words like "notation," "demonstration," "remark," and so on. The visitor would also notice that these texts are riddled with internal and external references and that these references obey a simple rule: they refer practically always to parts of the text situated above, that is, read beforehand, and to articles or books published previously.

Our mathematics visitor would therefore be led to observe that each mathematical text is like a step on a journey, or a path, as if it told a story in chronological order and, what is more, as if the specific story it appears to tell were part of a general step in mathematical science and in the history of that onward march.

However, the visitor would necessarily make a comment that seems to contradict the previous one: whereas any text is structured like a story and is explicitly linked to the wider story that mathematics as a whole appears to form, it is written in the present tense. As if it were a story without events, or rather a story telling events outside or beyond time.

Our visitor would then understand that mathematical texts belong to the writing and reading time frame, as well as to the publications time frame, but that the temporal structure of their neatly ordered storytelling mirrors the intemporal structure of what they are telling the story about. The chain of logical implications that weaves the fabric of deductive reasoning is displayed in the layers of linear reading over time and in carefully dated publications.

Through the linear progression of single stories they each expound, and in the vast story they all make up together, mathematical texts reveal logical implications as if there were causes and effects linked over time, as if logic were a form of the principle of causality, as if logical and structural structures identified one another. But the use of the present tense in the texts' verbs means that, in its very essence, mathematical logic does not depend on time.

And yet our visitor could wonder, any mathematical text is well and truly anchored in time: it not only includes a logical structure in the time frame of a story; it is itself included in the time frame of mankind as a moment and stage in the long history of the science it belongs to. Most concepts, results, and methods that are part of it or that make it possible are borrowed from other articles and books, or from other mathematicians, long gone or contemporaries. Any mathematical text is both a story, that is, a temporal form, of an intemporal mathematical story and the hinge—between past and present—of the history of mathematical science in its own time frame. This duality in the identity of mathematical texts would in fact be particularly manifest in our visitor's eyes in the fact that very many mathematicians' names are used to designate mathematical objects and results, which is another way of linking the intemporal substance of mathematics to their history made by mankind.

Our observant visitor could also discover that mathematical texts veer between, on the one hand, the use of prior methods, concepts, and results in new analyses in order to solve problems set since a specific time and, on the other, the development of new methods, the introduction of new concepts, the exploration of new territories, the formulation of new statements the demonstration of which follows or are suggested as conjectures. Each of these two models could then appear to be both narrative and speculative, but in reverse: the model using established theories in new analyses to prove well-known conjectures fits more easily in the history of mathematics, in the illustration, summary, and, in a way, the renewed telling of one of its pages. It is however more speculative from the point of view of the substance of mathematics, as it consists in solving given problems by working back in the chain of their causes, to find the implications that derive from them. On the contrary, the model of discovery and development of new theories is more speculative from the point of view of mathematical history, as it equates to going back to the source of ancient theories so that, from those sources, another path is followed, but more narrative from the point of view of mathematics, as it flows down the causal chain, just as water flows down a riverbed.

Mathematical texts that expound or introduce a theory are indeed similar to narratives, more specifically, to travel tales. The entirely discursive nature of speech or writing prevents an entire theory from being presented in one scene: its paths need to be traveled slowly, its crossroads negotiated, its towns, lands, and buildings need to be visited one by one.

Our still uninitiated visitor could finally ask himself if mathematical texts comprise events in the stories they unfold. He would conclude that, from the history of mathematics angle, this is certainly the case: the solution to an old problem or the emergence of a new concept represents historical events. But, from the substance of mathematics angle, do events exist? If it is true that mathematics are outside of time, can anything happen there? Our visitor would doubtless avoid answering such a strange question too quickly. He would simply note that when mathematicians talk through this or that theory or demonstration they often use such expressions as "Here is where something happens." As if striking statements, an unexpected simplification, a computation result, gave these mathematicians the feeling they were moving from one landscape to another, opening a new vista.

But if it is true that mathematicians' texts and speeches, each individually and all together, have the form of narratives, our visitor might well ask for whom are mathematicians telling their stories?

However paradoxical it may seem, given the manifestly unentertaining nature of these texts and the difficulty of understanding them, an objective fact would immediately spring to our visitor's mind: lectures are given so that students can follow them, seminar presentations are made for colleagues to listen to them, conversations are held so that mathematicians can enter into a dialogue with one another, articles are written to be published, and, finally, journals and specialized books are commercialized so that they can be bought—especially by university libraries—and read by mathematicians.

Our visitor would then ask what inclines mathematicians to teach students, give presentations for the attention of their colleagues or speak to them informally, to write articles or books intended for publication. He would then learn that what those institutions which employ mathematicians expect from them is that they give mathematics lectures and presentations and publish articles or books in exchange for the means of subsistence provided to them. This information would, however, doubtless only displace the question in his mind, and make him address those formative years, when longing to become a mathematician appears and takes shape: why would young people ever engage in careers of which the objective reality for them will consist of speaking to be listened to and writing to be read? It is obvious that this fact echoes far deeper human aspirations that dwell within them. So what can these aspirations be?

Our visitor could first recognize in most researchers in mathematics—as in all academic fields—the avatar of a desire, highly visible in children and probably still present in adults, although in a more concealed manner: the desire to obtain confirmation from others, to draw their attention, and to receive their approval of what they do, which is felt in part to be approval of who they are. In other words, the desire to be loved, more or less corrupted and confused by the tenacious illusion that it is possible to conquer love by merit. Young children seek their parents' approval of what they do every day; to grow, they need to feel their parents' benevolent and supportive gaze on them. Later and in parallel, the desire to receive positive judgments from their teachers and professors represents one of students' most powerful reasons for working diligently. Our visitor, discovering the world of mathematics, would not fail to liken this well-known characteristic of the human heart to the importance afforded to small and great honors in university life and the prestige attached to certain places, names, institutions, and journals, and so on.

Acknowledging this could lead our visitor to interpreting the obligation, which mathematicians and other academic researchers have placed upon themselves, to try to be listened to and read, as a sign of immaturity. Unless he realized that another very deep human longing dwelled in researchers side by side with the previous one, and in the purest hearts, dominated it: the longing to share. In other words, the need to offer others a form of love, by sharing with them objectively precious things, which we possess or hope to be able to discover and make known. People know deep in their hearts that giving brings more happiness than receiving. For mathematicians, there is no other possible gift than speech, and therefore, our visitor would think, no true happiness is possible unless the narrative content of mathematics is liable to be of considerable value. Mathematicians necessarily compose their articles and books—that is, the tales of their mathematical journeys—thinking that the regions these tales describe are beautiful and worthy of being known and visited by others. They are propelled by their desire to make known and loved their mathematics pathways and landscapes, the wealth and splendor of which they discover; in the same way are we happy to invite friends to a beloved country and try to share with them all the knowledge that this country gives us.

But our visitor would soon observe that the efforts deployed by mathematicians to share with others the truth and beauty they discover encounter obstacles and disappointments similar to those we suffer from when we invite dear friends to a familiar region, where everything speaks to our hearts but not to theirs. Nowadays especially, mathematicians seem to be moving away from one another at great speed, and whereas the number of published articles and books never ceases to increase, that of actual readers of almost all these articles and books is undoubtedly constantly decreasing.

Mathematicians expound their narratives in the hope of sharing, that is, of experiencing a form of love with their human brethren through mathematics; but most will know the secret misery of the fruit of their mind's labor awakening no particular interest, as if they were talking and writing in a desert without ears or eyes. Even the most highly regarded mathematicians, those whose presentations and writings are awaited, listened to, and read, generating other work, are not sheltered from self-doubt and despair; this can arise if they become conscious that, in the tokens of respect and admiration they are surrounded by, fascination for social glory and strength, or even jealousy, dominates and supplants the shared love for truth.

Our visitor could also ask mathematicians the difficult question of whether they prefer to read or write mathematics. Judging by the ever increasing flow of articles sent to the editorial boards of journals and by the matching increasing difficulty of finding reviewers for the articles submitted, our visitor would probably hear most mathematicians reply that they prefer to write mathematics. And this is humanly quite normal, the visitor would reflect, as there is more joy in giving than in receiving.

This clearly identified fact would then bring the visitor to ask himself whether writing a mathematical narrative intended to be read is indeed a form of gift to other mathematicians, if the latter do not in fact appear to be very interested in reading them. And if writing mathematical narratives represents a gift of questionable value to others, then why write?

Perhaps to write to one's self?

Our visitor would observe in any case that, as in any text, mathematical texts are prepared and drafted by their author before being read by others: at least chronologically, writing precedes reading, with the result that a mathematician who writes has no other witness than the narrative itself. This general nature of writing is particularly strongly marked in mathematics, because, when compared to other sciences, time flows in it slowly: the time taken to craft books and articles is measured in months, even years, and articles are generally published long after they have been submitted to a specialized journal. Today most articles are made available beforehand on the web; they are easier to download, but time is still needed to read them, and most are probably never read.

If he were to ask mathematicians, our visitor would in fact learn that when they write up their work mathematicians are not thinking about their future readers or anybody. They even forget themselves. They think of nothing but the narrative, from which they are trying, through their writing, to reveal in their minds the clearest possible picture. A mathematical narrative is like a travel story in which, in fact, the journey consists of the narrative itself, the attentive traveler is its author, and the pen, pencil, or keyboard are both instruments of the tale and instruments of the journey featured in the story. The paper or screen, a proxy for paper, is an ocean, and the pen or keyboard, the stereotyped form of a pen, is a boat on that ocean.

But if it is true that mathematicians first *themselves* tell their tales *for* themselves, our visitor could ask, what is the point of this?

The question deserves all the more to be asked that mathematical writing requires considerable efforts of concentration and attention, at the very limits of the possibilities offered by the human mind. Our visitor might then reflect that telling one's self a story is only of true value if it is apparent that the story is not one's own, in other words, that the story is inspired. The term *inspiration* is often used by widely differing mathematicians.

But most go no further. They talk of inspiration, without the idea entering their mind that it could come from an unknown person or author, from God, whose marvels every mathematician would praise and celebrate in writing and in speech.

Some mathematicians even say in the same breath that, to write mathematics, hearing needs to be finely tuned to the subtle, and very discreet, almost inaudible voice of mathematical truths that are waiting to be told, to receive form in language; most, however, do not think that anyone is speaking, and yet, in laying down on paper their mathematical narratives, they show that they are paying attention to a certain kind of words from this someone and that they find their only joy in becoming servants to these words, following them as faithfully as they can.

Translation by Hélène Wilkinson,
Institut des Hautes Études Scientifiques

NOTE

1. Mgr. Dominique Rey and Fabrice Hadjadj, *L'Héritage et la promesse* (n.p.: Éditions RCF Méditerranée, 2011).

PART III

Explanation in the Natural Sciences

CHAPTER FIVE

A Molecular Glimpse of How Mother Nature Can Regulate Our Being

THOMAS NOWAK

The concept of truth has been a philosophical topic of discussion and study for centuries. Truth can be attributed to various forms of questions, focus, and presentations that include truth emanating from reason, rhetoric, and religion. In these cases, "truth" arises from what might be logic, argument, or beliefs dictated by a formal religious conviction. Truth in the arena of science comes from different sources; those of research, observation, and discovery [1]. Even in this venue, the concept of truth has various meanings. With this in mind, two different types of truth are defined, objective truth and subjective truth. Objective truth is relatively easy to recognize; it appears absolute. If someone walks into the room and the light is on, we all recognize that is true. You are drinking coffee from a cup. It is clearly a fact. Subjective truth is much less distinct. It is how we perceive ideas, beliefs, and concepts. In general, subjective truth emanates from our perception based on arguments, prejudice, feelings, logic, and whatever means we use to foster our belief that our ideas are correct. Truth as "commonsense knowledge" is an example of subjective truth. It is rarely proven but often believed. Our individual belief in a political philosophy is subjective truth. In the Christian religion, one believes in the virgin birth. We cannot prove this to be true, but it is inherent in the belief. This *truth* or concept has been passed on through tradition over the centuries. Many would believe that a particular actor or actress is good-looking. Again, this is clearly subjective.

In science, objective truth normally takes the form of observation and experimental data. Objective truth is usually obtained by information collected: the observation of how fast a process occurs, the formation of a precipitate, the measurement of how tightly a drug binds to a receptor, the nuclear magnetic resonance (NMR) spectrum of a synthesized compound, and so on. The validity of experimental data is a critical part of science, and its *truth* or correctness is fundamental to attempting to answer the scientific question addressed. The basis of scientific ethics requires a clear description of experimental procedures and a correct representation of the data collected. This information, objective truth, is fundamental to the understanding of the mysteries of nature. This approach is clearly the opposite approach to understanding the universe suggested by Plato, who reputedly argued that "reason alone was the superior approach to unravel the mysteries of nature." How far we have come in understanding Mother Nature!

In the realm of science, subjective truth is usually the interpretation of observed data. Such interpretations are referred to as hypotheses or theories. The interpretation is based, in large part, on what scientists already know relative to the question addressed and how the data are consistent with conclusions proposed. Virtually all credible scientists believe in the phenomenon of evolution. This hypothesis, or theory, is consistent with biochemical, biological, and paleontological studies. The data collected and observed make scientific sense. Nearly all those who investigate this area of science believe this phenomenon to be true, but clearly evolution has not been proven beyond a shadow of a doubt. This might not even be possible. Interpretation of data is subjective truth, and this is a normal process, especially in mechanistic science. Mechanistic science attempts to determine how processes function and are controlled. The explanation of a process is based on the hypothesis being consistent with the data obtained. This is a processive process to obtain absolute scientific truth. In this scientific process, *truth* is almost always an asymptotic search. The normal search for scientific truth begins with an observation and the subsequent attempts to explain it. A hypothesis or theory is generated to explain the observation. There are often a number of reasonable theories that can explain the observation, and scientists may disagree on which theory is more correct. Subsequent experiments are performed to challenge the hypothesis, and if the consequent data are consistent with this hypothesis, it is retained. What is most often true is that hypotheses that are inconsistent with the data are clearly incorrect. One description of the scientific process is that it is the attempt to overthrow our current solution to the problem addressed. The choice of experiments to challenge the hypothesis depends, in part, on the technology available. Many refinements of theories have been made because newer technology has enabled the experimental scientist to address the question with greater speed, precision, detail, and accuracy. An important facet of this scientific process is the imagination of the experiment performed. Einstein commented that in science, "imagination is more important than knowledge. For knowledge is limited, whereas imagination embraces the whole world, stimulating progress, giving birth to evolution" [2]. In science, a hypothesis is rarely proven but is either supported or demonstrated to be inconsistent with the data. Continuing studies rule out other potential theories that are inconsistent with the data, and hypotheses that are consistent are retained or refined. A simple reflection of this scientific process comes from an appropriate quote by Sherlock Holmes to his colleague Watson, "It is a capital mistake to theorize before one has data. Insensibly one begins to twist facts to suit theories instead of theories to suit facts" [3]. When hypotheses have been challenged over an extended period of time and always found to be consistent, these then become "laws." Such scientific laws include the conservation of mass, the law of gravity, Boyle's law, and the laws of thermodynamics, among others.

The evolution of many theories has come from refinements of what were the current theories. There are many striking examples, however, where the challenge of current theory has led to total paradigm shifts in understanding nature and often given rise to new applications of the science, technology. Humans believed for centuries that physically we were the center of the universe until observations performed and analyzed first by N. Kopernik (1473–1543) and subsequently by Galileo Galilei (1564–1642) demonstrated that the sun was actually the center of our cosmos. Of course, this was highly controversial and both suffered from the authorities of the time as they expressed their interpretations of their observations. The Big Bang theory drastically changed our concepts of how the entire galaxy began and is still evolving. Significant cosmology data support this theory. Very early belief, expressed by the Greeks, was that there were four elements in nature: air, earth, fire, and water. This changed when experiments initially performed by Henry Cavendish (1731–1810) clearly described several elements that were found to be fundamental structures in nature. This work has continued so that we now can attribute the presence of 118 elements, even though several have been synthetically prepared. The infamous phlogiston theory of the late seventeenth century, described by G. Stahl (1660–1734), explained combustion of different fuels containing an immeasurable substance, phlogiston, which was emitted when combustion occurred. The more phlogiston a substance contained, the better the fuel. This theory held for a century before A. Lavoisier (1743–94) carefully quantified matter and demonstrated the presence of oxygen that was utilized in the combustive process. Although a creative chemist/alchemist, his career was cut short by the guillotine during the revolution in France. Atomic and molecular theory developed in the later part of the eighteenth century, giving rise to chemical synthesis that has enabled us to devise and synthesize new compounds such as drugs, plastics, fibers, fertilizers, explosives, and even computer chips. In the late nineteenth century, the germ theory of disease was described from the observations made by J. Lister and L. Pasteur who, in 1890, argued the practice of antisepsis. This work emanated from the observations of microorganisms that are present and correlated their presence with specific diseases. The ability to see these microorganisms was possible with the development of microscopes by A. van Leeuwenhoek (1632–1723). The attack on microorganisms to treat disease was initially performed by the early experiments of P. Ehrlich, who showed that certain arsenic-containing compounds could destroy the microorganisms that caused syphilis (1880), hence, chemotherapy. Although most of these concepts were slow to be accepted, the observations by A. Fleming in 1929 that mold prevented the growth of pus-producing bacteria in the laboratory gave rise to the recognition that the compound penicillin, found in this mold, cured a large number of infections. It took about ten years to implement this treatment as medical practice. These microorganisms, and subsequently human cells, were believed to have magical powers that existed only when cells were intact and living. This mysticism was used to explain the power and chemistry of life in organisms and required that cells be intact. Experiments performed in 1899 by the Büchner brothers showed that following lysis of yeast cells, the extract could also ferment grape juice to form wine, although at a slower rate than intact yeast. These observations gave rise to the discipline of biochemistry. This has allowed many new developments that include our current "logical approach" in drug design. We can target specific molecules, proteins, and nucleic acids that reside in cells as we now believe there is an understanding of the function of many of these molecules in living organisms. Molecular treatment of disease is currently a rapidly growing process. If light is a waveform, then it appears logical that something must be waving similar to water molecules moving up and down in (water) waves. It was believed that something immobile is present in space that allows light and gravity to be transmitted. This something, believed to be a rarefied gas, did not interfere with the motions of celestial bodies. It was an immobile constant of nature. This rarefied gas was called ether, a term used by Aristotle to describe the substance that makes up the heavens and heavenly bodies. It wasn't until July 1887 that the experiments of A. Michelson and E. Morley, who measured the speed of light, demonstrated by interferometry, that there was no "ether wind" that would affect the speed of light and consequently no absolute motion in the universe. In the early twentieth century, a number of observations by physicists and chemists could not be explained by the classical theories of Newton and others in physics. This required a revision of theory. M. Planck (1900) and N. Bohr (1914) developed quantum theory to explain a number of molecular events. This included the ability to describe light not only as a particle but also as a wave. Many of our most recent electronic devices and computers that are now common have evolved via applications of these recent theories. For centuries we understood the concept of genetics in that information about what we call genetic traits was passed down through progeny, whether plants (corn is a great example) or humans. These unknown materials were called genes. Early in the twentieth century it was thought that proteins were genes, but experiments in 1944 and shortly thereafter by F. Griffith and O. Avery demonstrated that compounds called nucleic acids carried genetic material. The characterization of genetic material as DNA gave rise to molecular biology where genetic analyses are now common and genetic engineering in plants and microorganisms is a fruitful applied technology. We have dreams of genetic treatment of diseases and possibilities of "curing" many diseases genetically in the near future.

The specific example to demonstrate the evolution of scientific *truth* that I develop in this essay is the attempt to clarify the biochemical mechanism for a key step in the regulation of the metabolic process of glycolysis in greater detail. This study reflects the asymptotic process of better understanding the details of how a specific regulatory process occurs. Glycolysis is the metabolic pathway where the carbohydrate metabolite glucose (and some other related carbohydrates) is degraded under anaerobic conditions to generate pyruvic acid. In this sequential metabolic process, chemical energy in the form of adenosine triphosphate (ATP) is generated. This process occurs in ten sequential steps, each step being catalyzed by a separate enzyme. This metabolic pathway is virtually ubiquitous in all living systems, is critical to life, and is one of the most well studied pathways in metabolism. Each of the individual enzymes in the pathway has now been isolated, purified, and characterized and the structures of each enzyme determined [4]. Most mechanistic details have been well investigated. Figure 5.1 outlines this pathway. The fate of the end product, pyruvate (pyruvic acid), depends upon the metabolic state of the organism. Pyruvate can undergo subsequent oxidative degradation that yields significantly more chemical energy (ATP), can go on to form fats to conserve and store chemical energy, can serve as a scaffold in the biosynthesis of some amino acids, and can be used in the biosynthesis of glucose, or temporarily form lactate (lactic acid) under anaerobic conditions. It should be clear that these, and virtually all other metabolic pathways, must be biochemically regulated to yield the most rapid, economical, and efficient set of processes for the living organism and to respond to the metabolic needs of the organisms in a rapid manner.

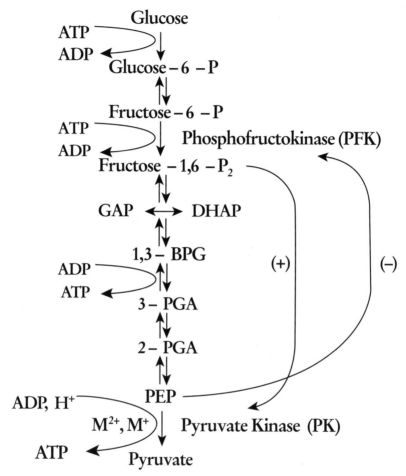

Figure 5.1. The Glycolytic Pathway

The glycolytic pathway, the primary, anaerobic path of carbohydrate metabolism. Abbreviations: ATP, adenosine-5'-triphosphate; ADP, adenosine-5'-diphosphate; GAP, glyceraldehyde-3-phosphate; DHAP, dihydroxyacetone-phosphate; 1,3-BPG, 1,3 bisphosphoglycerate; 3-PGA, 3-phosphoglycerate; 2-PGA, 2-phosphoglycerate; PEP, phosphoenolpyruvate. Glucose and fructose are 6 carbon carbohydrates and each of the subsequent metabolites along the pathway are 3 carbon metabolites. The (+) arrow demonstrates where the product FBP serves as a positive activator of PK and the (-) arrow demonstrates that the substrate PEP serves as an inhibitor of PFK.

Mother Nature has devised a vast array of regulatory mechanisms so that our biochemical ability to function allows us to rapidly respond to physiological challenges accordingly. Eating, fasting, exercise, stress, and so on, all require different biochemical responses. Control and regulation of key metabolic steps is critical. A number of methods for regulation and details of each control process often vary for each enzyme that is being modulated. The two general methods of control are an on/off process where the catalytic reaction is active or inactive (much like a light switch) or modulation of the reaction process so that the reaction rate catalyzed by the enzyme can proceed at a faster or slower rate to produce the reaction product. The analogy here is a rheostat. In the first case, the on/off process usually occurs by a covalent modification of the enzyme that can be subsequently reversed when required. This chemical modification is catalyzed by a specific enzyme, unrelated to the target enzyme, which results in the alteration of the target. The target enzyme might be phosphorylated, acetylated, glycosylated, and so on, and this modification either turns on or turns off its active form. Another separate enzyme can catalyze the reverse of this modification. The latter case of modulation often occurs via the reversible binding of some small molecule, usually another metabolite. As more of the regulator molecule binds the target protein, the greater the effect on the target enzyme. Some of these metabolic regulatory processes can be initiated by the secretion of metabolites or hormones that trigger a cascade of regulatory steps for the process to begin or to finish. Understanding how these mechanisms work is also the basis for a significant number of drug development studies.

The example chosen to demonstrate truth as a subjective scientific understanding and how the approach to obtaining this *truth* is asymptotic is the understanding of the mechanism of regulation of the enzyme pyruvate kinase (PK). PK catalyzes the nearly irreversible reaction of phosphoenolpyruvate (PEP) and adenosine diphosphate (ADP), requiring the presence of two divalent cations (Mg^{2+} or Mn^{2+} can serve this purpose) and a monovalent cation (K^+), to yield pyruvate and ATP [5]. The chemical process is shown in figure 5.2. This reaction results in a net formation of 2 moles of ATP per mole of glucose utilized under anaerobic conditions. Humans synthesize four different forms (isozymes) of this enzyme: fetal muscle (fPK), red blood cell (rPK), liver

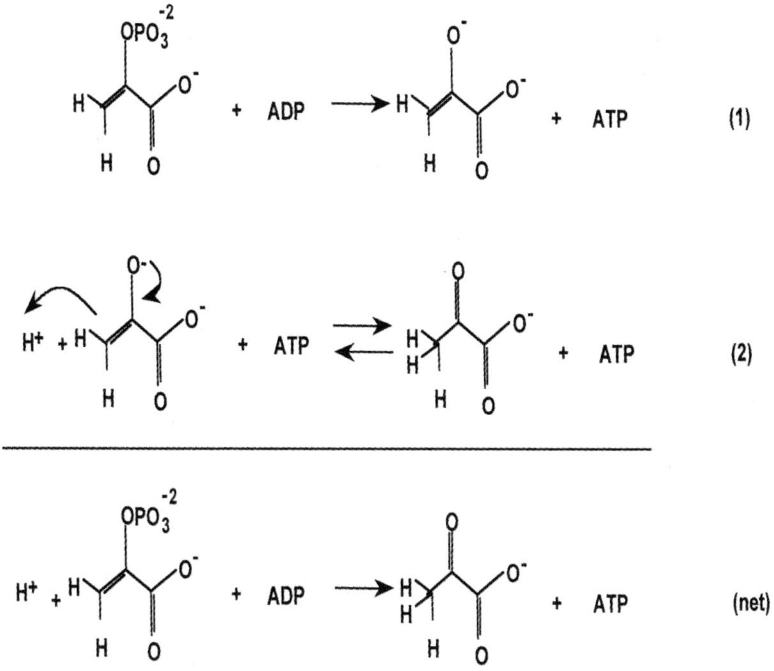

Figure 5.2. The Chemical Mechanism Catalyzed by Pyruvate Kinase

The figure shows that this enzymatic reaction occurs at least in two distinct, known steps on the enzyme. In the first step, the phosphoryl group of PEP is transferred to ADP resulting in the formation of ATP and the very unstable, enzyme-bound enolate form of pyruvate. In the second step, the enzyme catalyzes the addition of a proton to the enolate of pyruvate to yield the stable keto form of pyruvate [14]. The net reaction is the sum of the two partial reactions. Both steps require the presence of the divalent and monovalent cations.

(lPK), and skeletal muscle (mPK) pyruvate kinases. Each of these enzymes catalyzes the identical reaction, but their kinetic behavior differs. These differences in kinetic responses reflect specific metabolic requirements of the expressing tissues. These isozymes have very similar but distinct amino acid sequences that account for these differences. The first three forms of the enzyme display allosteric or sigmoidal kinetic behavior in product formation as a function of substrate (PEP) concentration, whereas the skeletal muscle enzyme displays "classical" hyperbolic kinetics (fig. 5.3). Hyperbolic kinetic responses are normally expected for a response of the initial velocity of the enzymatic

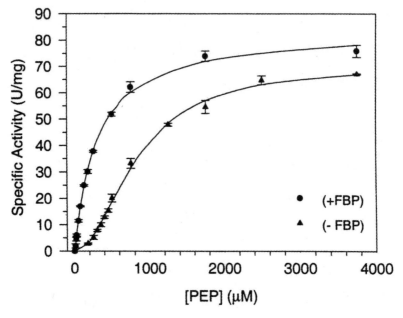

Figure 5.3. The Kinetic Responses of Allosteric Pyruvate Kinase in the Absence and Presence of the Heterotropic Activator, FBP

The response of the initial velocity of the enzyme-catalyzed formation of pyruvate as a function of the concentration of the substrate PEP in the absence (▲) and presence (●) of the heterotrotropic activator FBP. The hyperbolic curve (●) is the same form as seen with the mPK.

reaction as a function of the concentration of the substrate, PEP (as demonstrated, fig. 5.3). In some tissue cancers such as prostate or breast, the PK that is normally present is mPK, whereas in tumors, the mPK that would normally be present is replaced by fPK [6]. In part, the anaerobic metabolic process of generating energy as ATP differs. It was observed many years ago that the rate of the glycolytic process increases in tumor cells [7].

The key facet to the control mechanism of the allosteric form of PK from most species is that the kinetic response of the enzyme to the concentration of PEP is altered from the sigmoidal response to a hyperbolic response by the interaction of the enzyme with the product of an earlier reaction in the pathway. Sigmoidal kinetics and/or binding is described as positive cooperativity. The explanation for this phenomenon is that initial binding of the substrate to the enzyme is weak, but subsequent binding, once some substrate has bound, is enhanced. This implies multiple binding sites on the enzyme. Since PK from most species is a tetramer, there are four binding sites in the active enzyme complex. In most species of PK, the metabolite that induces a hyperbolic kinetic response is fructose-1,6-bisphosphate (FBP, or sometimes known as FDP, fructose-1,6-diphosphate) that is formed by the reaction catalyzed by the enzyme phosphofructokinase (PFK), the third reaction in the pathway (see fig. 5.1). This activation process is known as "feedforward activation," where a metabolite formed early in the pathway activates an enzyme farther down the pathway so the rate of the pathway increases. Of course, the change from sigmoidal to hyperbolic response is not an all-or-none phenomenon but a gradual process as the enzyme PK becomes saturated with the activator FBP. There are four FBP binding sites on tetrameric PK. From these observations, it appears clear that the activation process of allosteric PK arises by the binding of FBP as the transition of the kinetic effect takes place. Earlier studies demonstrated that the binding of FBP to the enzyme causes some alterations in the three-dimensional structure of PK [8]. Recent crystallographic studies of PK from yeast, very homologous to lPK, have demonstrated that FBP binds at a site that is about 40Å from the active site of the enzyme where the catalytic reaction occurs [9]. This is consistent with the general idea that allosteric modulation of activity by a ligand that is not the substrate (a heterotropic modulator) is an "action at a distance," an indirect effect on kinetic responses. The current hypothesis for the action of FBP on PK activation is that the binding of FBP to allosteric PK induces a subtle structural change at the reactive site of the enzyme that results in enhanced binding of the substrate PEP to the enzyme that is identical for each of the four binding sites on the enzyme. This results in a hyperbolic kinetic response. This description is given in most biochemistry textbooks. This kinetic response is then the same as found for mPK. This activation process is considered to be due entirely to FBP binding. As the activation process occurs, the $K_{M, apparent}$ value, the concentration of substrate that gives half maximal activity, decreases. This transformation results in metabolic activation because the physiological concentration of PEP in the cell is roughly 25μM where enzymatic activity is very slow for the sigmoidal form of the enzyme. Activity increases by as much as an order of magnitude when hyperbolic kinetics occur (see fig. 5.3).

It has been observed that one divalent cation (either Mg^{2+} or Mn^{2+}) plays a key role in the binding of the substrate PEP to PK by serving as a bridge for the substrate to interact with the enzyme. This metal ion also assists in the activation process for catalysis [10, 11].

A more detailed investigation was initiated on the impact of both the activator FBP on the interaction of PEP to PK and the role of the divalent cation in these interactions. Two approaches to these interactions have been taken. One approach was kinetic where the effects of varying concentrations of the divalent metal, FBP, and PEP on the initial rates of the enzyme reaction are measured. A second approach is thermodynamic in nature where the effects of the divalent metal, FBP, and PEP on the mutual binding of each ligand are determined. Both sets of studies take what were three-dimensional experiments (e.g., measurement of kinetics vs. variable concentrations of PEP and metal) and extend them to four dimensions (measurements of kinetics vs. variable concentrations of PEP, metal, and FBP). The theoretical treatments of both the thermodynamic and the kinetic studies and subsequent mathematical treatments to fit the data are given in appendixes A and B.

In the first series of studies, a three-dimensional approach to the putative synergism between ligands that bind the enzyme might occur as shown in scheme I. In this example, the interaction of the divalent metal (M) and the substrate PEP (S) can independently interact with the enzyme (E) to form the resultant EM and ES binary complexes, respectively. Each interaction is characterized by a kinetic or thermodynamic constant, depending on the experiments performed. The terms K_m and K_s are used here to designate the strength of the formation of complexes with metal and substrate, respectively. (The nomenclature for thermodynamic and kinetic constants differs, but the fundamental concept for synergism is the same.) In this formalism, the enzyme is active only in the E-M-S complex since the metal is absolutely necessary for catalysis to form the product of the reaction, P. In this scheme, one can easily observe the identity $K_m \cdot K_{m,s} = K_s \cdot K_{s,m}$. Any synergism in the interaction of substrate to the enzyme can be quantified via the ratio Q where $Q_{s,m} = K_s/K_{m,s}$. In thermodynamic nomenclature, the free energy change in binding, $\Delta(\Delta G^{o'}_{s,m}) = -RT \ln Q_{s,m}$.

SCHEME I

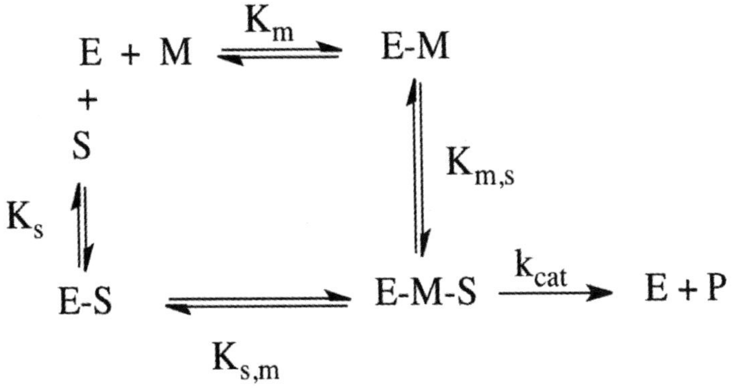

$$E + M \; \underset{}{\overset{K_m}{\rightleftharpoons}} \; E\text{-}M$$

$$+$$

$$S$$

$$K_s \updownarrow \qquad\qquad\qquad \updownarrow K_{m,s}$$

$$E\text{-}S \; \underset{K_{s,m}}{\rightleftharpoons} \; E\text{-}M\text{-}S \; \xrightarrow{k_{cat}} \; E + P$$

$$K_m \cdot K_{m,s} = K_s \cdot K_{s,m}$$

The results of a kinetic analysis of the effect of the divalent metal Mn^{2+} on the kinetic response of the enzyme to variable concentrations of PEP and the converse is shown in figure 5.4. The data demonstrate that an increase in the concentration of the metal decreases the value of $K_{m,s}$ and an increase in the concentration of PEP decreases the value of $K_{s,m}$. Synergy occurs.

Fluorescence measurements were used to determine the effect of the metal on direct binding of PEP to the enzyme and its converse. The binding of either the metal ion to the enzyme or of PEP to the enzyme results in a change in the intrinsic fluorescence of the enzyme. The data reflect binding and are shown in figure 5.5. From both kinetic and thermodynamic studies, the data clearly demonstrate that the metal ion has a substantial positive synergistic effect on the interaction of PEP to the enzyme. The expected converse of the effect of PEP on the interaction of the metal to the enzyme is also observed. This fits the model outlined in scheme I, and the extent of synergism is quantified. It is clear from the kinetic studies that sigmoidal kinetic responses are observed throughout these experiments since FBP is not present in these studies.

These studies have been extended to another dimension by the investigation of the interaction of FBP to the formation of the E-M-FBP-PEP complex for catalysis [8, 12]. The studies have been extended

Figure 5.4. The Results of the Kinetic Study to Analyze the Effect of Increasing Concentrations of Mn²⁺ on the Response of Enzyme Activity as a Function of Variable Concentrations of PEP

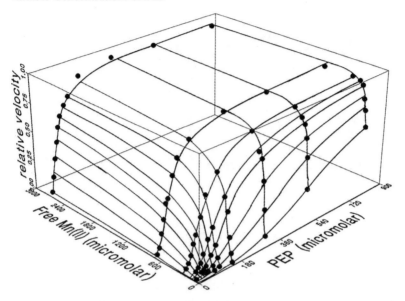

A. The steady state kinetic rate profiles of PK as a function of variable concentrations of PEP at fixed, variable concentrations of Mn²⁺ [8]. The curves are best fits to the data using the last equation given in Appendix B.

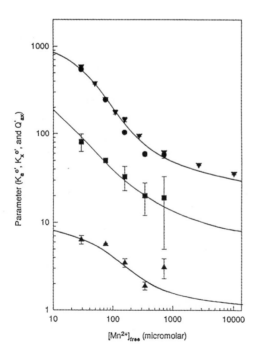

B. The calculated values of the K_m of PEP (●) (from fig. A), FBP (■) (data not shown), and $Q'_{PEP-FBP}$ as a function of free Mn²⁺ concentration. Note that the data are plotted as a log-log plot.

to analyze the respective effects of both the metal and the heterotropic activator (an activator that is not the substrate) FBP on both ligand binding and kinetic responses. In this case, scheme I is extended to give scheme II. In scheme II, the activator, FBP is designated as F.

The analysis of this study is partially simplified kinetically since $k_{cat} \approx k_{cat}'$. The experiments were performed by a series of three-dimensional studies with fixed variable concentrations of the free metal ion resulting in the fourth dimension. The results of one such set of experiments are shown in figure 5.6. In these studies, it is clear that both FBP and M^{2+} have an influence on both the kinetics and the binding (similar to the kinetic data but not shown) of PEP to the enzyme.

The analysis of both the kinetic and the thermodynamic results were analyzed in a sequential manner to determine values for the interaction of a single ligand to the enzyme in the absence of the second ligand X (K_A°) and the value in the presence of various concentrations of the second ligand, X, (K_A). These studies were extended to where both other ligands, X and Y, were present. The binding of each ligand in the absence of any other is designated as K_{PEP}°, K_{FBP}°, and K_{Mn}°. The extent of couplings for the ligand pairs, synergistic effects, are measured as $Q_{PEP-FBP}$, Q_{PEP-Mn}, and Q_{FBP-Mn}. The free energy change in binding is calculated as $\Delta G_{PEP-FBP}$, and so on. These results are shown in table 5.1.

Table 5.1   Kinetic and thermodynamic properties of ligand interactions to pyruvate kinase [8]

Parameter	Kinetic Values (μM)	Thermodynamic Values (μM)
K_{PEP}° (μM)	2440 ± 540	1106 ± 187
K_{FBP}° (μM)	150 ± 56	321 ± 7
K_{Mn}° (μM)	860 ± 333	7180 ± 930
$\Delta G_{PEP-FBP}^{\circ}$ (kcal/mol)	0	-0.22 ± 0.03
$\Delta G_{PEP-Mn}^{\circ}$ (kcal/mol)	-2.75 ± 0.14	-3.88 ± 0.08
$\Delta G_{FBP-Mn}^{\circ}$ (kcal/mol)	-1.55 ± 1.03	-1.09 ± 0.02

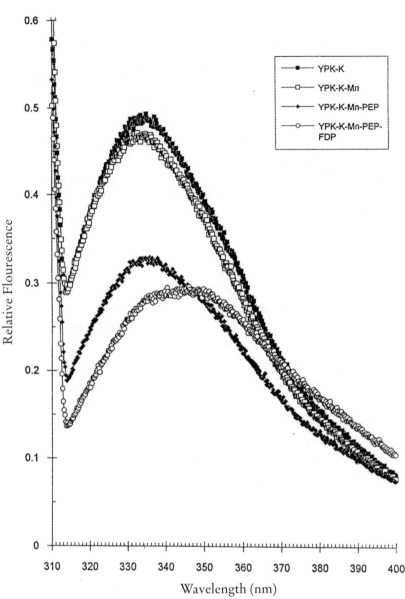

Figure 5.5. The Fluorescence Spectra of Yeast PK (YPK) and YPK in the Presence of Various Ligands

In figure 5.5A (above), the emission spectra of free YPK and the enzyme in the presence of various ligands and combination of ligands are shown. In figure 5.5B (right), the emission spectra for the enzyme with additional ligands are shown. In these cases, the emission spectra of the enzyme in the presence of PEP, PEP + FBP and PEP + FBP + Mn^{2+} all give virtually the same emission spectra [12].

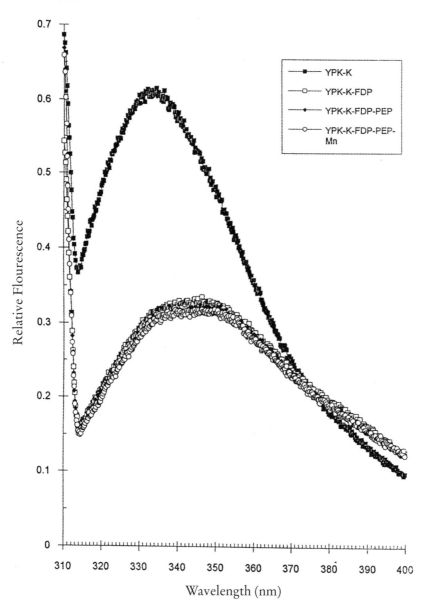

SCHEME II

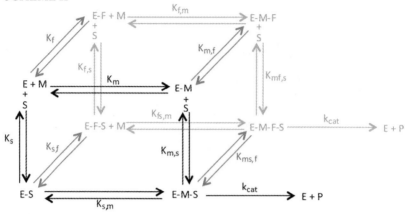

The values for the synergy among the three ligands that interact with the enzyme are similar whether measured by kinetic methods or by direct binding, reflected in thermodynamic values. The values for the interactions of Mn^{2+} to the free enzyme vary significantly, but weaker binding and the inability to perform "simple" kinetic analyses at low concentrations of Mn^{2+} give rise to these variations. It appears that the activator FBP itself does not have a significant effect on the interaction of PEP to the enzyme. The primary synergistic effect is the mutual effect of the substrate PEP and the metal on their respective interactions to the enzyme. From a brief survey of the literature, this is the largest synergistic effect measured for two ligands interacting to an enzyme. Such a qualitative effect is not surprising since structural information demonstrates that the metal interacts with the enzyme and PEP also interacts with the enzyme-metal complex to form the E-M-S complex [9]. From the level of the synergy, binding for both metal and substrate is enhanced by approximately two orders of magnitude. The synergy between the activator FBP and the metal is also relatively large. This is not obviously expected since the binding of these two ligands occurs in different segments of the protein, approximately 40Å apart [9]. Synergism is not an obvious result. These data demonstrate that ligand binding to a protein may certainly have long-distance structural effects that can alter the activity or behavior of the protein.

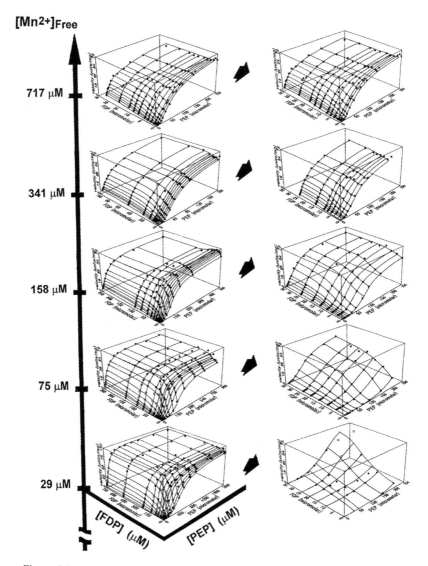

Figure 5.6

The apparent four-dimensional plot of the steady state kinetic rate profiles of pyruvate kinase as a function of variable concentrations of the substrate PEP at fixed variable concentrations of FBP and various fixed, variable concentrations of Mn^{2+}. The series of plots on the left show the full set of data, and the plots on the right are expanded to demonstrate, in greater detail, the changes in kinetics at the lower concentrations of both PEP and of FBP prior to saturation effects occurring.

The measured steady state kinetic results are shown in the vertical axis as a function of both variable PEP concentrations at fixed variable concentrations of FBP. These experiments were all performed at fixed variable concentrations of free Mn^{2+} as indicated at the far left. Concentrations of free Mn^{2+} below 29 μM were too difficult to calculate with any degree of sensitivity and accuracy [12]. All data showing sigmoidal behavior were fit to the Hill equation, whereas the data that showed hyperbolic behavior were fit to the "classical" Michaelis-Menten equation, both given in Appendix B.

The global analysis of the four-dimensional experiments of ligand interactions by both kinetic and thermodynamic studies was also analyzed. In this treatment, all the data were utilized together in a general, four-dimensional analysis. In this case K_A was the value for PEP, K_x for Mn^{2+}, and K_y for FBP. One additional value that is obtained is the combined coupling, Q_{AXY} for the ligands together. A comparison of the kinetic values determined by either using a sequential analysis of three-dimensional studies (1) or a global analysis in four dimensions (mathematically) (2) is shown in table 5.2.

Table 5.2   Steady state kinetic parameters describing the influence of Mn^{2+} and FBP on the interaction of PEP to pyruvate kinase [8]

Parameter	1	2
K_{PEP}° (μM)	2466 ± 1352	2440 ± 541
K_{FBP}° (μM)	129 ± 15	150 ± 56
K_{Mn}° (μM)	880 ± 685	860 ± 33
$Q_{PEP-FBP}$	1.0	1.0
$\Delta G_{PEP-FBP}$ (kcal/mol)	0	0
Q_{Mn-PEP}	105 ± 56	105 ± 25
ΔG_{Mn-PEP} (kcal/mol)	-2.75 ± 0.36	-2.75 ± 0.14
Q_{Mn-FBP}	20 ± 4	14 ± 1.4
ΔG_{Mn-FBP} (kcal/mol)	-1.77 ± 0.12	-1.55 ± 1.03
$Q_{PEP-Mn-FBP}$	1278 ± 154	1520 ± 880
$\Delta G_{PEP-Mn-FBP}$ (kcal/mol)	-4.22 ± 0.07	-4.32 ± 0.40

The results demonstrate that if one uses either the simpler (1) or the more global treatment (2) of the data, virtually identical results are obtained. The major synergistic effect on binding is between the divalent metal and the substrate PEP. A smaller but significant synergistic effect is observed between the metal ion and the allosteric activator FBP. There is no effect of FBP on the interaction of the substrate PEP, unlike that initially assumed from simpler experiments. A major enhancement of the synergism among these three ligands for binding to the enzyme is observed when each of these three ligands is present. The free energy of interaction for the presence of all ligands is increased by about another -1.5 kcal/mol or another order of magnitude in binding to form the activated form of the enzyme.

The results of this investigation demonstrate that when a more detailed study of the effects of both the activating divalent metal ion and the allosteric activator on the interactions of the substrate PEP with PK is measured, it is the metal ion that serves as the key to enhancing the interactions of PEP and FBP to the enzyme. The activator FBP is not solely responsible for the activation process. The theory behind the mechanism of how PK is activated by FBP has been refined.

This study is a great example of how *truth* in science progresses. We believe in a particular hypothesis that serves as an understanding of how and why particular processes occur. This theory is believed because it is consistent with the data that have been obtained relative to the question raised. That belief is held as it continues to be consistent with the information provided. As those beliefs are challenged by further experimentation, they continue to be held unless the results of further studies become inconsistent with the current theory. If that occurs, the theory is subsequently expunged or refined such that the new, revised *truth* is consistent with all the data. Truth in science often appears ephemeral as we continue to explore Mother Nature. Science is an ongoing search for clear, objective truth, the goal of those who continue to pursue scientific truth.

Appendix A:
A Brief Introduction to Thermodynamics as Applied to Ligand Binding to Proteins

The reversible binding of a ligand X to an enzyme E to form the EX complex can be described as follows:

$$E + X \rightleftharpoons EX$$

The equilibrium for this binding is quantified via an equilibrium constant K_{eq} where

$$K_{eq} = \frac{[E_f]\ [X_f]}{[EX]}$$

and $[E_f]$ and $[X_f]$ represent the free concentrations of E and X respectively and $[EX]$ is the concentration of the complex formed at equilibrium. The concentration of total enzyme and total ligand are determined prior to the experiment then $[E_f] = [E_t] - [EX]$ and $[X_f] = [X_t] - [EX]$. In the experiment, either the concentration of the EX complex or either $[E_f]$ or $[X_f]$ are measured, giving sufficient information to measure K_{eq}.

To understand the meaning and quantitative value of K_{eq}, if a fixed value of E_T is used in the experiment and $[EX]$ is measured at various concentrations of X_T, the K_{eq} value is the concentration of free X that gives half saturation of the enzyme ($[E_f] = [EX]$). Mathematically this can be shown as follows:

$$K_{eq} = \frac{[E_f]}{[EX]}\ [X_f]$$

This relationship demonstrates that when $[E_f] = [EX]$, then the ratio $[E_f]/[EX] = 1$ and $K_{eq} = [X_f]$. The equilibrium constant, also called dissociation constant, K_d can be related to the free energy of binding $(\Delta G^{o'})$ by the relationship

$$\Delta G^{o'} = -RT \ln K_{eq}$$

R is the gas constant ($R = 1.987$ cal/mol $\bullet °K = 0.001987$ kcal/ mol $\bullet °K$). $°K$ is the temperature in degrees Kelvin. If the temperature is $37°$ C ($98.7°$ F) then $T = 310°K$. Thus, $\Delta G^{o'} = -0.616 \ln K_{eq}$ (kcal/mol).

To give a quantitative feel for the data, if an alteration in binding occurs and is enhanced by an order of magnitude, the change in free energy change is -1.4 kcal/mol.

$$\Delta(\Delta G^{o'}) = \Delta G^{o'}{}_1 - \Delta G^{o'}{}_2$$

If $\Delta(\Delta G^{o'}) = 0$ there is no alteration in binding.
If $\Delta(\Delta G^{o'}) > 0$ weaker binding, negative synergy, occurs
If $\Delta(\Delta G^{o'}) < 0$ stronger binding, positive synergy, occurs.

Thus we can quantify the extent of ligand binding and any alteration thereof via thermodynamic measurements and units.

For most of the measurements made in this study, the binding of a ligand, PEP, FBP, or the metal ion has an influence on the fluorescence (Φ) of the enzyme PK. The measure of a change in fluorescence as a function of ligand added gives rise to a change in fluorescence. From these data, the equilibrium constant can be quantified via the mathematical model

$$\Phi_{obs} = \Phi_{max} [L] / (K_d + [L]) \qquad \text{eq. a}$$

where [L] is the concentration of ligand added, Φ_{obs} is the observed fluorescence at a given ligand concentration and Φ_{max} is the maximum fluorescence observed when the enzyme is saturated with L. If Φ_{obs} is observed as a function of variable [L], this gives rise to a hyperbolic response and Φ_{max} is the asymptote. If the binding is cooperative, giving rise to a sigmoidal response, the data are then fit to a variant of the above mathematical model

$$\Phi_{obs} = \Phi_{max} [L]^n / K_d + [L]^n \qquad \text{eq. b}$$

where the coefficient n is a measure of the cooperativity in binding. Equation b is the same form as the Hill equation [13] used to fit oxygen binding to hemoglobin.

Appendix B: Enzyme Kinetics

The measure of the initial rate of an enzyme-catalyzed reaction is a critical tool for examining how a catalytic process works. The treatment of the data is based on a fundamental model where chemistry only occurs when the substrate is bound to the enzyme ([ES]), the concentration of substrate is significantly greater than the concentration of enzyme ([S] >> [E]) and the steady state occurs. In the steady state, the *rate of change* of the concentration of the ES complex (d[ES]/dt) is 0. The rate of the initial velocity of the reaction at steady state, v_i is measured as a function of the concentration of the substrate. The following model and mathematical treatment is obtained.

$$E + S \xrightleftharpoons[k_{-1}]{k_1} ES \xrightarrow{k_2} E + P$$

$[S] \gg [E]$

$$v_i = \frac{d[P]}{dt} = k_2 [ES]$$

$$\frac{d[ES]}{dt} = k_1[E_f][S] - k_{-1}[ES] - k_2[ES]$$

@ steady state, $\dfrac{d[ES]}{dt} = 0$ & $[E_f] = [E_t] - [ES]$ $\therefore$

$$[ES] = \frac{k_1[E_t][S]}{k_1[S] + k_{-1} + k_2} = \frac{[E_t][S]}{\dfrac{k_{-1} + k_2}{k_1} + [S]}$$

since $v_i = k_2[ES] = \dfrac{k_2[E_t][S]}{K_M + [S]} = \dfrac{V_{max}[S]}{K_M + [S]}$

When $[S] \gg K_M$, $v_i = V_{max}$ & when $[S] = K_M$ $v_i = 0.5 V_{max}$

The final equation shown, known as the Michaelis-Menten equation, is the same form as for a rectangular hyperbola if v_i is measured as a function of the variable concentration of substrate, $[S]$. The rate of the reaction $(d[P]/dt)$ is measured as a function of $[S]$ and the concentration of total E and S are both known to a high degree of accuracy. The concentration of ES is rarely known via normal measurements, and that value is very small and difficult to directly measure. Although individual rate constants k_1, k_{-1} and k_2 are not determined by these methods, a combination of these constants gives rise to a functional constant, referred to as a Michaelis Constant K_M. This constant has units of concentration (as does $[S]$) and has the functional meaning that it is the substrate concentration that gives ½ maximal velocity of the reaction. Most enzymes follow this general model. This is the identical mathematical form used to analyze classic measured binding data. If "nonclassical" kinetics are observed that reflect cooperativity, a variant of this equation normally fits that data:

$$v_i = \frac{V_{max}[S]^n}{K_M + [S]^n}$$

where, as with cooperative binding, the coefficient n is a quantitative value of the extent of cooperativity. When n > 1, positive cooperativity, sigmoidal kinetics, are observed. The data are well fit via the Hill equation. Even in the case of cooperative kinetics, the K_M value, regardless of its microscopic meaning, is the concentration of substrate that gives half maximal activity, V_{max}.

References

1. Gardener, W. M. (2012) *Handling Truth*. Fairhope, AL: Logica Books.
2. Einstein, Albert. (1931) *Cosmic Religion: With Other Opinions and Aphorisms*. New York: Covici-Friede, 97.
3. Doyle, A. C. (1892) "A Scandal in Bohemia." *The Adventures of Sherlock Holmes*. London: George Newnes, 163.
4. Voet, D. & Voet, J. G. (2011) *Biochemistry*. 3rd ed. New York: John Wiley & Sons.
5. Nowak, T. & Suelter, C. (1981) Pyruvate Kinase: Activation by and Catalytic Role of the Monovalent and Divalent Cations. *Mol. Cell. Biochem.* 35, 65–75.
6. Imamura, K., Noguchi, T. & Tanaka, T. (1986) *Markers of Human Neuroectodermal Tumors* (Staal, G. E. & van Veelen, C. W. M.). New York: CRC Press, 191–222.
7. Warburg, O. (1956) On the Origin of Cancer Cells. *Science* 123, 309–14.
8. Mesecar, A. D. & Nowak, T. (1997) Metal Ion Mediated Allosteric Triggering of Yeast Pyruvate Kinase II. A Multidimensional Thermodynamic Linked Function Analysis. *Biochemistry* 36, 6803–13.
9. Jurica, M. S., Mesecar, A. D., Heath, P. J., Shi, W., Nowak, T. & Stoddard, B. L. (1998) The Allosteric Regulation of Pyruvate Kinase by Fructose-1,6-bisphosphate. *Structure* 6, 195–210.
10. Mildvan, A. S. & Cohn, M. (1966) Kinetic and Magnetic Resonance Studies of the Pyruvate Kinase Reaction: II. Complexes of Enzyme, Metal and Substrates. *J. Biol. Chem.* 241, 1176–93.
11. Nowak, T. & Lee, M. J. (1977) Reciprocal Cooperative Effects of Multiple Ligand Binding to Pyruvate Kinase. *Biochemistry* 16, 1343–50.
12. Mesecar, A. D. & Nowak, T. (1997) Metal Ion Mediated Allosteric Triggering of Yeast Pyruvate Kinase I. A Multidimensional Kinetic Linked Function Analysis. *Biochemistry* 36, 6792–6802.
13. Hill, A. V. (1913) XLVII. The Combinations of Haemoglobin with Oxygen and with Carbon Monoxide. I. *Biochemistry* 7, 471–80.
14. Kuo, D. J. & Rose, I. (1978) Stereochemistry of Ketonization of Enolpyruvate by Pyruvate Kinase. Evidence for Its Role as an Intermediate. *J. Amer. Chem. Soc.* 100, 6288–89.

CHAPTER SIX

What Light Does Biology Shed on the Social Sciences and the Humanities?

FRANCISCO J. AYALA

Humans are animals but a unique and very distinct kind of animal. Our anatomical differences include bipedal gait and enormous brains. But we are notably different also, and more important, in our individual and social behaviors and in the products of those behaviors. With the advent of humankind, biological evolution transcended itself and ushered in cultural evolution, a more rapid and effective mode of evolution than the biological mode. Products of cultural evolution include science and technology; complex social and political institutions; religious and ethical traditions; language, literature, and art; and electronic communication.

Here, I explore ethics and ethical behavior as a model case to illuminate the interplay between biology and culture. I propose that our exalted intelligence—a product of biological evolution—predisposes us to form ethical judgments, that is, to evaluate actions as either good or evil. I further argue that the moral codes that guide our ethical behavior transcend biology in that they are not biologically determined; rather, by and large, they are products of human history, including social and religious traditions.

HUMAN ORIGINS

Humankind is a biological species that has evolved from species that were not human. Our closest biological relatives are the great apes and, among them, the chimpanzees and bonobos, who are more closely related to us than they are to the gorillas, and much more than they are to the orangutans. The hominid lineage diverged from the chimpanzee lineage 6 million to 8 million years ago (Mya) and evolved exclusively in the African continent until the emergence of *Homo erectus*, somewhere around 1.8 Mya. Shortly after their emergence in tropical or subtropical eastern Africa, *H. erectus* dispersed to other continents of the Old World, where their descendants eventually became extinct. Modern humans first arose in Africa (or in the Middle East) between 150,000 years ago (kya) and 100 kya. Starting around 60 kya modern humans spread throughout the world, eventually replacing in the Old World any surviving *Homo* populations, including *Homo neanderthalensis*.

HUMAN DISTINCTIVE TRAITS

Erect posture and large brain are the two most conspicuous human anatomical traits. We are the only vertebrate species with a bipedal gait and erect posture; birds are bipedal, but their backbone stands horizontal rather than vertical (penguins are a minor exception). Brain size is generally proportional to body size; relative to body mass, humans have the largest (and most complex) brain. The chimpanzee's brain weighs less than a pound; a gorilla's, slightly more. The human male adult brain has a volume of 1,400 cubic centimeters (cc), about three pounds in weight.

Until recently, evolutionists raised the question whether bipedal gait or large brain came first, or whether they evolved consonantly. The issue is now resolved. Our *Australopithecus* ancestors had, since four million years ago, a bipedal gait, but a small brain, about 450 cc, a pound in weight. Brain size starts to increase notably with our *Homo habilis* ancestors, about 2.5 Mya, who had a brain about 650 cc and also were prolific toolmakers (hence the name *habilis*). Between one and two million years afterward, *Homo erectus* had adult brains about 1,200 cc. Our species, *Homo sapiens*, has a brain about three times as large as that of *Australopithecus*, 1,300 to 1,400 cc, or some three pounds of gray matter. Our brain is not only much larger than that of chimpanzees or gorillas but also much more complex. The cerebral cortex, where the higher cognitive functions are processed, is in humans disproportionally much greater than the rest of the brain when compared to apes.

Erect posture and large brain are not the only anatomical traits that distinguish us from nonhuman primates, even if they may be the most obvious. A list of our most distinctive anatomical features includes the following:

- Erect posture and bipedal gait (which entail changes of the backbone, hipbone, and feet)
- Opposing thumbs and arm and hand changes (which make possible precise manipulation)
- Large brain
- Reduction of jaws and remodeling of face
- Cryptic ovulation (and extended female sexual receptivity)
- Slow development
- Modification of vocal tract and larynx

Humans are notably different from other animals not only in anatomy but also, and no less important, in their behavior, both as individuals and socially. A list of distinctive human behavioral traits includes the following:

- Intelligence: abstract thinking, categorizing, and reasoning
- Symbolic (creative) language
- Self-awareness and death awareness
- Toolmaking and technology
- Science, literature, and art
- Ethics and religion
- Social organization and cooperation (division of labor)
- Legal codes and political institutions

Humans live in groups that are socially organized, and so do other primates. But primate societies do not approach the complexity of human social organization. A distinctive human social trait is culture, which may be understood as the set of human activities and creations that are not strictly biological. Culture includes social and political institutions, ways of doing things, religious and ethical traditions, language, common sense and scientific knowledge, art and literature, technology, and in general all the creations of the human mind. The advent of culture has brought with it cultural evolution, a superorganic mode of evolution superimposed on the organic mode, which has, in the last few millennia, become the dominant mode of human evolution. Cultural evolution has come about because of cultural change and inheritance, a distinctively human mode of achieving adaptation to the environment and transmitting it through the generations.

BIOLOGICAL ROOTS OF ETHICAL BEHAVIOR

I want to now discuss ethics and ethical behavior as a model case of how we may seek the evolutionary explanation of a distinctively human trait. The objective is to ascertain whether an account can be advanced of ethical behavior as an outcome of biological evolution and, if such is the case, whether ethical behavior was directly promoted by natural selection or has rather come about as an epigenetic manifestation of some other trait that was the target of natural selection.

People have moral values; that is, they accept standards according to which their conduct is judged either right or wrong, good or evil. The particular norms by which moral actions are judged vary to some extent from individual to individual and from culture to culture (although some norms, like not to kill, not to steal, and to honor one's parents, are widespread and perhaps universal), but value judgments concerning human behavior are passed in all cultures. This universality raises two related questions: whether the moral sense is part of human nature, one more dimension of our biological makeup; and whether ethical values may be products of biological evolution rather than being given by religious and other cultural traditions.

When philosophers consider theories of morality they distinguish between metaethics, normative ethics, and practical ethics (Copp 2006). Theories of metaethics seek to justify why we ought to do what we ought to do. They are the primary concern of philosophers, who favor different theories, such as "divine command" (God's commanding is what makes a particular kind of action moral); "moral realism" (there are moral facts; our moral judgments are made valid or not by the moral facts); "utilitarianism" (the moral value of an action is determined by the expected benefit to the largest number of people); "positivism" (there are no objective rational foundations for morality, but rather moral norms are determined by social agreement or, in the individual, by emotional decisions); "libertarianism" (moral values are measured by the extent to which they maximize personal freedom and limit the role of the state to the protection of individual freedoms); and several others.

Normative ethics refers to the rules or laws that determine what we ought to do. Practical ethics considers the application of moral norms to particular situations, which often involve conflicting values: will abortion be justified in order to save the life of the mother?

Aristotle and other philosophers of classical Greece and Rome, as well as many other philosophers throughout the centuries, held that humans hold moral values by nature. A human is not only *Homo sapiens* but also *Homo moralis*. For the past twenty centuries, the foundations of morality were an important subject for Christian theologians, as in the case of Thomas Aquinas, but also for philosophers, such as, in the eighteenth and nineteenth centuries, Hume, Kant, and others familiar to Darwin, including notably William Paley (*The Principles of Moral and Political Philosophy*, 1785) and Harriet Martineau (*Illustrations of Political Economy*, 1832–34).

The theory of evolution brought about the need to reconsider the foundations of morality. We do not attribute ethical behavior to animals (surely, not to all animals and not to the same extent as to humans, in any case). Therefore, evolution raises distinctive questions about the origins and tenets of moral behavior. Is the moral sense determined by biological evolution? If so, when did ethical behavior come about in human evolution? Did modern humans have an ethical sense from the beginning? Did Neandertals hold moral values? What about *H. erectus* and *H. habilis*? And how did the moral sense evolve? Was it directly promoted by natural selection? Or did it come about as a by-product of some other attribute (such as rationality, for example) that was the direct target of selection? Alternatively, is the moral sense an outcome of cultural evolution rather than of biological evolution?

DARWIN AND THE MORAL SENSE

Darwin's most sustained discussion of morality is in chapter 3 of *The Descent of Man* (Darwin 1871, 67–102). The keystone significance of morality in human distinctness is clearly asserted by Darwin in that chapter's first sentence: "I fully subscribe to the judgment of those writers who maintain that of all the differences between man and the lower animals the moral sense or conscience is by far the most important" (67).

Darwin's two most significant points concerning the evolution of morality are stated early in chapter 3 of *The Descent of Man*. The two points are (1) that moral behavior is a necessary attribute of advanced intelligence as it occurs in humans, and thus that moral behavior is biologically determined; and (2) that the norms of morality are not biologically determined but a result of human collective experience, or human culture as we would now call it.

After the two initial paragraphs of chapter 3, which assert that the moral sense is the most important difference "between man and the lower animals" (see quotation above), Darwin states his view that moral behavior is strictly associated with advanced intelligence: "The following proposition seems to me in a high degree probable—namely, that any animal whatever, endowed with well-marked social instincts, would inevitably acquire a moral sense or conscience, as soon as its intellectual powers had become as well developed, or nearly as well developed, as in man" (68–69). Darwin is affirming that the moral sense, or conscience, is a necessary consequence of high intellectual powers, such as exist in modern humans. Therefore, if our intelligence is an outcome of natural selection, the moral sense would be as well an outcome of natural selection. Darwin's statement further implies that the moral sense is not by itself directly promoted by natural selection but only indirectly as a necessary consequence of high intellectual powers, which are the attributes that natural selection is directly promoting.

In the ensuing paragraph of chapter 3, before proceeding to a discussion of how morality might evolve, Darwin makes an important distinction: "It may be well first to premise that I do not wish to maintain that any strictly social animal, if its intellectual faculties were to become as active and as highly developed as in man, would acquire exactly the same moral sense as ours. . . . [T]hey might have a sense of right and wrong, though led by it to follow widely different lines of conduct" (70). According to Darwin, having a moral sense does not by itself determine what the moral norms would be: which sorts of actions might be sanctioned and which ones would be condemned.

Darwin's distinction between the moral sense or conscience, on the one hand, and the moral norms that guide the moral sense or conscience, on the other, is fundamental. It is a distinction I will elaborate. Much of the post-Darwin historical controversy, particularly between scientists and philosophers, as to whether the moral sense is or is not biologically determined, has arisen owing to a failure to make that distinction. Scientists often affirm that morality is a human biological attribute because they are thinking of the predisposition to make moral judgments: that is, to judge some actions as good and others as evil. Some philosophers argue that morality is not biologically determined but rather comes from cultural traditions or from religious beliefs, because they are thinking about moral codes, the sets of norms that determine which actions are judged to be good and which are evil. They point out that moral codes vary from culture to culture and, therefore, are not biologically predetermined.

DARWINIAN AFTERMATH

Herbert Spencer (1820–1903) was among the first philosophers seeking to find the grounds of morality in biological evolution. In *The Principles of Ethics* (1893), Spencer seeks to discover values that have a natural foundation. He argues that the theory of organic evolution implies certain ethical principles. Human conduct must be evaluated, like any biological activity whatsoever, according to whether it conforms to the life process; therefore, any acceptable moral code must be based on natural selection, the law of struggle for existence. According to Spencer, the most exalted form of conduct is that which leads to a greater duration, extension, and perfection of life; the morality of all human actions must be measured by that standard. Spencer proposes that, although exceptions exist, the general rule is that pleasure goes with that which is biologically useful, whereas pain marks what is biologically harmful. This is an outcome of natural selection: thus, while doing what brings them pleasure and avoiding what is painful, organisms improve their chances for survival. With respect to human behavior, we see that we derive pleasure from virtuous behavior and pain from evil actions, associations which indicate that the morality of human actions is also founded on biological nature.

Spencer proposes as the general rule of human behavior that people should be free to do anything that they want, so long as it does not interfere with the similar freedom to which others are entitled. The justification of this rule is found in organic evolution: the success of an individual, plant or animal, depends on its ability to obtain that which it needs. Consequently, Spencer reduces the role of the state to protecting the collective freedom of individuals so that they can do as they please. This laissez-faire form of government may seem ruthless, because individuals would seek their own welfare without any consideration for others' (except for respecting their freedom), but Spencer believes that it is consistent with traditional Christian values. It may be added that, although Spencer sets the grounds of morality on biological nature and on nothing else, he admits that certain moral norms go beyond that which is biologically determined; these are rules formulated by society and accepted by tradition.

Social Darwinism, in Spencer's version or in some variant form, was fashionable in European and American circles during the latter part of the nineteenth century and the early years of the twentieth century, but it has few or no distinguished intellectual followers at present. Spencer's critics include the evolutionists J. S. Huxley and C. H. Waddington who, nevertheless, maintain that organic evolution provides grounds for a rational justification of ethical codes. For Huxley (1953; Huxley and Huxley 1947), the standard of morality is the contribution that actions make to evolutionary progress, which goes from less to more "advanced" organisms. For Waddington (1960), the morality of actions must be evaluated by their contribution to human evolution.

Huxley's and Waddington's views are based on value judgments about what is or is not progressive in evolution. But, contrary to Huxley's claim, there is nothing objective in the evolutionary process itself (i.e., outside human considerations) that makes the success of bacteria, which have persisted as such for more than two billion years and which consist of a huge diversity of species and astronomical numbers of individuals, less valuable than that of the vertebrates, even though the latter are more complex. The same objection can be raised against Waddington's human evolution standard of biological progress. Are the insects, of which more than one million species exist, less successful or less valuable from a purely biological perspective than humans or any other mammal species? Waddington fails to demonstrate why the promotion of human biological evolution by itself should be the standard to measure what is morally good.

More recently, numerous philosophers as well as scientists have sought to give accounts of moral behavior as an evolutionary outcome (e.g., Blackmore 1999; Hauser 2006; Maienschein and Ruse 1999; Ruse 1995; Sober and Wilson 1998; Wilson 2012). Particularly notable are the early contributions of Edward O. Wilson (1975, 1978, 1998), founder of sociobiology as an independent discipline engaged in discovering the biological foundations of all social behavior. Sociobiologists, as well as the derivative subdisciplines of evolutionary psychology (e.g., Barkow, Cosmides, and Tooby 1992) and memetics (Blackmore 1999), have sought to solve the naturalistic fallacy by turning it on its head. They assert that moral behavior does not exist as something distinct from biological, or biologically determined, behavior. As Ruse and Wilson (1985) have asserted, "Ethics is an *illusion* put in place by natural selection to make us good cooperators" (emphasis added).

MORAL JUDGMENT VERSUS MORAL NORMS

The question whether ethical behavior is biologically determined may, indeed, refer to either one of the following two issues. First, is the capacity for ethics—the proclivity to judge human actions as either right or wrong—determined by the biological nature of human beings? Second, are the systems or codes of ethical norms accepted by human beings biologically determined? A similar distinction can be made with respect to language. The question whether the capacity for symbolic creative language is determined by our biological nature is different from the question whether the particular language we speak—English, Spanish, Chinese, and so on—is biologically determined, which in the case of language obviously it is not.

I propose that the moral evaluation of actions emerges from human rationality or, in Darwin's terms, from our highly developed intellectual powers. Our high intelligence allows us to anticipate the consequences of our actions with respect to other people and, thus, to judge them as good or evil in terms of their consequences for others. But I will argue that the norms according to which we decide which actions are good and which actions are evil are largely culturally determined, although conditioned by biological predispositions, such as parental care to give an obvious example.

The moral sense refers first and foremost to our predisposition to evaluate some actions as virtuous, or morally good, and others as evil, or morally bad. Morality, thus, consists of the urge or predisposition to judge human actions as either right or wrong in terms of their consequences for other human beings. In this sense, humans are moral beings by nature because their biological constitution determines the presence in them of the three necessary conditions for ethical behavior. These conditions are (i) the ability to anticipate the consequences of one's own actions; (ii) the ability to make value judgments; and (iii) the ability to choose between alternative courses of action. These abilities exist as a consequence of the eminent intellectual capacity of human beings.

The ability to anticipate the consequences of one's own actions is the most fundamental of the three conditions required for ethical behavior. Only if I can anticipate that pulling the trigger will shoot the bullet, which in turn will strike and kill my enemy, can the action of pulling the trigger be evaluated as nefarious. Pulling a trigger is not in itself a moral action; it becomes so by virtue of its relevant consequences. My action has an ethical dimension only if I do anticipate these consequences.

The ability to anticipate the consequences of one's actions is closely related to the ability to establish the connection between means and ends, that is, of seeing a means precisely as a means, as something that serves a particular end or purpose. This ability to establish the connection between means and their ends requires the ability to anticipate the future and to form mental images of realities not present or not yet in existence.

The ability to establish the connection between means and ends happens to be the fundamental intellectual capacity that has made possible the development of human culture and technology. An evolutionary scenario, seemingly the best hypothesis available, proposes that the remote evolutionary roots of this capacity to connect means with ends may be found in the evolution of bipedalism, which transformed the anterior limbs of our ancestors from organs of locomotion into organs of manipulation. The hands thereby gradually became organs adept for the construction and use of objects for hunting and other activities that improved survival and reproduction, that is, which increased the reproductive fitness of their carriers. The construction of tools depends not only on manual dexterity, but on perceiving them precisely as tools, as objects that help to perform certain actions; that is, as means that serve certain ends or purposes: a knife for cutting, an arrow for hunting, an animal skin for protecting the body from the cold. According to this evolutionary scenario, natural selection promoted the intellectual capacity of our bipedal ancestors because increased intelligence facilitated the perception of tools as tools, and therefore their construction and use, with the ensuing improvement of biological survival and reproduction.

The development of the intellectual abilities of our ancestors took place over several million years, gradually increasing the ability to connect means with their ends and, hence, the possibility of making ever more complex tools serving more diverse and remote purposes. According to the hypothesis, the ability to anticipate the future, essential for ethical behavior, is therefore closely associated with the development of the ability to construct tools, an ability that has produced the advanced technologies of modern societies and that is largely responsible for the success of humans as a biological species.

The second condition for the existence of ethical behavior is the ability to advance value judgments, to perceive certain objects or deeds as more desirable than others. Only if I can see the death of my enemy as preferable to his survival (or vice versa) can the action leading to his demise be thought of as moral. If the consequences of alternative actions are neutral with respect to value, an action cannot be characterized as ethical. Values are of many sorts: not only ethical but also aesthetic, economic, gastronomic, political, and so on. But in all cases, the ability to make value judgments depends on the capacity for abstraction, that is, on the capacity to perceive actions or objects as members of general classes. This makes it possible to compare objects or actions with one another and to perceive some as more desirable than others. The capacity for abstraction requires an advanced intelligence such as it exists in humans and apparently in them alone.

I will note at this point that the model that I am advancing here does not necessarily imply the ethical theory known as utilitarianism (or, more generally, consequentialism). According to the "act consequentialism," the rightness of an action is determined by the value of its consequences, so that the morally best action in a particular situation is the one the consequences of which would have the most benefit to others. I am proposing that the morality of an action depends on our ability (1) to anticipate the consequences of our actions and (2) to make value judgments. But I am not asserting that the morality of actions is exclusively measured in terms of how beneficial their consequences will be to others.

The third condition necessary for ethical behavior is the ability to choose between alternative courses of actions. Pulling the trigger can be a moral action only if you have the option not to pull it. A necessary action beyond conscious control is not a moral action: the circulation of the blood or the process of food digestion are not moral actions. Whether there is free will is a question much discussed by philosophers, and the arguments are long and involved (e.g., Fischer 2006; Bok 1998; Ekstrom 2000; Kane 1996; see also Greene and Haidt 2002; Haidt, Bjorklund, and Murphy 2000; Hauser 2006). Here, I will advance two considerations that are commonsense evidence of the existence of free will. One is personal experience, which indicates that the possibility to choose between alternatives is genuine rather than only apparent. The second consideration is that when we confront a given situation that requires action on our part, we are able mentally to explore alternative courses of action, thereby extending the field within which we can exercise our free will. In any case, if there were no free will, there would be no ethical behavior; morality would only be an illusion. A point to be made, however, is that free will is dependent on the existence of a well-developed intelligence, which makes it possible to explore alternative courses of action and to choose one or another in view of the anticipated consequences.

MIND TO MORALITY

The capacity for ethics is an outcome of gradual evolution, but it is an attribute that exists only when the underlying attributes (i.e., the intellectual capacities) reach an advanced degree. The necessary conditions for ethical behavior come about only after the crossing of an evolutionary threshold. The approach is gradual, but the conditions appear only when a degree of intelligence is reached such that the formation of abstract concepts and the anticipation of the future are possible, even though we may not be able to determine when the threshold was crossed. Thresholds occur in other evolutionary developments—for example, in the origins of life, multicellularity, and sexual reproduction—as well as in the evolution of abstract thinking and self-awareness. Thresholds occur in the physical world as well; for example, water heats gradually, but at 100°C boiling begins and the transition from liquid to gas starts suddenly. Surely, human intellectual capacities came about by gradual evolution. Yet, when looking at the world of life as it exists today, it would seem that there is a radical breach between human intelligence and that of other animals. The rudimentary cultures that exist in chimpanzees do not imply advanced intelligence as it is required for moral behavior.

A different explanation of the evolution of the moral sense has been advanced by proponents of the theory of gene-culture coevolution (Richerson and Boyd 2005; Strimling, Enquist, and Eriksson 2009; Richerson, Boyd, and Henrich 2010; see also Greene et al. 2001; Haidt 2007). It is assumed that cultural variation among tribes in patriotism, fidelity, sympathy, and other moralizing behaviors may have occurred incipiently in early hominid populations, starting at least with *H. habilis*.

This cultural variation may have, in turn, selected for genes that endowed early humans with primitive moral emotions. Primitive moral emotions would in turn have facilitated the evolution of more advanced cultural codes of morality. Repeated rounds of gene-cultural coevolution would have gradually increased both the moral sense itself and the systems of moral norms. That is, the evolution of morality would have been directly promoted by natural selection in a process where the moral sense and the moral norms would have coevolved.

The gene-culture coevolution account of the evolution of morality is, of course, radically different from the theory I am advancing here, in which moral behavior evolved not because it increased fitness but as a consequence of advanced intelligence, which allowed humans to see the benefits that adherence to moral norms bring to society and to its members. The extreme variation in moral codes among recent human populations and the rapid evolution of moral norms over short time spans would seem to favor the explanation I am proposing. Gene-culture coevolution would rather lead to a more nearly universal system of morality, which would have come about gradually as our hominid ancestors evolved toward becoming *Homo sapiens*.

Empathy, or the predisposition to mentally assimilate the feelings of other individuals, has recently been extensively discussed in the context of altruistic or moral behavior. Incipient forms of empathy seem to be present in other animals. In humans, increasing evidence indicates that we automatically simulate the experiences of other humans (Gazzaniga 2005, 158–99; 2008). Empathy is a common human phenomenon, surely associated with our advanced intelligence, which allows us to understand the harms or benefits that affect other humans, as well as their associated feelings. Empathic humans may consequently choose to behave according to how their behavior will affect those for whom we feel empathy. That is, human empathy occurs because of our advanced intelligence. Humans may then choose to behave altruistically, or not, that is, morally or not, in terms of the anticipated consequences of their actions to others.

The question remains, when did morality emerge in the human lineage? Did *Homo habilis* or *Homo erectus* have morality? What about the Neandertals, *Homo neanderthalensis*? When in hominid evolution morality emerged is difficult to determine. It may very well be that the advanced degree of rationality required for moral behavior may only have been reached at the time when creative language came about, and perhaps in dependence with the development of creative language. (When creative language may have come about in human evolution is discussed in Cela-Conde and Ayala 2007).

MORAL CODES

I have distinguished between moral behavior—judging some actions as good, others as evil—and moral codes—the precepts or norms according to which actions are judged. Moral behavior, I have proposed, is a biological attribute of *H. sapiens*, because it is a necessary consequence of our biological makeup, namely, our high intelligence. But moral codes, I argue, are not products of biological evolution, but of cultural evolution.

It must, first, be stated that moral codes, like any other cultural systems, cannot survive for long if they prevailingly run in outright conflict with our biology. The norms of morality must be by and large consistent with human biological nature, because ethics can exist only in human individuals and in human societies. One might therefore also expect, and it is the case, that accepted norms of morality will often, or at least occasionally, promote behaviors that increase the biological fitness of those who behave according to them, such as child care. But the correlation between moral norms and biological fitness is neither necessary nor indeed always the case: some moral precepts common in human societies have little or nothing to do with biological fitness, and some moral precepts are contrary to fitness interests.

How do moral codes come about? The short answer is, as already stated, that moral codes are products of cultural evolution, a distinctive human mode of evolution that has surpassed the biological mode, because it is a more effective form of adaptation: it is faster than biological evolution, and it can be directed. Cultural evolution is based on cultural heredity, which is Lamarckian, rather than Mendelian, so that acquired characteristics are transmitted. Most important, cultural heredity does not depend on biological inheritance, from parents to children, but is transmitted also horizontally and without biological bounds. A cultural mutation, an invention (think of the laptop computer, the cell phone, or rock music), can be extended to millions and millions of individuals in less than one generation.

In chapter 5 of *The Descent of Man*, titled "On the Development of the Intellectual and Moral Faculties during Primeval and Civilized Times," Darwin writes: "There can be no doubt that a tribe including many members who, from possessing in a high degree the spirit of patriotism, fidelity, obedience, courage, and sympathy, were always ready to give aid to each other and to sacrifice themselves for the common good, would be victorious over most other tribes; and this would be natural selection. At all times throughout the world tribes have supplanted other tribes; and as morality is one element in their success, the standard of morality and the number of well-endowed men will thus everywhere tend to rise and increase" (159–60).

Darwin is making two important assertions. First, he is saying that morality may contribute to the success of some tribes over others, which is natural selection in the form of group selection. Second, he is asserting a position of moral optimism, namely, that the standards of morality will tend to improve over human history precisely on grounds of group selection, because the higher the moral standards of a tribe, the more likely the success of the tribe. This assertion depends on which standards are thought to be "higher" than others. If the higher standards are defined by their contribution to the success of the tribe, then the assertion is circular. But Darwin asserts that there are some particular standards that, in his view, would contribute to tribal success: patriotism, fidelity, obedience, courage, and sympathy.

MORAL NORMS AND NATURAL SELECTION

Parental care is a behavior generally favored by natural selection that may be present in virtually all codes of morality, from primitive to more advanced societies. There are other human behaviors sanctioned by moral norms that have biological correlates favored by natural selection. One example is monogamy, which occurs in some animal species but not in many others. It is also sanctioned in many human cultures but surely not in all. Polygamy is sanctioned in some current human cultures and was to a greater extent in the past. Food sharing outside the mother–offspring unit rarely occurs in primates, with the exception of chimpanzees—and, apparently, in capuchin monkeys (Brosnan and de Waal 2003)—although even in chimpanzees food sharing is highly selective and often associated with reciprocity. A more common form of mutual aid among primates is coalition formation; alliances are formed in fighting other conspecifics, although these alliances are labile, with partners readily changing partners.

Those moral codes tend to be widespread that lead to successful societies. Since time immemorial, human societies have experimented with moral systems. Some have succeeded and spread widely throughout humankind, like the Ten Commandments, although other moral systems persist in different human societies. Many moral systems of the past have surely become extinct because they were replaced or because the societies that held them became extinct. The moral systems that currently exist in humankind are those that have been favored by cultural evolution. They were propagated within particular societies for reasons that might be difficult to fathom but that surely must have included the perception by individuals that a particular moral system was beneficial for them, at least to the extent that it was beneficial for their society by promoting social stability and success (Gazzaniga 2005, 2008). Cultures, of course, do not evolve as completely differentiated units. Rather, cultures often incorporate elements from other cultures. "Far from being self-preserving monoliths, cultures are porous and constantly in flux. Language . . . is a clear example" (Pinker 2002; see Pinker 2011).

The norms of morality, as they exist in any particular culture, are felt to be universal within that culture. Yet, similar to other elements of culture, they are continuously evolving, often within a single generation. As Steven Pinker has pointed out, Western societies have recently experienced the moralization and amoralization of diverse behaviors. Thus, "smoking has become moralized [and is] . . . now treated as immoral. . . . At the same time many behaviors have become amoralized, switched from moral failings to lifestyle choices. They include divorce, illegitimacy, working mothers, marijuana use and homosexuality"

(Pinker 2002, 34). Acceptance by individuals or groups of particular sets of moral norms is often reinforced by civil authority (e.g., those who kill or commit adultery will be punished) and by religious beliefs (God is watching and you'll go to hell if you misbehave). But it is worth noticing that the legal and political systems that govern human societies, as well as the belief systems held by religion, are themselves outcomes of cultural evolution, as it has eventuated over human history, particularly over the last few millennia.

REFERENCES

Barkow, J., L. Cosmides, and J. Tooby, eds. 1992. *The Adapted Mind: Evolutionary Psychology and the Generation of Culture*. Oxford: Oxford University Press.

Blackmore, S. 1999. *The Meme Machine*. Oxford: Oxford University Press.

Bok, H. 1998. *Freedom and Responsibility*. Princeton: Princeton University Press.

Brosnan, S., and F. de Waal. 2003. "Monkeys Reject Unequal Pay." *Nature* 425: 297–99.

Cela-Conde, C. J., and F. J. Ayala. 2007. *Human Evolution: Trails from the Past*. Oxford: Oxford University Press.

Copp, D., ed. 2006. *The Oxford Handbook of Ethical Theory*. Oxford: Oxford University Press.

Darwin, C. R. 1871. *The Descent of Man, and Selection in Relation to Sex*. London: John Murray. Reprint New York: Appleton and Company, 1971.

Ekstrom, L. 2000. *Free Will: A Philosophical Study*. Boulder, CO: Westview Press.

Fischer, J. M. 2006. "Free Will and Moral Responsibility." In *The Oxford Handbook of Ethical Theory*, ed. D. Copp, 321–24. Oxford: Oxford University Press.

Gazzaniga, M. S. 2005. *The Ethical Brain*. New York: Dana Press.

———. 2008. *Human: The Science behind What Makes Us Unique*. New York: HarperCollins.

Greene, J. D., and J. Haidt. 2002. "How (and Where) Does Moral Judgment Work?" *Trends in Cognitive Science* 6: 517–23.

Greene, J. D., R. B. Sommerville, L. E. Nystrom, J. M. Darley, and J. D. Cohen. 2001. "An fRMI Investigation of Emotional Engagement in Moral Judgment." *Science* 293: 2105–8.

Haidt, J. 2007. "The New Synthesis In Moral Psychology." *Science* 316: 998–1002.

Haidt, J., F. Bjorklund, and S. Murphy. 2000. "Moral Dumbfounding: When Intuition Finds No Reason." Working Paper, University of Virginia.

Hauser, M. 2006. *Moral Minds: How Nature Designed Our Universal Sense of Right and Wrong*. New York: HarperCollins.

Huxley, J. 1953. *Evolution in Action*. New York: Harper.

Huxley, T. H., and J. Huxley. 1947. *Touchstone for Ethics*. New York: Harper.

Kane, R. 1996. *The Significance of Free Will*. Oxford: Oxford University Press.

Maienschein, J., and M. Ruse, eds. 1999. *Biology and the Foundations of Ethics*. Cambridge: Cambridge University Press.

Martineau, H. 1832–34. *Illustrations of Political Economy,* 3rd ed., in 9 vols. London: Charles Fox.

Paley, W. 1785. *The Principles of Moral and Political Philosophy*. Dublin Exshaw.

Pinker, S. 2002. *The Blank Slate: The Modern Denial of Human Nature*. New York: Viking.

———. 2011. *The Better Angels of Our Nature: Why Violence Has Declined*. New York: Viking.

Richerson, P. J., and R. Boyd. 2005. *Not by Genes Alone: How Culture Transformed Human Evolution.* Chicago: University of Chicago Press.

Richerson, P. J., R. Boyd, and J. Henrich. 2010. "Gene-Culture Coevolution in the Age of Genomics." *Proc. Natl. Acad. Sci. USA* 107 (Suppl. 2): 8985–92.

Ruse, M. 1995. *Evolutionary Naturalism*. London: Routledge.

Ruse, M., and E. O. Wilson. 1985. "The Evolution of Ethics." *New Scientist* 108: 50–52.

Sober, E., and D. S. Wilson. 1998. *Unto Others: The Evolution and Psychology of Unselfish Behavior*. Cambridge, MA: Harvard University Press.

Strimling, P., M. Enquist, and K. Eriksson. 2009. "Repeated Learning Makes Cultural Evolution Unique." *Proc. Natl. Acad. Sci. USA* 106: 13870–74.

Waddington, C. D. 1960. *The Ethical Animal*. London: Allen and Unwin.

Wilson, E. O. 1975. *Sociobiology, the New Synthesis*. Cambridge, MA: Belknap Press.

———. 1978. *On Human Nature*. Cambridge, MA: Harvard University Press.

———. 1998. *Consilience: The Unity of Knowledge*. New York: Knopf.

———. 2012. *The Social Conquest of Earth*. New York: Norton/Liveright.

CHAPTER SEVEN

What Is the Nature of Perception?

ZYGMUNT PIZLO

There have been two broad definitions of *perception*. The conventional, largely content-free definition says that "to perceive means to be aware of the external world through the medium of the senses." This definition is rooted in Fechnerian psychophysics in which the percept is the passive result of a causal chain of events (Fechner [1860] 1966). Fechner recognized that studying perception requires establishing relations among three different types of phenomena. One is the *distal* stimulus (an object "out there"), which is a physical phenomenon (event) described in the language of physics and geometry, such as weight, inertia, surface reflectance, stiffness, size, and shape. This also holds for the *proximal* stimulus, which is a physical distribution of the stimulus energy on the surface of the receptors. In visual perception, the proximal stimulus is a distribution of light on the surface of the retina, where the light energy is transduced (translated) into the bioelectrical messages used by the nervous system. In auditory perception, the proximal stimulus is a distribution of mechanical energy on the basilar membrane in the inner ear, and in tactual perception, the proximal stimulus is a distribution of mechanical energy on the surface of the skin. Taste and smell are different; the proximal stimulus is a distribution of chemical energy. Receptors in all the sensory systems translate the energy of the stimulus into the electrical energy used in the nervous system. It is at this stage, at the proximal stimulus, that physiological, rather than physical, phenomena come into play, but it is only after the stimulus is analyzed in the brain that the percept, a mental phenomenon, arises. When the Fechnerian causal chain is described in this way, the events between the distal stimulus and the percept can be characterized as a sequence of "pushes," a deterministic process in which the knowledge of the cause allows one to compute its effect.

A more recent, and quite different, definition states that "perception is an *inference* that provides the observer with accurate information about the external world." This definition is very similar to Thomas Reid's ([1764] 2000) understanding of the nature and role of perception. Why am I calling the percept an "inference"? I am calling it an inference because sensory data is *never* sufficient to completely describe an object "out there." This is particularly clear in visual perception because the proximal stimulus, a retinal image, is two-dimensional (2D), but the distal stimulus "out there" in the physical world is three-dimensional (3D). The mapping from the object (model) to its image (data) is many-to-one. Such problems in the contemporary theory of inverse problems are called "forward" or "direct" problems. Under this rubric, the opposite problem, mapping from the data to the model is one-to-many, and it is called an "inverse" problem. Because of the nature of the mapping, the inverse problem, unlike the forward problem, is ill-posed and/or ill-conditioned. In plain English, this means that the solution of the inverse mapping may not exist, and if it does exist, it may not be unique, and when it is unique, it will be unstable in the presence of noise and uncertainty in the data. It follows that solving an inverse problem of perceptual inference is not easy. The only way to produce a unique and accurate interpretation is to impose a priori constraints on the family of possible interpretations (the nature and role of these constraints are discussed later). Reid's understanding of what he meant by perception is relevant here because he was the first to be credited with distinguishing "sensations" from "perceptions." Sensations, in his usage, *do not* refer to any object, making it impossible to talk about their veridicality. Perceptions, on the other hand, *always* refer to an object, and they are *always* veridical. In the psychology of perception, we often use the term *veridicality* when we refer to the fact that the percept agrees with (is a faithful copy of) things "out there." It is easy to see that Reid's *sensations* correspond, in contemporary language, to what we call "sensory coding," the activities described as a forward problem (above). The perception of hue, brightness, and loudness is a good example of sensory coding (forward problems). Reid's *perceptions* are different. They correspond to the kind of perceptual inference described as an inverse problem (above). The perception of 3D shapes and 3D scenes are good examples of such inverse problems (inferences). Reid insisted that perceptions are accurate, but he could not explain how this is accomplished. He did know that for this to happen the human mind must have some innate, hardwired intuitions of space, time, and causality. Reid anticipated Kant (1781) when he published these views seventeen years before Kant did. For skeptics, those who eschewed a role for in-built intuitions such as Bishop Berkeley ([1709] 1910), Reid offered this oft-cited rebuttal: "I have never seen a skeptic who would walk into the fire because he did not trust his senses." Unfortunately, Reid's views on perception, with his emphasis on the importance of veridicality and arguments against a role for illusions in the study of visual perception, have largely been forgotten.

Can We Trust and Can We Study Our Perceptions?

Perception is the oldest branch of experimental psychology. Systematic observations and theorizing about the nature and veridicality of perception started at least a thousand years ago (Alhazen [1083] 1989). This should come as no surprise. There was very good reason for the natural philosophers, physicians, and alchemists, who would become physicists, astronomers, and physiologists, to wonder about the veridicality of their perceptions. For most of recorded history, scientific observations were made simply by looking at, listening to, touching, smelling, and tasting things. If you could not be sure that you were perceiving (or sensing) things accurately, you would not be able to take your data seriously. Fortunately, their commitment to taking their observations seriously was buttressed by their common sense (another concept emphasized by Reid), so the early physicists and astronomers had no difficulty convincing themselves that our perceptions are, or are almost always, veridical. This allowed them to lay the foundations of modern science. Perceptionists, who jumped on this bandwagon shortly after the Renaissance and stayed there until the Age of Enlightenment, managed to fall off, and stay off, since then. It is surprising, if not simply irrational and self-contradictory, that many contemporary perceptionists who argue that perceptions are never veridical trust the data they collect. How do they manage to use their senses in designing their experiments and collecting and interpreting their data, then go on to refusing to accept the fact that their subjects' perceptions can be veridical? Paraphrasing Reid, what possible basis do you have to trust your reasoning about perception but not to trust your perception itself? Both are produced by the same wetware!

But there is even a more fundamental question that needs to be examined. Once we are willing to assume that we can trust our perception, the question remains as to whether we can study perception "scientifically"? Why is this a problem? Well, perceptions, as mental events, are "private" in the sense that each of us has a special, privileged access to our thoughts and perceptions. I know that I think (at least part of the time), but there is no objective way I can verify that the reader of this chapter ever experiences "thinking." Actually I, and I suspect you, take it for granted that most if not all other people think and perceive in the same way you do. This belief is often supported by the following kind of folk argument (reasoning), the walking, talking duck metaphor you have heard so often. Other people look like me, and they react to events as I do (or as I might). When I talk to them, they respond as I would. In other words, I can easily put myself in their shoes. This is why I believe that other people have perceptions and thoughts like mine. But assuming that other people think and perceive as we do does not tell us how to study them scientifically. Science can only deal with "public" events, so in order to do science when we study perception, we must obtain behavioral data (activities we can observe) about people's perceptions. We ask an observer (now called a "subject") to compare two objects and respond (tell us) whether they are the same or different. This is what Brindley (1960) called a "Class A" experiment. The scientist will infer the subject's "private" perceptions from these behavioral ("public") responses. It follows that studying perception can, in engineering terminology, be called a "black box" problem. This problem is difficult because the subject's responses *always* confound perceptions with response biases produced by the subject's preferences, opinions, guesses, and even social pressures. Fortunately, we have an experimental methodology, called signal detection (Green and Swets 1966), that allows the scientist to estimate perceptions and response biases separately. So folk arguments about perception have been replaced by signal detection experiments that allow one to study perception scientifically. But note that if a signal detection experiment is not used to study perception, and not everyone uses it today, the possibility remains that the result of such efforts does not belong in science.

NATIVISM VERSUS EMPIRICISM

The *origin of perceptual mechanisms* comes next on our list of questions about the nature of perception. The empiristic view in perception is expressed well by what is called the "peripatetic axiom," which states, "Nihil est in intellectu quod non prius in sensu" (There is nothing in the mind that was not in the senses first). So, for those perceptionists who are empiricists, the mind of a newborn human baby is like a blank slate, and the 3D percepts of an adult human being, which are produced by a 2D retinal image, are the result of comparing the adult's retinal data with his memory traces of previous images. So we are not able to recover 3D shapes and scenes when we are born. We must learn how to do this through dozens and hundreds and even thousands of interactions with objects in the external world. It was also assumed that learning to perceive required motor actions and active haptic exploration (manipulating objects with one's hands). Note that if perceptions actually had to be learned this way, people who grew up in different parts of the world would see objects differently. People who had never had a chance to handle a quarter-inch drill as they looked at it, or a violin, would know nothing about their shapes. These days we know quite well that there are actually very, very few individual differences in perception. We know that the role of personal experience in perception is negligible. This fact makes it practical, as well as profitable, for a high-tech manufacturer to move production of his product to a region where indigenous people are still using wooden plows and spears. Furthermore, if we actually had to learn how to perceive veridically, we would probably have to practice seeing to maintain it and to improve our ability to use it. This, obviously, is not the case. Now, consider the well-known Müller-Lyer illusion shown in figure 7.1. The line segment on the right appears to be longer than the segment on the left by about 15 percent. The magnitude of this illusion is roughly the same for everyone, and it does not get smaller if the subject keeps looking at it and even when he is allowed to measure the lengths with a ruler. No matter how hard you think about the fact that the length of these two lines is identical and no matter how many times you measure them, the magnitude of the illusion remains the same. Empiricists have tried to remove this illusion since it came into vogue in the nineteenth century by asking subjects to make long series of saccadic (scanning) eye movements among the three corners in the display. They reported small reductions in the illusion's size that did not persist beyond the experimental session, and, to my knowledge, even these small effects have not been confirmed with signal detection methodology. This illusion, which is robust, as well as vivid, provides convincing evidence against a role for learning in visual perception. It is hard to understand why empiricism has persisted in visual perception as long as it has despite such observations.

The commitment to perceptual learning, characteristic of the empiristic point of view, usually goes together with a commitment to an important role for cognitive and social factors in perception. This idea loomed large just after World War II when what was called the New Look movement in perception came into vogue (Bruner 1957, 1973; Bruner and Goodman 1947). This fad was supposedly "supported" by the following kinds of observations: (i) poor, but not rich, children in Boston were found to overestimate the sizes of coins, and (ii) percep-

Figure 7.1. Müller-Lyer illusion. The two horizontal line segments demarcated by the three corners are exactly the same length, but the line on the right looks longer than the line on the left.

tual thresholds were higher for taboo words, including such threatening words as *penis* and *KOTEX*. This fad still has adherents as evidenced by recent papers showing that (iii) a hill looks steeper when a backpack is heavy and (iv) a glass of water appears farther away when the observer is thirsty. We now know that all of the effects "discovered" by New Lookers derive from bad experimental methodology combined with bad statistical analyses. All of these effects go away completely when the experiments are done correctly. Unfortunately, empiricism in perception shows no signs of disappearing, despite the recognition of these problems in psychology. It is actually gaining popularity thanks to the "contributions" of our colleagues from engineering. Most contemporary efforts in computer vision and artificial intelligence focus on learning. We cannot blame these engineers for their scientific ignorance. There is nothing in the traditional engineering curriculum, unlike the curriculum in experimental psychology, that requires graduate students to read the history of sensation and perception. I will add a few classical results here that speak against empiricism for the benefit of engineers who do not have this background, namely, a newborn chicken has good depth perception: it will not jump off a post one meter above the ground plane, and the time it takes for it to decide to jump varies directly with the height of the post (Thorndike 1899); a newborn chick's monocular and binocular space perception is accurate: it is good enough to allow it to find and peck accurately at grains scattered on the ground (Hess 1956); a newborn human infant perceives both visual and auditory directions in space accurately (Wertheimer 1961); a crawling human infant has good depth perception: it prevents it from crawling off a "visual cliff" (Gibson and Walk 1960); and newborn infants recognize planar (flat) shapes slanted differently in 3D space (Slater and Morrison 1985). These examples should be sufficient to encourage engineers, as well as others, who want to study perception, and who come to it with an empiristic bias, to at least look into what is already known about the problems inherent in empiricism. Those of us who have this knowledge are convinced that perceptual mechanisms are much more likely to be innate than learned. We also know that it is very difficult (if possible at all) to demonstrate appreciable and significant effects of learning in perception. If perceptions are innate and hardwired, all humans are likely to see things the same way, and there should be few if any qualitative individual differences in perception. I believe that both of these claims are true. This verity, once accepted, provides a useful tool for verifying whether an experimental result reflects the operation of the perceptual system that is not confounded with response biases. If results of several subjects, both naive and not naive, are very similar, the confounding effects of response bias are likely to be absent. An important caveat follows from this observation, namely, the results of individual subjects should be reported in perception experiments. Subjects' results should not be combined before they are averaged. Unfortunately, this kind of averaging is still an all too common practice. It should be discontinued because it is the absence, or at least the relative insignificance, of individual differences in the data that lends confidence to any conclusions drawn about what has been perceived.

There is an additional, surprising difference between empiricists and nativists. Nativists assume that the visual system uses computational algorithms, while empiricists assume that the visual system uses look-up tables. Those who advocate perceptual learning are simply not interested in discovering the perceptual algorithms at work in the visual system. According to them, perceptual learning depends entirely on getting more and more experience with the visual world. This experience translates into better and better "priors" (likely outcomes). This is the only role for experience in the empiristic approach. Empiricists believe that computational algorithms are superfluous. The Bayes rule, which is used in the contemporary empirical approach, *is* "the" mechanism. This observation brings us to considering why perception should be viewed as an inverse problem and how it should be studied once this is done.

The Nature of A Priori Constraints in Solving an Inverse Problem in Perception

Consider the 2D image of the 3D indoor scene shown in figure 7.2. There are several pieces of furniture in the center of the floor, a floor that was chosen because its texture was quite complex visually. The first task for the visual system is to determine whether there is an object "out there," how many of them are there, and where are they located. This analysis is called figure-ground organization (FGO). FGO is not an easy task, in no small measure, because the human retina has six million receptors (cones), the receptors used for the perception of shape and details. Without any a priori constraints, the visual system would have to try all partitions of the set of six million receptors. The number of partitions of a set with N elements is called a Bell number (B_N). The number of partitions B_N of N elements grows faster with N than 10^N but slower than N factorial (N!). Consider a low-resolution camera with only 10x8 pixels. Not much can be done with so few receptors, but to appreciate the enormity of the task at hand, you must realize that the number of all partitions of eighty receptors is already larger than the number of atoms in the universe, which is currently estimated to be 10^{80}. The number of partitions of six million receptors is between $10^{6,000,000}$ and $10^{38,000,000}$, which is many, many orders of magnitude larger than the number of atoms in the universe. One cannot even begin to try to imagine how big this number is. Even if you could evaluate billions of partitions each second, there would not be enough time to train the 10x8 camera during the 13.7 billion years that have elapsed since the Big Bang. There is simply no way to take Lotze's ([1852] 1886) theory of local signs seriously. By way of reminder, Lotze's empiristic theory of local signs says that when the human infant is born, its visual system *already knows* that there are individual receptors and that its visual system can also distinguish among the stimulations of the different receptors, but the visual system at birth has no spatial information about the world "out there." Even, a straight line segment on the retina is not "understood" by a newborn infant as a straight line segment, nor as any other geometrical entity.

According to Lotze, and then according to Helmholtz ([1910] 2000), and then to Hebb (1949), the visual system learns the meaning of all

Figure 7.2. One of the 3D indoor scenes used to test our human subjects and our robot, Čapek.

spatial arrangements of visual stimuli. Lotze, Helmholtz, and Hebb simply forgot to run the numbers. Permutations had been known for at least a century when Helmholtz wrote the first edition of his *Handbüch* in 1866. He apparently never thought to check the number of permutations that would be required to perform the computations required by any empiristic theory of vision. Had he done this, he would surely have realized that each of us must have some writing on our "slates" when we are born. Were the tabula rasa anywhere near blank or clean, the task of training feature detectors in our visual system would be hopeless. This should give pause to anyone thinking about or getting into the learning of natural images or into natural scene statistics (Fei-Fei and Perona 2005; Long and Purves 2003; Simoncelli and Olshausen 2011). Learning particular configurations or features is an impossible approach. The only way to go is to extract abstract characteristics of the visual stimulus such as smooth pieces of curves, colinearity and the parallelism of edges, and 3D symmetry by a geometrical analysis of the stimulus, *not* by using look-up tables. Algorithms, not look-up tables, is how the visual system works.

Conventionally, FGO is considered to be the first step in visual processing, whose output is used for higher-level computing, such as the recovery of 3D shape and space. As you will see, this is not how things actually work, so I will discuss the nature of the 3D recovery problem before saying anything more about FGO. We humans evolved in a three-dimensional space well before the physicists added the eight dimensions needed in their theories, so, if evolution taught us anything

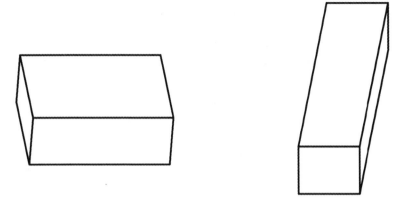

Figure 7.3. "Shepard boxes." The two parallelograms representing the top faces of these boxes are geometrically identical on this page. The only difference is that one of them has been rotated through 90°. They look very different because they are perceived as residing in 3D, not in 2D. From Pizlo 2008.

about the world "out there," we surely learned that it had three dimensions and this important fact was surely written on our slates before we were born. The presence, as well as the compelling nature, of this information can be demonstrated easily because you *always* see objects as three-dimensional. Look at figure 7.3. It shows two boxes whose top faces (2D parallelograms) are identical on the 2D page of this book (except for a 90° rotation on this page), but they do not look the same. The fact that these two parallelograms are geometrically identical is easy to verify by cutting a parallelogram that matches one and then checking that it matches the other. You do not see things in the 2D space of the page in front of you, but note that this is *not* an illusion. The two 3D boxes are really different, so when you see them as different your percept is actually veridical, not illusory! Your visual system recovered the 3D shapes in a single computational step without any access to the 2D image on the page or on your retina. We cannot see our retinal images no matter how hard we try.

Recall that the 3D recovery from a 2D image is a difficult inverse problem. It is difficult because each retinal point could have been produced by any of the infinite number of points on the projecting ray of light (Berkeley [1709] 1910). Now that we appreciate this, let us make some simplifying assumptions. First, assume that the visual system can produce a 3D recovery by using ten bits of information for the direction of depth. This amount of information permits a precision of one millimeter for an object whose range in depth is one meter. Next, if the object occupies the central 20° of the visual field, as many as three million cones will be stimulated (one-half of all the cones on the retina). It follows that for any given 2D image of a 3D object there are $1000^{3,000,000}$ possible 3D interpretations. This amounts to $10^{9,000,000}$ interpretations. This number is not very different from the number estimated earlier in the discussion of the computational complexity of FGO. Both problems seem to be computationally impossible. This seeming curse of computational intractability could actually be a blessing for a vision scientist. The veridical perception of 3D shapes and scenes is so very difficult that it seems possible that there might be *only* one way to solve such a problem. If this is true and if you can develop *a* theory of vision that actually solves it, it seems likely that this theory would be *the* theory of vision. We all know that this "impossible" problem can be solved because our visual system does it nearly perfectly every day. We do recover 3D shapes from 2D images veridically. Until recently, no one knew how this was done, but now that we have built a machine that can see like us, we have moved a bit closer to having *the* theory of vision (see Li at al. 2011, 2012; Pizlo et al. 2010, 2014).

So how does our machine work, and can the answer to this question help us understand how the human visual system works, too? I will start by pointing out that the only way to produce a unique and veridical perceptual interpretation is to use a priori knowledge about what we perceive. This idea was first emphasized by the Gestalt psychologists (Koffka 1935; Köhler 1920; Wertheimer [1923] 1958). They conjectured that the visual percept is the simplest possible interpretation of the retinal image. The rest of this section illustrates why and how this claim works.

Figure 7.4 is a 2D image of a 3D cube. All human observers will see a 3D cube within a fraction of a second rather than any of the remaining $10^{9,000,000}-1$ possible 3D interpretations. We know that no look-up table is, or could be, used in such a case. There simply is not enough time to build a useful look-up table for even a fraction of the possible 3D interpretations: and even if sufficient time could be provided, there is no way that all humans, old and young, born in Asia, Europe, or the Americas, would have at their disposal an identical look-up table permitting them to see the same 3D object. And even if, miraculously, all of our look-up tables were identical, what chances are there that the resulting percept would have been a *perfect* 3D cube! There are no *perfect* cubes in the physical environment, so if experience was actually driving our perceptions, we could never perceive *perfectly* regular (symmetrical) shapes. Plato knew this well. Plato, and those who agreed with him, namely, Descartes, Reid, and the Gestalt psychologists, held that *universals* such as symmetry can exist independently from *particulars* like the characteristics possessed by concrete objects. This should surprise no one, because symmetry, as a mathematical concept, can be defined (formulated) without ever seeing a single object. What might be surprising to a reader but is not surprising to me is that our 3D perceptions of concrete objects are driven by abstract universals rather than by experience with such objects (i.e., particulars). This is the only possible way for us to perceive 3D scenes and 3D objects veridically (see Pizlo 2008 for support of this claim). In the physical world of objects where symmetry is the rule rather than the exception, the best, perhaps the only, way to deal with the prohibitive computational complexity inherent in vision is to use symmetry to recover the 3D shapes of objects. Symmetry, the abstract mathematical construct, permits the visual system to use a single universal prior, instead of an empirically derived prior that would have to be defined for all possible objects, all possible depths, all possible 3D viewing orientations, and all possible partitions of the retinal image. While working on this problem, we discovered that if the 3D object is not perfectly symmetrical, the visual system has the ability to add a correction, but it will only do this if it matters. This becomes obvious once one realizes how easy it is to recognize the asymmetrical posture of a flamingo standing on one leg and how difficult it is to detect the asymmetry present in all human faces. So, contrary to what empiricists, beginning with Aristotle, claimed, not everything that is in the mind had to be in the senses first. Concrete objects are instantiations of the abstract concept of symmetry rather than symmetry being abstracted (derived) from particular objects.

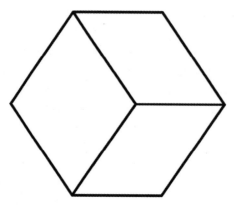

Figure 7.4. An orthographic image of a cube. When your line of sight is orthogonal (at 90°) to the plane of this page and your viewing distance is at least 10 times the size of the image, this 2D image will produce the percept of a 3D cube.

The result of implementing this approach in a robot that can see is shown in figure 7.5 (Li et al. 2012). A scene containing many common objects is at the top. This scene was viewed and interpreted by our robot, called Čapek. The result of Čapek's interpretation of this scene is shown on the bottom, with the floor plan on the left and the regions in the image that Čapek chose to represent, where individual objects were located, shown on the right. More examples of scenes recovered by Čapek's visual system can be found at http://web.ics.purdue .edu/~li135/ObjDetect.html. Note that Čapek, like us, solved the figure-ground organization problem in this 3D scene and in its 2D image in a *fraction of a second*, using cameras whose resolution was only 600x400 pixels. These results suggest that we are on our way to having a theory of vision that actually works. I also suspect that this is the road that will end with *the* theory of human vision, alluded to earlier. I am somewhat confident about this claim because we have obtained considerable psychophysical evidence to support it. This evidence comes from both 3D shape and 3D scene recovery experiments, as well as from the more traditional signal detection experiments. I have reason to believe that the newer recovery experiments provide a better way to study perceptions scientifically than the older signal detection approach. The new recovery methodology works as follows. You begin by specifying a computationally intractable problem of perception, like perceiving 3D

Figure 7.5. Top: A 2D image of a 3D scene containing children's furniture. Bottom left: A top view of the 3D scene shown on top. The black rectangles represent the actual sizes and positions of furniture. The gray rectangles represent Čapek's perception of the individual pieces of furniture. Bottom right: The white polygons indicate the distinct 2D regions Čapek "saw" as representing individual objects.

shapes and 3D scenes. You then test human observers in the task and verify that they can solve it perceptually, quickly, and accurately, despite the fact that this task cannot be solved mathematically. With this done, you formulate a computational algorithm (model) that transforms this ill-posed problem into a well-posed problem by using effective a priori constraints. You then implement the algorithm in a machine, testing the model with the same 3D scenes and 3D shapes you used with your observers. Then (i) if the performance of your computational model is as good as the performance of your subjects, (ii) if the computational complexity of your model is similar to the computational complexity of the perceptual mechanisms, and finally (iii) if the model

fails in the same way as the humans when faced with degenerate viewing conditions, you can be sure that you have a model of the observer's
perceptual mechanisms rather than his response biases. This new approach to studying and explaining perception is very similar to what
Craik (1943) advocated seventy years ago, around the time when the
first computers were being built. Craik realized even then that computer simulation might become the method of choice for explaining
cognitive functions. The time has come to concentrate on implementing Craik's suggestion.

Let me conclude by summarizing how we understand perception today.
Perception is an inference that provides the observer with a veridical
representation of the external world. Illusions almost never happen in
everyday life. Perception is based on algorithms, not look-up tables.
These algorithms are automatically applied to the incoming sensory
stimulation. This automaticity gives us the impression that perception
is easy and effortless. Computationally, it is not. Perception algorithms
are innate; we are born with them. It is possible, perhaps even likely,
that some parameters of these algorithms are estimated or tuned after
birth. This makes sense because the genes that convey the information
about these algorithms are communication channels with finite information capacity. The parameters may have to be tuned to varying input
as the child grows up and ages. It is very unlikely, however, that the algorithms themselves are either learned or modified through learning
during life. This permanence and innateness allows all human beings
to perceive the external world the same way from their first day to their
last. This is crucial for successful interaction among humans and with
objects in the world "out there." The key to understanding how perception algorithms work is to recognize the critical role a priori simplicity constraints play in perception. The sensory data that come in
are always ambiguous, and they are subjected to the simplest possible
interpretation. It so happens that the simplest interpretation is almost
always the correct interpretation. This predilection for choosing the
simplest interpretation suggests that the human mind is solving an "optimization problem." Unlike the numerical methods most scientists

use for solving optimization problems with conventional computers, the human mind uses physiological mechanisms that probably implement what is called the "least action" principle of physics (Lanczos 1970). The concept of optimization, which is widely used in explaining physical and biological systems, as well as in designing engineering systems, is becoming popular in explaining cognitive systems, where it is likely to shed light on the relationship between the mind and the brain. It may also demystify the perennial question about whether machines can see and think.

Note

The author is grateful to Robert M. Steinman for suggestions and comments on earlier versions of this essay. But even more important, I am grateful to Professor Steinman for directing my interest to the history of science and emphasizing the importance of reading firsthand sources. He also convinced me that I should not be afraid to think about the most fundamental aspects of science and philosophy.

References

Alhazen. [1083] 1989. *The Optics.* Books 1–3. Trans. A. I. Sabra. London: Warburg Institute.

Berkeley, G. [1709] 1910. *A New Theory of Vision.* New York: Dutton.

Brindley, G. S. 1960. *Physiology of the Retina and Visual Pathway.* Baltimore: Williams & Wilkins.

Bruner, J. S. 1957. "Going beyond the Information Given." In *Contemporary Approaches to Cognition,* ed. J. S. Bruner, E. Brunswik, L. Festinger, F. Heider, K. F. Muenzinger, C. E. Osgood, and D. Rapaport, 41–69. Cambridge, MA: Harvard University Press.

———. 1973. *Beyond the Information Given.* New York: Norton.

Bruner, J. S., and C. C. Goodman. 1947. "Value and Need as Organizing Factors in Perception." *Journal of Abnormal and Social Psychology* 42: 33–44.

Craik, K. J. W. 1943. *The Nature of Explanation.* Cambridge: Cambridge University Press.

Fechner, G. [1860] 1966. *Elements of Psychophysics.* New York: Holt, Rinehart & Winston.

Fei-Fei, L., and P. Perona. 2005. "A Bayesian Hierarchical Model for Learning Natural Scene Categories." In *IEEE Conference on Computer Vision and Pattern Recognition,* vol. 2: 524–31. San Diego, CA: IEEE Computer Society.

Gibson, E., and R. Walk. 1960. "The 'Visual Cliff.'" *Scientific American* 202: 64–71.

Green, D. M., and J. A. Swets. 1966. *Signal Detection Theory and Psychophysics.* New York: Wiley.

Hebb, D. O. 1949. *The Organization of Behavior.* New York: Wiley.

Helmholtz, H. von. [1910] 2000. *Treatise on Physiological Optics.* Trans. J. P. C. Southall. Bristol: Thoemmes.

Hess, E. H. 1956. "Space Perception in the Chick." *Scientific American* 195: 71–80.

Kant, I. [1781] 1990. *Critique of Pure Reason.* New York: Prometheus Books.

Koffka, K. 1935. *Principles of Gestalt Psychology.* New York: Harcourt, Brace.

Köhler, W. [1920] 1938. "Physical Gestalten." In *A Source Book of Gestalt Psychology,* ed. W. D. Ellis, 17–54. New York: Routlege & Kegan.

Lanczos, C. 1970. *Variational Principles of Mechanics.* Toronto: University of Toronto Press.

Li, Y., T. Sawada, L. J. Latecki, R. M. Steinman, and Z. Pizlo. 2012. "A Tutorial Explaining a Machine Vision Model That Emulates Human Performance When It Recovers Natural 3D Scenes from 2D Images." *Journal of Mathematical Psychology* 56: 217–31.

Li, Y., T. Sawada, Y. Shi, T. Kwon, and Z. Pizlo. 2011. "A Bayesian Model of Binocular Perception of 3D Mirror Symmetric Polyhedra." *Journal of Vision* 11 (4): 11, 1–20.

Long, F., and D. Purves. 2003. "Natural Scene Statistics as the Universal Basis of Color Context Effects." *Proceedings of the National Academy of Sciences* 100: 15190–93.

Lotze, H. [1852] 1886. *Outlines of Psychology.* Boston: Ginn.

Pizlo, Z. 2008. 3D *Shape: Its Unique Place in Visual Perception.* Cambridge, MA: MIT Press.

Pizlo, Z., Y. Li, T. Sawada, and R. M. Steinman. 2014. *Making a Machine That Sees Like Us.* New York: Oxford University Press.

Pizlo, Z., T. Sawada, Y. Li, W. G. Kropatsch, and R. M. Steinman. 2010. "New Approach to the Perception of 3D Shape Based on Veridicality, Complexity, Symmetry and Volume." Minireview. *Vision Research* 50: 1–11.

Reid, T. [1764] 2000. *An Inquiry into the Human Mind and the Principles of the Common Sense.* University Park: Pennsylvania State University Press.

Simoncelli, E. P., and B. A. Olshausen. 2001. "Natural Image Statistics and Neural Representation." *Annual Review of Neuroscience* 24: 1193–1216.

Slater, A., and V. Morrison. 1985. "Shape Constancy and Slant Perception at Birth." *Perception* 14: 337–44.

Thorndike, E. 1899. "The Instinctive Reactions of Young Chicks." *Psychological Review* 6: 282–91.

Wertheimer, M. [1923] 1958. "Principles of Perceptual Organization." In *Readings in Perception,* ed. D. C. Beardslee and M. Wertheimer, 115–35. New York: D. van Nostrand.

———. 1961. "Psychomotor Coordination of Auditory and Visual Space at Birth." *Science* 134: 1692.

PART IV

Introspection and Understanding
in the Humanities

CHAPTER EIGHT

Is Introspection (a First-Person Perspective) Indispensable in Psychology?

OSBORNE WIGGINS

THE SUBJECT MATTER OF PSYCHOLOGY

It might seem rather odd that before I can begin to address the issue of introspection in psychology, I must first stipulate what I take the discipline of psychology to be *about.* That is to say, I must first indicate what I take to be the *subject matter* of psychology. Before the question of method can be asked, the question of subject matter must be answered. This may seem rather odd, I say, because for most intellectual disciplines we usually do not have to begin by ferreting through competing proposals in order to define their topics of study. Psychology, however, has spent most of its history in disagreements regarding its specific topic. The proposals have ranged from the mind to overt behavior to the brain. Most recently interesting arguments have been developed claiming that it is all three and showing us how we might conceive of these three as something of a unity. I would like to cut though all these arguments by first taking my stand with those people who speak of the "subjective brain" (Gillett) or "symbolic brain" (Coakley and Shelemay) and then, while admitting fully that such a subjective brain is the

181

reality, confessing a preference for beginning with the "subjective" or "symbolic" side of that reality.

Another way of framing this issue of subject matter is Thomas Nagel's way (Nagel, 165–80). Just as he asks, "What is it like to be a bat?," we might ask, "What is it like to be a human being?" And then in examining this question we discover that there is indeed something it is like to be a human being for the human being himself or herself. There is something it is like to me for me to be me. This is what I shall stipulate is an important part of the subject matter of psychology. And, following Nagel, I shall switch from this awkward phraseology "what it is like" to employing the traditional terms of mind and its cognates. Still, this does not carry us far toward defining our subject matter. But we cannot go far without utilizing a *method* for defining this subject matter. Therefore I now turn my attention to the role of "introspection" in providing cognitive access to this subject matter.

The Mind/Body Problem and "Introspection"

In my presentation I shall use terms *other than introspection* to designate the kind of self-awareness I shall propose. The word *introspection* carries traditional connotations that I wish to avoid. The assumptions on the basis of which it arose were those of a mind/body dualism; and it was thought that there were dual methods for studying these dual realities: introspection provides direct access to the "inner" mind, while sense perception furnishes direct access to the "outer" world. On the solid foundation of these two distinct modes of self-givenness, lawlike statements and whole theories could be devised.

Many writers in the modern period exemplify these assumptions. Here I shall cite only the case of William James in his *Principles of Psychology*. Regarding mind/body dualism, James writes:

Nature in her unfathomable designs has mixed us of clay and flame, of brain and mind, [such] that the two things hang indubitably together and determine each other's being, but how or why, no mortal may ever know. (182)

And James's characterization of psychological *method* seems to follow almost automatically from his commitment to dualism:

> *Introspective Observation is what we have to rely on first and foremost and always.* The word introspection need hardly be defined— it means, of course, the looking into our own minds and reporting what we there discover. *Everyone agrees that we there discover states of consciousness.* So far as I know, the existence of such states has never been doubted by any critic, however skeptical in other respects he may have been. (185; original emphasis)

The grip of these traditional presuppositions regarding both the subject matter and the method for studying it was so strong that James was committed to them despite the positivism which otherwise determined his approach. William Lyons in his book *The Disappearance of Introspection* wonders why, given James's positivism, this could have been the case. He replies to his own question as follows:

> Part of the answer lies in the fact that, besides being influenced by the European positivists, he was also influenced by the heirs to British empiricism, such as John Stuart Mill, and particularly the Scottish philosophical psychologists, James Mill and Alexander Bain. These nineteenth-century empiricists took for granted, assuming rather than arguing, that introspection was the method for studying anything to do with the mind. (Lyons, 7)

I mention this history and quote James to illustrate it because from it I want to retain the notion of modes of *direct access* to the subject matter of psychology and, correlatively, a notion of the *direct givenness* of it. On the other hand, I set aside the traditional understanding of a metaphysical dualism of inner mind and external world. Consequently, my avoidance of the traditional term *intro*spection. In its place I shall employ terms like *first-person perspective* or, simply and more often, *self-awareness*. However, my analysis will lead to a distinction between two different forms of first-person perspective, two kinds of self-awareness.

Self-Awareness and What It Is Aware Of

Let me explain further why the term *introspection* troubles me. I shall claim that the subjective realm given to us in self-awareness is not just a sphere of mental processes. It is a sphere of mental processes which are *experiences of* something. In particular, they are experiences *of my body* and experiences *of the world.* Readers who have heard something about phenomenology will probably recognize this as an adherence to Edmund Husserl's notion of intentionality (Gurwitsch 2009, 139–56). The world that is the object is the world *as experienced by the subject.* Similarly, the body is precisely the body *as experienced by the subject.* And here body and mind are not experienced as separate: the mind given through self-awareness is an *embodied mind.* Moreover, it is an embodied mind *situated* or *embedded* in the world (Merleau-Ponty; Rowlands, 51–84). In insisting that this is the body *as experienced* and the world *as experienced,* I am not propounding an idealism: I am not denying that there is a world and body other than the world and body as experienced by the subject. I am rather claiming that the subject matter for the psychologist is first of all the world and body *as experienced by the subject under study.*

Perhaps the need for such a claim can be recognized more readily if I shift to that subdiscipline within psychology called "psychopathology." When the psychopathologist studies schizophrenia, for instance, she will not make much progress comprehending the experiences of someone who suffers from delusions and hallucinations unless she seeks to understand the spatiotemporal and causal world as the schizophrenic subject experiences it. I speak of the spatiotemporal and causal world, but this is not the space, time, and causality experienced by us so-called normal individuals. Space, time, and causality as experienced by the person with schizophrenia are different, strikingly different. Nonetheless the psychopathologist must try to make as much sense as she can of them in order to make some sense even of what the words *delusion* and *hallucination* mean, and these are essential technical concepts for understanding schizophrenia. Similar remarks could be offered about the patient's experienced body (Wiggins and Schwartz, 269–81).

So let me sum up the point I have just sought to make. When I am aware of myself in the two different forms of self-awareness I am about to describe, I am aware not just of some sphere of mental events. I am rather aware of mental processes that are themselves aware of something, namely, aware of their embodiment and aware of a world. As a result, it makes no sense to contend any longer that self-awareness gives us only an "inner" realm of "inner" mental occurrences. Hence the misleading connotations of "*intro*spection."

PRESCIENTIFIC SELF-AWARENESS: THE TACIT EXPERIENCE OF SELF IN EVERYDAY LIFE

Two different levels of self-awareness must be distinguished, however. The first I shall call "prescientific" or "everyday" self-awareness. Perhaps the second phrase, everyday self-awareness, is more fitting because by "prescientific" I mean merely that this mode of self-awareness goes on continuously, throughout our wide-awake lives. It requires no special effort, no turning of our focal attention toward ourselves, as is required for the more careful and intellectually rigorous self-awareness that I shall term scientific self-reflection. We human beings become initially acquainted with the basic phenomena of psychology through our own prescientific experience of ourselves as we grow up and as we continually experience ourselves in our everyday lives. This prescientific self-awareness involves *a direct, although indistinct, givenness of ourselves to ourselves.* In this everyday experience we are also aware of the experiences of other people, and these experiences of others also shape our understanding of ourselves and of mental life in general. This awareness of the experiences of other people is *indirect*, but it is integral to forming our familiarity with the human mind. Hence in our prescientific lives, we *directly* experience our own subjective lives and *indirectly* experience the subjective lives of other persons; and these intertwined and comingled experiences of the subjective teach us, in a manner suitable for everyday communication and understanding, the workings of human subjectivity as such. For example, you, as you read this essay, are attending to what I am saying. But during the entire time you are also inattentively aware of your own experiencing life, however indefinite this ongoing self-awareness may be (Zahavi; Gallagher and Zahavi, 45–68).

It is crucial to note that this sort of self-awareness is *not* an *explicit* or *focused* awareness. It is rather *implicit* and *tacit*. It occurs "on its own," we might say; I do not have to actively bring it about. Of course, at any given moment of our experience we are usually focused on or attending to something or other. Something is the "explicit topic" of our awareness. As the Gestalt psychologists have pointed out, however, this explicit theme appears to us within an implicit field. We always have some awareness of this field, however marginal this awareness may be in comparison with our active absorption in the theme. And whatever the changing themes of my consciousness may be, this flowing self-awareness persists as a part of the *field* within which the various themes appear. Not *focusing on* my experience, my attention is directed elsewhere: I may be actively attending to the sentence in the essay I am writing. Nonetheless, at a far more automatic or passive level my experiencing life is indistinctly aware of its own ongoing experiencing (Gurwitsch 2010, 413–537).

Prescientific self-awareness is *essential* for our learning the nature of psychological events and thus for our comprehension of psychological concepts. Moreover, this prescientific learning and understanding continue to inform the inquiries of the scientific psychologist. However far the conceptualizations of the scientific psychologist extend beyond what is experienced at the prescientific level, these more sophisticated concepts draw some of their meaning from it.

These last statements may appear dubious, however. So let me attempt to shore them up. An experimental psychologist is concerned, let us say, to pinpoint the neuronal processes in the brain that correlate with certain visual experiences the research subject is having. Throughout the investigation, the psychologist assumes she knows what it is like to visually perceive something. We are back to Nagel's question, "What is it like to have an experience of a certain kind?" The psychologist can know what it is like to visually perceive something because she herself has visually perceived many things in the past and this pervasive experience was something that she herself, at a tacit and automatic level, was vaguely aware of. Hence her experiment, to herself and to her readers, will make sense because they all are aware of visual perception through their own implicit self-awareness of it.

Let me cite just one other example. In our daily lives, apart from ever being schooled in the science of psychology, we possess an understanding of various emotional words. We use the terms, *remorse, regret,* and *guilt.* Of course, in everyday speech distinctions among these words may remain somewhat obscure. But we do assume that we know generally what they mean, and we may on occasion find the word *remorse* appropriate when we would reject the term *guilt* as not truly designating the feeling meant. Such words represent only a small sampling of the broad vocabulary we employ in speaking of mental processes, and they usually serve well in making ourselves understood by others. My claim is that this mentalistic vocabulary of nontechnical language derives much of its meaningfulness from the tacit but direct awareness we have of our own experiences, as well as from the indirect awareness we have of the experiential lives of others.

Explicit Self-Reflection: A Step into Psychological Science

The continuous occurrence of ordinary, implicit self-awareness makes possible an *explicit* act of reflection on precisely the experiences occurring at this first level. In other words, I can explicitly thematize the experiences that previously occurred without being explicitly noticed. As a matter of fact the descriptions I proposed earlier of what was happening at this implicit level would have been impossible if I had not at that time been explicitly reflecting on this implicit level.

I want to stress, in addition, that the "self" that is disclosed in such reflection is an *embodied self,* just as it is at the first, implicit level. And moreover, this embodied self now brought into explicit focus as my theme is seen by me as itself aware of the world.

In such explicit self-reflection it is possible for the self to be *directly given* to one's reflective attention. To assert such direct givenness of something is not, however, to say that this givenness is *uninterpreted.*

I agree that, on the one hand, there are no "uninterpreted data." There are nevertheless "data," that is, items that are directly observable. A datum can be both *seen as* something (interpreted) and at the same time *directly present itself as* precisely this something. And it can as well directly present itself as *something other* than what it was interpreted as being.

The main advantage of self-reflection for the science of psychology is that it is the only mode of examination in psychology in which the topic being examined is directly given to the inquirer. Hence it enjoys the epistemological advantage involved in direct evidence: the subject matter is directly presented to our direct inspection. We need not engage in inferences regarding our topic of study: we have *it itself* directly given to our observing reflection.

Now I need to substantiate as best as I can these claims regarding the self-givenness of intentional processes to reflection. Assertions regarding the possibility of self-givenness, however, can be substantiated in only one way: by inviting one's critic to try to directly see for himself. Attempting to prove direct givenness by argument is pointless because the propositions in an argument will themselves ultimately have to find their justification in things that are directly given. In brief, direct givenness is the ultimate court of appeal for rational discourse.

Now in self-reflection, I may, of course, simply examine various particular features of my experiences. I can, however, go beyond such inspection of particulars and their particular features and begin to focus on features of my own several experiences as *examplars* of a *more general kind* of experience. Of course, a question of epistemological justification arises here: How can I generalize from features of my own individual experiences to all human experiences of a specific kind? How can I assure myself that my own experiences do exemplify features that can be found in *all* experiences of the selected class? For after all a critic might intervene at this juncture to point out that the lack of justification for any such generalization has always constituted the Achilles' heel of a psychological science utilizing "introspection."

In an attempt to reply to such a critic we might begin by examining what theorists *in fact do* when they make general claims on the basis of self-reflection. This examination will not, of course, provide an epistemological justification, but it may help us infer what these theorists assume will convince us, their readers, that their general claims are cogent.

The Uses of Self-Awareness in Present-Day Psychological Theory

Let us first look at an example developed by Mark Rowlands, in his 2010 book, *The New Science of the Mind: From Extended Mind to Embodied Phenomenology*. Rowlands seeks to persuade his readers of the thesis advanced only recently that the human mind is "extended" in a manner not previously recognized (Clark and Chalmers; Rowlands). His example is using his car's GPS to direct him to a desired address. He begins his example in the manner that philosophers often do: "Consider, for example, a relatively new acquaintance of mine: my car's GPS (global positioning system)" (Rowlands, 13). Rowlands invites us to "consider" his example. What is involved in "considering" it? I suggest that as Rowlands develops his example we are supposed to *imagine ourselves doing* what he is describing. He is not saying, "*Really* go out and *really* get in your car, *really* start it up, and *really* program your GPS and *really* follow it as it directs you to the destination." In other words, we are not required to *actually* follow the instructions of our car's real GPS. We are rather supposed to *imagine ourselves* programming the GPS, listening to its instructions, and following these instructions as we drive our car. Having imagined ourselves having such a set of experiences, we are supposed to reflect on them and determine whether we can detect in those experiences the features to which Rowlands then directs us. We may or may not detect those features, and this seems to serve for Rowlands as a "test" for the claims he seeks to advance.

In order to indicate that this argumentative practice is not rare, I shall cite the original 1998 article by Andy Clark and David J. Chalmers that introduced their "extended mind" thesis. After a first paragraph which starts by posing the question, "Where does the mind stop and the rest of the world begin?" (Clark and Chalmers, 10), they outline three examples of the sorts of experiences they will analyze in order to develop their novel position. These examples are introduced this way: "Consider three cases of human problem solving: . . ." (10–11). The reader is supposed to *imagine* a "person" having the experiences they describe, although, of course, none of the readers is *actually having* those experiences at that time. The last of their examples is indisputably imaginary since it begins: "Sometime in the cyberpunk future, a person sits in front of a similar computer screen" (10–11).

Now there are (at least) two attitudes in which we can read and make sense of their examples. We can read the examples as if they were characterizing the activities of *someone else*. In other words, we could understand the "person" they describe from a third-person point of view. We would still be able to grasp that other person's experiences but only indirectly, "from the outside," as it were. This sort of indirect awareness fails to present us with the presence of the experience in its definite and graphic detail. Only the direct givenness of the experience would do that. Consequently, if we really wish to examine the precise features of this experience, we must, each of us, imagine ourselves having the experiences of the "person" they portray. I must put myself in this person's place and exactly imagine the experiences they depict "him" as having. I must turn "his" experiences into my own by precisely creating in myself the experiences Clark and Chalmers describe him as having. I need not actually sit in front of my computer and rotate the figures as they say: I need rather only graphically *imagine* myself sitting in front of a computer rotating the figures in that way. But such imaginings must produce the experiences precisely as Clark and Chalmers state.

Once I do this, I can take the next step: I can *directly reflect* on these imagined experiences of mine and see if they do in fact exhibit the properties Clark and Chalmers attribute to them. This is a first-person perspective. Such reenacting of the experiences depicted in the authors' examples is required if I wish even to understand the claim they are making. The imagined experience I reflect upon gives their claim meaning by exemplifying it and thereby adding concreteness to their propositions. And such self-reflection is necessary, moreover, if I wish to *determine for myself the truth* of their statements. In this self-reflection I may find that the experience exhibits features inconsistent with the ones they assert. In this case I have some evidence—at least some provisional evidence—for disagreeing with them. And it just so happens that, when I do reflect carefully on my own imagined experiences, I find that I disagree with Clark and Chalmers. I maintain, against Clark and Chalmers, that these properties should be characterized in a different manner in order to describe them correctly.

But the determination of truth has not proceeded far: we have at this point only two sets of people disagreeing. Hence any claims to truth or falsity must remain modest. Its main right to be deemed a test of truth at all arises from its appeal to others to do the same and then to critically examine their findings. In other words, it appeals to intersubjective confirmation or disconfirmation. Obviously, empirical studies in cognitive science or neuroscience must be brought to bear on this theory of extended mind if its evidential support is to gain strength. Indeed evidence of any kind that has been rigorously developed and bears relevance to the hypothesis should be sought. And in fact Clark and Chalmers and Rowlands do draw on research studies in psychology to buttress their assertions (Clark and Chalmers; Rowlands). But these findings could help to decide our disagreement only if we correctly interpret the psychological experiences the subjects had. And here again it would seem to require that we imagine ourselves in the same experimental situation as the subjects and ask ourselves what they must have been experiencing. In slightly different words, we are seeking to imagine ourselves having experiences similar in all relevant respects to what the subjects experienced so that we can examine reflectively and carefully the properties of those experiences.

I mentioned above one advantage that explicit self-reflection brings to psychology when I stressed the epistemological value of the direct givenness of psychological processes to reflection. Having now portrayed the role that imagination plays in providing this reflection with its direct object, I would like to indicate the *second advantage* provided by this procedure. By imagining myself engaged in an experience of a certain sort, I bring into being the experience I shall examine. To the extent that I bring into being an experience of exactly that sort, I can then have directly given to my reflective perceiving the exact and definite features that I wish to scrutinize. I have a detailed and graphic exemplar of my object of study. This precise and definite givenness of the features of the experience furnishes a reliable basis for reflective examination. Without such a graphic imagining of the experience, my reflection on it, no matter how careful, would find in it only indefinite and inexact features.

Now if we are still considering something analogous to the traditional concept of introspection, it is indeed an untraditional kind. For this sort of self-reflection is reflection on a self that generates new experiences through imagining itself having them. Imagination plays a far more central role here than it did in traditional psychological methods. The psychologist must first graphically imagine himself or herself having certain kinds of experiences and then reflect on them and seek features they might share with others.

The Need for Expertise

The ability to employ this method in a reliable manner requires that the psychologist cultivate, through repeated practice, an *expertise* in doing so. Almost all sciences require an expertise that draws on but surpasses "book learning." Such expertise develops gradually as scientists immerse themselves in the daily practice of their science. Being able to graphically imagine oneself performing certain mental acts is not the ability of a beginner, a novice. It requires someone who has lived through all the frustrations, failures, and accomplishments of a seasoned practitioner (Collins).

And the work of acquiring expertise is even more crucial for the success of self-reflection. For purposes of simplicity I have spoken thus far about the *direct* givenness of one's own experiences through *direct* reflection on them. But such *direct* givennness in *direct* reflection can be achieved only as the fruit of much practice, effort, and study. I cannot directly observe my own experience as easily as I can directly perceive the color of the wall. It is more like the expert radiologist's direct perception of the two small cancerous masses on the X-rays of a patient's lungs (Polanyi, 49–65). *Direct* self-reflection is a hard-earned achievement. It is an ability that requires and reveals the attainment of expertise.

CONCLUSION

I realize that the novelty of some of my proposals is likely to leave them seeming dubious. In the final resort any appeal I may make for their cogency must take the form of an appeal to the reader to try it for himself or herself. Especially the claim regarding the productive function that imagination can provide may seem to deviate much too far from a reliance on reality as the source of all evidence.

For a brief defense of my position I would like to suggest that all, or almost all, of the social sciences employ the methods of imagination far more than we have yet recognized. History, anthropology, sociology, hermeneutics, and so on, all have ample need to imagine the experiences of their subjects. Of course, any such imaginings must ultimately be tested through confrontation with the evidence given in reality. But this very evidence is a manifestation, an externalization (we might say), of the experiences of peoples, experiences the social scientist aims to know.

REFERENCES

Clark, Andy, and David J. Chalmers. "The Extended Mind." *Analysis* 58 (1998): 10–23.

Coakley, Sarah, and Kay Kaufman Shelemay, eds. *Pain and Its Transformations.* Cambridge, MA: Harvard University Press, 2007.

Collins, Harry, and Robert Evans. *Rethinking Expertise.* Chicago: University of Chicago Press, 2007.

Gallagher, Shaun, and Dan Zahavi. *The Phenomenological Mind: An Introduction to Philosophy of Mind and Cognitive Science.* London: Routledge, 2008.

Gillett, Grant. *Subjectivity and Being Somebody: Human Identity and Neuroethics.* Charlottesville, VA: Imprint Academic, 2008.

Gurwitsch, Aron. *The Collected Works of Aron Gurwitsch (1901–1973). Vol. II: Studies in Phenomenology and Psychology.* Ed. F. Kersten. Dordrecht: Springer, 2009.

———. *The Collected Works of Aron Gurwitsch (1901–1973). Vol. III: The Field of Consciousness: Theme, Thematic Field, and Margin.* Ed. Richard M. Zaner. Dordrecht: Springer, 2010.

James, William. *The Principles of Psychology.* Cambridge, MA: Harvard University Press, 1983.

Lyons, William. *The Disappearance of Introspection.* Cambridge, MA: MIT Press, 1986.

Merleau-Ponty, Maurice. *Phenomenology of Perception.* London: Routledge, 2000.

Nagel, Thomas. *Mortal Questions.* Cambridge: Cambridge University Press, 1979.

Polanyi, Michael. *Personal Knowledge: Towards a Post-Critical Philosophy.* New York: Harper Torchbooks, 1964.

Rowlands, Mark. *The New Science of the Mind: From Extended Mind to Embodied Phenomenology.* Cambridge, MA: MIT Press, 2010.

Wiggins, Osborne P., and Michael Alan Schwartz. "'The Delirious Illusion of Being in the World': Toward a Phenomenology of Schizophrenia." In *Founding Psychoanalysis Phenomenologically: Phenomenological Theory of Subjectivity and the Psychoanalytic Experience,* ed. D. Lohmar and J. Brudinska, 269–81. Dordrecht: Springer, 2012.

Zahavi, Dan. *Self-Awareness and Alterity: A Phenomenological Investigation.* Evanston, IL: Northwestern University Press, 1999.

CHAPTER NINE

Could Normative Insights Be Sources
of Normative Knowledge?

———

ALLAN GIBBARD

The nineteenth-century English philosopher Henry Sidgwick, Derek
Parfit (2011, xxxiii) tells us, wrote "the best book on ethics ever written." This was Sidgwick's treatise *The Methods of Ethics*, whose first
edition was 1874. I think I agree with Parfit's assessment. Sidgwick, like
Jeremy Bentham (1789) and John Stuart Mill (1863), was a utilitarian:
Sidgwick's version of utilitarianism holds that an act is right if it produces the greatest net happiness, the greatest balance of enjoyment over
suffering. Opponents of utilitarianism have often thought that moral
requirements like the duty to speak truthfully and to keep one's promises have a strength that goes beyond what they draw from happy consequences. Utilitarians like Mill prided themselves on finding an empirical basis for morality, whereas their opponents—William Whewell
(1845) prominent among them—claimed a basis for morality in intuition. Sidgwick, as I say, was a utilitarian, but he argued that utilitarianism too needs intuition.

Why would he think this? Sidgwick, and his student G. E. Moore
after him, argued that moral claims differ in nature from scientific

claims. Moral claims aren't naturalistic and empirical. Findings of what we approve of contrast with this: they are psychological, and experimental psychologists can study them empirically, testing their hypotheses by observing people's responses and the like. The claim that something is morally wrong, though, isn't that people disapprove. Neither is it a more complex psychological claim. Against this, someone might contend that when we call something "wrong," we mean that we would disapprove if we rehearsed, vividly and repeatedly, everything involved. This, if it were correct, would make questions of right and wrong a topic for psychologists to study: the question of what we would approve of under those conditions is a psychological question that can be investigated by designing and running experiments. But Sidgwick denied that moral questions are empirical, scientific questions, and Moore (1903, chap. 1) constructed elaborate arguments against all such "naturalistic definitions" of moral terms. Moral questions, they argued, can't be answered by empirical methods of experiment and observation alone.

Moore argued in addition that no metaphysical definition will capture what we mean by "good." Plato long ago had Socrates arguing to Euthyphro that *pious* can't mean "loved by the gods." The gods love pious things because they are pious, Euthyphro asserts—and this can't mean that they love them because they love them. Such arguments may be controversial among theologians, but it seems clear that *good* can't mean "approved by an all-powerful being," since it's not a sheer matter of meaning that an all-powerful being will approve good things.

Moore concluded that good is, as he put it, "a simple, non-natural property." It is simple in that it can't be analyzed into component concepts. Quite what he meant by "non-natural" might be hard to characterize, but according to Moore, good isn't a physical property, and it isn't a psychological property such as that of being approved. An alternative to Moore's view would make good a definable property, but still non-natural. The term *good* means "desirable," we can say, and *desirable* means something like "fittingly desired." As I myself would put it, that something is good means that desiring it is *warranted*. When we say that stealing is wrong, we can try saying, we mean that feelings of disapproval toward stealing are warranted. That leaves another nonempirical element, warrant for such things as desires or feelings of disapproval. People desire fame even to continue after they are dead, for its own sake and not just as a means to something else—but, we can ask, is such a desire warranted? One view of moral questions is that they boil down to questions of which acts and attitudes are warranted. Does a lie to spare a person embarrassment warrant feelings of approval or of disapproval? On this analysis, there indeed is a simple non-natural property that characterizes ethics, but it is not the goodness but the property of being warranted. This qualifies as a form of non-naturalism but a form that is different from Moore's.[1]

In recent decades, various moral philosophers have come to see ethics as part of a broader subject matter involving warrant or something of the sort. The broader category is labeled "normative," and we can perhaps define normative issues as questions of what warrants what. Normative questions will include not only ethical questions, but such questions as what beliefs are warranted in light of one's evidence. In science, we can ask what degrees of credence are warranted for various hypotheses, such as the hypothesis that depression is a genetic adaptation. The philosopher Wilfrid Sellars characterized normative claims as "fraught with ought," and Kevin Mulligan calls them "oughty." I have been suggesting that we explain normative concepts as concepts involving a primitive concept of being warranted. Other philosophers, including Derek Parfit (2011) and T. M. Scanlon (1998), propose that the basic normative concept is that of a *reason* to do something or to believe something or the like. When we ask, for instance, whether a correlation between taking a drug and death is causal, we face the question of whether the correlation is reason to believe that the drug tends to kill. Normative ethics, then, the study of what makes acts morally right or wrong, counts as a normative subject matter. So do such other subfields of philosophy as normative epistemology. Epistemology, as a branch of philosophy, is the theory of knowledge, and normative epistemology is that major part of epistemology which addresses normative questions concerning knowledge and belief, such as what degrees of credence in a claim are warranted by what sorts of evidence.

According to non-naturalists, these normative fields of inquiry deal with properties that are non-natural. The *probability* of a claim, for example, we can define, in one sense, as the degree of credence in it that is warranted by the evidence. This concept of probability is normative in that it concerns warrant, and so according to normative non-naturalists, the probability of a claim, in light of a given body of evidence, is a non-natural property of the claim. (This is one sense among many that the term *probability* can be given, but I'll stick to this sense in my use of the term in my examples.)

All this brings us to a fundamental and baffling problem: if normative properties aren't ordinary empirical properties which we can investigate via sense experience, how could we know about them? This has long seemed the deepest problem in ethical theory. Ethical properties aren't natural properties, arguments like those of G. E. Moore seem to show. Still, we take ourselves to know things about them. It would be wrong to extort money from a couple by torturing their child; that seems as clear as anything could be. But to say this, according to non-naturalists, is to ascribe a non-natural property to such an act. How could we know that the act has this property, if it isn't one that we can learn about through empirical, scientific investigation? This, I'm now saying, is a kind of problem that extends far beyond ethics. Normative epistemology is another normative subject matter. If normative non-naturalists are right, the theory of justified credence studies properties that are non-natural: probabilities in the normative sense that I just defined. If you flip a coin twenty times and it comes up heads every time, you have reason to believe strongly that this is no fluke and the coin is fixed. Perhaps it has two heads, or perhaps it is weighted to land heads always or almost always, but surely, we can conclude, this is not a fair coin fairly flipped which just happened to come out that way. In light of how the coin has landed, its being fair has negligible probability. The warranted degree of credence that it is fair is close to zero. The coin thus has a non-natural property, normative non-naturalists will say, a property that statisticians can investigate. But again, we must ask, how can we learn about non-natural properties? Even if we should be skeptical of seeming ethical properties and reject them as mysteriously non-natural, can we be skeptical that there's any such normative property as that of being justified as a scientific conclusion? Or more precisely, the question is normative: *should* we be skeptical in this way? And if we should, is this "should" itself something non-natural, and so something we should banish from our thinking?

I have presented this problem of normative knowledge in a way that skips past a host of philosophical controversies. To many philosophers, the claims I have been presenting about non-natural properties that we can know about will seem implausible and even absurd. Many outside academic philosophy may respond the same way. I'll be asking later about alternative ways of regarding normative questions—alternatives to non-naturalism—and I'll be searching myself for an alternative. I want first, though, to spend some time with the problem of how we can have normative knowledge as it arises within non-naturalist thinking.

The Need for Intuitions

Sidgwick and Moore, as I say, agreed that ethical knowledge can only rest on intuitions. It's as clear as clear could be that it's wrong to torture a child to extort money to pay for a vacation, but we couldn't know this without intuition. We can investigate what it's like for the child and for the parents and how the workings of society must rest on a social trust that requires security from such things happening. Still, no normative conclusion follows from such non-normative facts alone. How do we establish that if all these non-normative facts obtain, then such an act is heinous? There is strong moral reason not to impose suffering on people—surely this is right. How, though, could we know such a fact if it is non-natural? And how can we investigate such questions if the methods of the empirical sciences aren't up to the job? The source of our knowledge of fundamental normative facts, Sidgwick concluded, can only be an ethical intuition.

What, then, is an *intuition*? The term is used in ordinary language, and it is used both by some philosophers and by some psychologists. In this essay I consider the term as used in the non-naturalist tradition of Sidgwick and his successors and as it is used by some social psychologists. My prime example in social psychology is the book *The Righteous Mind* by the social psychologist Jonathan Haidt (2012).

When Sidgwick spoke of "intuition," he meant a self-evident judgment that, by its nature, delivers knowledge—and so delivers a truth. Sidgwick worried about how to distinguish genuine intuitions from seeming intuitions or states we might confuse with them. A state can seem to deliver knowledge but fail to do so, and Sidgwick's question was how we can tell when this is the case. Psychologists too sometimes speak of "intuitions" but in an importantly different sense. A mental state is classified as an "intuition" by its psychological nature, regardless of whether it yields knowledge, and regardless even of whether it is true. Intuition in the psychologist's sense has come to be seen as one of the two basic types of thinking; the other is reasoning. Intuition is rapid and effortless, whereas reasoning is slow and effortful.[2] Haidt, in *The Righteous Mind*, gives as instances of intuition the "rapid, effortless moral judgments that we make every day" as, for instance, we read the newspaper (45). These are flashes of affect directed at things one is thinking about—newsmakers and their deeds, for example. These flashes of directed affect constitute moral intuitions in the psychologists' sense whether or not they correctly fit the rights and wrongs of matters.

It is no part of the psychologist's job as psychologist to ask whether a flash of affect conveys a truth, or even to make sense of the question of whether it does. Still, as human beings apart from anyone's role as a psychologist, we can ask this question: Can such flashes of moral affect tell us right from wrong? Are they sometimes intuitions in Sidgwick's sense, sources of fundamental moral knowledge? And what would it mean, if anything, to say that they can be? If we learn that a professor has stolen a book from the library, our immediate response is a flash of feeling which might lead us to exclaim "That's wrong!" He has betrayed his calling, undermining an institution established to serve our common goals. How, though, can we assess whether such an act is really wrong—whether the flash of affect gets matters right?

How we can learn moral truths and indeed whether or not we can are of course highly contentious questions among philosophers. I have been focusing on non-naturalism, which says that being wrong is a non-natural property, and we can know about such properties in ways that depend in part on moral intuition. A great deal of ethical theory, though, has been devoted to finding alternatives. The part of ethical theory that studies the nature of ethical claims and how they can be justified is known as *metaethics*. If ethics is a subdivision of normative studies more generally, then some problems in metaethics will turn out to be special instances of more general problems in what we could call *meta-normative theory*. This will include such questions as these: Are there normative facts? If so, are normative facts non-natural, or how else are they to be conceived? If there indeed are such things as non-natural, normative facts, can we know them or be justified in believing them to obtain? If so, how?

These questions concern what's normative fundamentally. Often, to be sure, ethical difficulties arise from the difficulties of knowing the non-normative facts of a situation. What economic system is ethically best, for example, depends on how the various alternative systems that one might support tend to work. Still, knowing the natural facts, the facts that can be studied by scientific method, won't by itself give the answers to ethical questions. That a system produces misery tells against it ethically, we can all agree, but a finding that it does goes beyond the natural facts of what misery is like. How do we know even such obvious things as that misery is bad? It's not just that misery is bad because of something further about it—that it makes people ill, say, or detracts from economic production. Those aren't the only things that make misery bad; misery is bad in itself. The claim that misery is bad in itself is fundamentally ethical, and so it is fundamentally normative. The puzzle of normative knowledge is how we can have fundamental normative knowledge, such as the knowledge that misery is bad in itself. This puzzle applies as well to questions that are normative but not fundamentally. The lesson often drawn from the experience of the English Jamestown colony is that private property is a good thing. The initial, communal regime of the colony produced hunger and misery, and so was a bad system. If it's true, though, that without private property there is greater misery than with it, that doesn't by itself establish that private property is a good thing. We still need the normative finding that misery is bad. Nonfundamental knowledge must rest in part on normative knowledge that is fundamental—and so again we are led to the question of how we can have fundamental normative knowledge.

That misery is bad in itself is obvious and little disputed, but other fundamental normative questions are contentious. Are happiness and misery all that matters in itself? Or are such things as deceit and coercion bad in themselves, even apart from whatever suffering they engender? Here again we face the puzzle of normative knowledge: Can we know answers to the fundamental normative questions that are disputed—and if so, how?

NON-NATURALISM AND ITS ALTERNATIVES

Whether and how we can know the answers to questions will depend on the natures of the questions. Normative non-naturalists like Sidgwick and Moore say that ethical questions concern fundamental normative properties that are non-natural, and our knowledge rests ultimately on fundamental normative intuitions. Many philosophers, as I say, reject this non-naturalist, intuitionist package. Indeed for a long time, this package was regarded as philosophically naive and not to be taken seriously. Among leading ethical theorists, it has undergone a revival only in the past couple of decades (with such writers as Russ Shafer-Landau, T. M. Scanlon, David Enoch, Ronald Dworkin, and Derek Parfit).[3] Still, even in the wake of this revival, many philosophers still find intuitionistic non-naturalism unacceptable. How, though, can we avoid it? A recent extensive scrutiny of alternatives comes in Derek Parfit's giant two-volume work, *On What Matters* (2011). Parfit argues that every position but his own non-naturalism has defects that are fatal, and non-naturalism is what's left standing. I won't attempt an exhaustive survey of the alternative positions that have been proposed, but I will say a few words about why I find some of the most prominent ones unsatisfactory. I'll then turn to the best answer I can give to the puzzle of normative knowledge.

Critics of non-naturalism maintain that we have no reason to think that there are any such things as non-natural properties, and that even if there were, we would have no way of knowing about them. Why would normative intuitions yield knowledge? A frequent response looks to mathematics. Mathematical knowledge too isn't empirical. Observation tells us how things are but not how they must be of necessity. My own view is that each of these kinds of knowledge must be explained separately, and an explanation of how we can have kinds of mathematical knowledge won't carry over to ethical knowledge. Mathematical knowledge is of structures that things in the natural world approximate. Genetic evolution could account for our potential abilities to have such knowledge. It shaped our species to be fairly reliable about some aspects of the natural world—the shapes and numbers of things, for instance—and the easiest way to be reliable about these things is to get matters of abstract structure right and suppose that the objects of our experience have such structures at least roughly. A story like this doesn't transfer over to fundamental questions of ethics. Take, for example, the question, Do wrongdoers deserve fundamentally to suffer? Parfit claims that at base, no one deserves to suffer, whereas retributivists like Kant think us morally required to impose suffering on wrongdoers, not because of the further evil it will avert, but for the pure purpose of apportioning recompense to desert. How would anything like abilities to think about structures enable us to discern the right answer in a dispute like this?

Many philosophers today appeal to "reflective equilibrium." This was John Rawls's term for a state where one has eliminated sources of bias or bad judgment, like partiality or fatigue, and has considered carefully all the arguments that could be brought to bear (Rawls 1971, 46–63). Reflective equilibrium is what we try to work toward in any philosophical inquiry, said Rawls, and this goes for ethics as much as for any other area of philosophy. Now I agree that a state of perfect ethical discernment would be a state of reflective equilibrium. That leaves us, though, with the question of why a state of reflective equilibrium would be one in which one got the layout of non-natural properties right.

An alternative to non-naturalism is moral skepticism. We can try saying that there is no such thing as moral knowledge. This is the "error theory" of the philosophers John Mackie (1977), Richard Joyce (2001), and others. Moral judgments are systematically mistaken, because there are no such properties as moral rightness or wrongness. Once we extend our puzzles to normative knowledge in general, though, the price of such blanket skepticism becomes very high. Do we never have reason to do anything or to believe anything? Or does talk of reasons to do things or to believe things make no real sense? Can we not assess whether one has reason not to hit one's thumb with a hammer or reason to believe that we are descended from apes? It seems that we have evidence for many of our beliefs, and by "evidence" for a conclusion, don't we mean observations that give us reason to believe that conclusion— not completely, perhaps, but at least with more confidence that we would have reason to have without the observation? Whether or not having reason to believe a thing is a non-natural property, the claim that, in light of our evidence, we have reason to believe the theory of natural selection is a normative claim, and it is hard to know how to proceed with any inquiry if such claims make no sense. And if normative claims like this make sense, why not ethical claims? I have reason not to stick my hand in a flame; if claims like this make sense, why not the claim that I have moral reason not to force someone else's hand into a flame? All these retorts are quick and need further exploration, but at the very least, a moral skeptic faces a challenge: if we deny all sense to moral claims, what are we to say about other sorts of normative claims, claims we seem to need in order to proceed with our lives? Must we deny that any normative claims whatsoever make sense?

Proponents of naturalism in ethics have far more sophisticated theories to offer than any I have mentioned. One prominent genre is "ideal response" theories, which I alluded to earlier. To say that an act is wrong is to say that feelings of moral disapproval toward it are warranted; our question is then what *warranted* means. It means, ideal response theorists say, such as would be had in an ideal state of mind. That disapproval is warranted means that in an ideal state of mind, one would disapprove. (Here and from now on, I'll use the term *approve* for having feelings of approval—and correspondingly with *disapprove*. Sometimes by the term *disapprove* we mean to believe to be wrong, but I won't use the term in that sense, since it would be circular to try to define *wrong* to mean "such as would be believed wrong in an ideal state of mind.") That said, we now have to say what it is for a state of mind to be "ideal." That a state of mind is ideal for judgment, some ideal response theorists say, means that the thinker has gotten the facts of the situation correctly, considered matters vividly and repeatedly, and is impartial—and some other conditions are added. Different accounts fill out this list differently. That makes for a problem: that conditions on a state of mind are "ideal" for judgment seems itself to be a normative claim, and we could dispute what conditions are ideal. What, we can ask, is at issue in such a dispute? The same sorts of arguments that G. E. Moore aimed at naturalistic definitions of *good* can be directed at naturalistic definitions of *ideal.* Suppose, for example, that responses are affected by upbringing, so that sparing the rod or not in childhood makes a difference to later, adult responses. Then people who agree on whether a person satisfies a given list of criteria that includes having been spared the rod may disagree on whether that makes the person's responses ideal. If so, we have to ask what is at issue among them.

Some philosophers reject addressing this question and trying to answer it. Instead, they propose, let's change the question. Let's change the question to one we know how to answer, redefining it as an empirical, scientific question, amenable to the methods of science. Sidgwick and Moore rejected trying to make normative questions empirical; it is changing the subject, they argued. Proponents of "reform definitions" of moral terms, though, advocate precisely that: changing the subject. We should regard our original questions, they say, as confused and ill formed and find a substitute that speaks to our needs (see Brandt 1979).

We should bear this alternative in mind as we proceed with this inquiry, asking whether some naturalistic reform of our language could serve the intelligible purposes of moral language. Before we settle on reform, though, we should look further for what we might already be asking with our moral questions.

MORAL EPISTEMOLOGY

Whether stealing a library book is wrong, I suggested, amounts to the question of whether condemnatory moral affect toward such an act is warranted. How can we address such questions? How can we evaluate whether a way of feeling toward an act is warranted? In his 1959 book, *Ethical Theory,* Richard Brandt formulated what he called the "qualified attitude method" (250) as our standard procedure for answering ethical questions. I'll sketch this method as an example of a moral epistemology, a theory of moral knowledge. We have no way to answer moral questions, Brandt took it, that is independent of moral attitudes such as feelings of obligation or feelings of moral condemnation. Particular moral questions we decide by exercising our affective capacities. We also decide them by applying moral principles, but moral principles too need testing, and we test moral principles too by our moral attitudes. If a principle clashes with our attitudes, we may revise it or reject it. We don't, though, regard our feelings as infallible. Not everything they seem to tell us is true. Brandt, then, offered some tests for attitudes. They must be discounted if they fail to be impartial or informed. They must be discounted if they stem from an abnormal state of mind. They must be discounted if they can't be made to accord with some tractable set of general principles. Attitudes that pass such tests we might call *qualified*. We judge principles by bringing to bear our qualified attitudes. And when principles conflict—for example, that one shouldn't lie and shouldn't cause pain, where only a lie will avoid pain—we resolve the conflict by bringing to bear our qualified attitudes. An act is morally required, we can try saying, if and only if feeling obligated to perform it would pass all the tests of the qualified attitude method, and thus constitute a qualified attitude.

Brandt meant this not as a definition of what the term *morally required* means but as an account of what it is for an act to be morally required. His endorsement of the qualified attitude method, then, doesn't violate G. E. Moore's strictures against naturalistic definitions, since the purported definitions Moore inveighed against were ones meant to say what moral terms mean. Brandt considers a claim something like the following:

> An act is morally required if and only if the attitude of feeling obligated to perform it passes the following tests (and then the tests of the qualified attitude method are listed).

If this is not intended as a definition that gives the meaning of the term *morally required*, what does it mean? We can also attribute to Brandt this claim about warrant:

> An attitude is warranted if and only if it passes the tests of the qualified attitude method.

Again, Brandt would not put this forth as a claim about what the term *warranted* means. What the claim does mean, then, will depend on what *warranted* means.

I'll now sketch an account of what *warranted* means, an account that could give sense to these claims. (It isn't Brandt's account; rather, it is an account that I have advocated.) Then I'll use this account to ask whether normative intuitions could ground normative knowledge.

EXPRESSIVISM

A kind of position now called "expressivism" was first broached in the 1930s and has been developed substantially since then. Non-naturalists are right, expressivists say, that no naturalistic definition will capture what a normative term means. We cannot give a correct naturalistic definition of a basic normative term like *good* or *warranted* or *ideal*. That's not, though, expressivists say, because normative terms stand for non-natural properties. Rather, their meaning is to be explained by characterizing the states of mind that normative terms are used to express. According to A. J. Ayer's emotivism in his provocative 1936 book, *Language, Truth and Logic*, to say "Stealing is wrong" is to express disapproval of stealing. (Again, here and subsequently, I use *disapproval* to mean feelings of disapproval, not the belief that the thing in question is wrong.) In saying this, we give the meaning of the term *wrong*.[4] Ayer's theory of moral meanings is powerful but unsatisfactory, in my view: I can feel disapproval toward a thing—a sexual practice, say—and yet think it isn't really wrong. What is it to believe that the practice isn't really wrong? It is to believe that disapproving of it isn't really warranted—which brings us back to what the term *warranted* means.

I propose explaining the meaning of *warranted*, in this sense, in an expressivistic way. What does it mean to say that a state of mind such as approval is "warranted"? We explain it, I proposed, by explaining the kind of state of mind that calling a state of mind "warranted" expresses. In my 1990 book, *Wise Choices, Apt Feelings*, I called this state of mind "accepting a system of norms," and I tried to explain this state of mind by its role in a psychological theory. Accepting a system of norms that says to feel disapproval is what stands behind a syndrome that includes tending to be in the state of mind and tending to avow one's acceptance in discussion. In my later book *Thinking How to Live* (2003), I described this state of mind as akin to planning how to feel. When I believe disapproval of stealing to be warranted, I "plan," in a certain sense, for the feelings to have toward stealing. This "planning" here isn't planning for action, since one can't feel disapproval at will, and even if one could act to get oneself to disapprove of a practice, planning to get oneself to disapprove wouldn't constitute believing the practice to be wrong. Planning a state of mind isn't in general planning to will being in it. Even with planning for action, something like this holds. The direct effect of my having the plan is on the will, true enough, but not because I will to will. My having the plan tends to bring it about directly that I will accordingly. Similarly, when I believe that disapproval is warranted, the direct effect isn't that I will to disapprove but that I disapprove.

Can normative insights, then, give us normative knowledge? Normative insights, I am taking it, consist of flashes of moral affect which prompt us to moral conclusions like "That's wrong!" Do these conclusions constitute knowledge? They do, we can say, if they deliver truths in a way that is nondefective—but what does it mean for a way of coming to beliefs to be "defective" or not? For a belief to constitute knowledge, we can try saying, it must be true, it must be warranted, and the processes that eventuate in true belief must be reliable. A chief question, then, is whether, in one's epistemic circumstances, the belief is warranted. I have tried to explain the belief that a state of mind is warranted, in a thinker's epistemic circumstances, as something like a plan to be in that state of mind if in those circumstances. The question of whether a belief is warranted in the circumstances thus amounts to the planning question of whether to have that belief in those circumstances. One way I might plan, for example, is to plan to feel toward things in ways that meet the standards of Brandt's qualified attitude method. To plan this way, I am saying, is to believe that moral feelings are warranted just when they meet the standards of Brandt's qualified attitude method. This is to adopt a thesis in the epistemology of normative beliefs.

Is it true that moral feelings are warranted if and only if they meet Brandt's standards? Nothing I have said so far speaks to this. Rather, I have been explaining the meaning of this claim—the claim that an attitude is warranted if and only if it meets the standards of Brandt's qualified attitude method. I explained it in the expressivist's way, by saying what believing the claim consists in. To believe the claim, I said, is to plan (in my special sense) to have moral feelings that meet Brandt's standards. Coming to believe the claim thus consists in a kind of planning. If you ask me whether the claim is true, I come to my answer by planning how to feel about things.

What happens, then, when I attempt this? I don't come to a plan that is fully worked out, but I do come to a plan roughly. Brandt's account of how to test moral attitudes strikes me as on the right track, and so in my planning for what moral feelings to have, I at least roughly adhere to Brandt's standards. I can now express the state of mind I am in, saying this:

> At least roughly, moral feelings are warranted if and only if they meet the standards of Brandt's qualified attitude method.

MORAL KNOWLEDGE

When, then, do moral feelings yield moral knowledge? Brandt discusses southwestern American Indians of a century ago playing a game of burying a chicken up to its neck and riding by on horseback trying to pull the chicken out of the ground. They accepted that this hurts the chicken but didn't see this as making the game wrong. I myself, though, have feelings of moral condemnation for playing this game of tormenting an animal. Do these feelings give me knowledge that playing the game is wrong?

Responding to this question requires an account of when a belief constitutes knowledge, and a prominent kind of account is the one I already gave roughly. First, a belief constitutes knowledge only if the belief is true. For it to constitute knowledge, moreover, it must be warranted. Finally, it must stem from processes that deliver truths reliably and have the features, in this particular instance, in virtue of which the process is reliable in general.

Suppose I am right, then, that moral feelings are warranted when they satisfy the standards of Brandt's qualified attitude method. What should we say of the case where I consider the chicken-pull game and come to believe it wrong by relying on my qualified attitudes? I have a qualified attitude of moral condemnation toward playing the game, and accordingly I come to the belief that playing the game is wrong. This belief constitutes knowledge if it is true and warranted and it stems from a process that reliably produces true moral beliefs, operating in the ways in virtue of which it tends to produce true moral beliefs. If these conditions obtain, then an affect-laden moral insight—my feeling of condemnation toward playing the game—has yielded moral knowledge.

What, though, if the moral insights of one person clash with the moral insights of another? Brandt's investigations into memories of playing chicken-pull indicate that this is such a case. Cultures, it appears, disagree fundamentally in their attitudes toward cruelty to animals, and I have drawn the chicken-pull example from Brandt's study of Hopi ethics; the game he reports was from the early twentieth century, as recalled in midcentury.[5] We readers abhor games that torment animals, but young Hopi men of a century ago had no such response. There is no indication that their qualified attitudes would be different—that if their attitudes met the standards of Brandt's qualified attitude method, they would disapprove.

Moral claims that contradict each other can't all be true, and moral insights that clash with moral truths can't be said to deliver moral knowledge. People whose qualified attitudes disagree, though, won't agree on which moral claims are true, or which psychic processes are reliable in coming to feelings that are warranted. I do claim to know that tormenting animals for fun is wrong, but I don't have arguments that will bring everyone's qualified attitudes into accord with mine. A Hopi of a century ago might reason with perfect coherence, in a way that satisfies every reasonable epistemic standard, and reject my contention that playing the game is wrong. (Or perhaps the right epistemic standards for moral beliefs include a requirement to abhor cruelty, but maintaining this would beg the question on which these two cultures disagree.)

TEMPERED MORAL REALISM

In making moral judgments, we must rely ultimately on our moral intuitions. Sidgwick was right to maintain this. The intuitions should be scrutinized critically, but there is no way to jettison them and respond to moral questions independently of them. There appear to be cases, though, I am worrying, where cultures differ in their moral attitudes and would continue to differ even if their attitudes satisfied all of Brandt's standards. Could one group be right in such a case and the other group be wrong? It is happenstance, in a way, whether I belong to one group or another, an accident of fate. How can a belief that I arrive at by such happenstance count as knowledge?

In parallel cases, after all, we wouldn't ascribe knowledge. Suppose two groups of medical doctors disagree as to which of two treatments will cure me of a disease. Ignorant of this conflict, imagine, I choose one group by chance and trust what they tell me. Even if I luckily consulted the right group, I didn't thereby come to know which treatment would cure me. I might have come to a true and warranted belief but not to a state of knowledge. As for the group with the right answer, for them to count as knowing which cure will work, they must lack some epistemic defect that accounts for the other group's disagreeing with them. If, for example, the group with the wrong answer can't even understand some of the pertinent arguments, then the fact that they don't agree doesn't impugn the claim of the group with the right answer to know. Doesn't the same go for my belief that tormenting an animal for fun is wrong? If we qualify as knowing that playing the game is wrong and the Hopi of a century ago whom Brandt studied didn't qualify as knowing that it isn't wrong, that can only be because they suffered some epistemic defect.

Metaethical debates are often couched in terms of "moral realism" versus "moral antirealism." A crucial development in expressivism has been the rise of what Simon Blackburn labels "quasi-realism." This is the doctrine that we can start out with the materials of a moral antirealist and earn the right to speak as a moral realist does. Moral realists, for example, claim that moral statements can be true or false. This, however, doesn't distinguish a moral realist from a moral expressivist, for the quasi-realistic expressivist agrees that moral statements can be true or false. He accepts a "deflationary" account of truth: the claim "It's true that snow is white," he says, is equivalent to the plain claim that snow is white. Likewise, he says, "It's true that stealing is wrong" is equivalent to "Stealing is wrong." Thus if an Ayer-like emotivist says that "Stealing is wrong" means "Boo for stealing!" he'll say the same for the claim "It's true that stealing is wrong." Expressivists can also account for realists' claims to moral objectivity: A moral realist might say, "Chicken-pull would be wrong whether or not anyone disapproved," and an Ayer-like emotivist can agree. This means, the emotivist can say, "Boo for chicken-pull, whether or not anyone disapproves!"

In considering claims to knowledge, though, we have found a respect in which expressivists should side against moral realists of an extreme kind. A strong moral realist might claim that true moral claims state moral facts, and that moral facts are factlike in every way. Here, though, we encounter a way in which moral "facts" and the cases that are most clearly matters of fact differ. With facts like whether the propensities of our species were shaped by millions of years of natural selection, if two people disagree fundamentally and neither has a clear epistemic defect that is independent of who happens to be right, then even the side with the right doctrine fails to know. Moral knowledge differs in this regard: we know that tormenting an animal for fun is wrong even if those who disagree have no epistemic defect apart from failing to recognize that such cruelty is wrong.

Are we warranted in this moral judgment? The judgment, I am saying, amounts to a plan for how to feel about chicken-pull. In judging that playing the game is wrong, I am coming to a plan for how to feel about playing the game. I am planning to feel obligated not to play such a game, even for the hypothetical case of being a Hopi of a century ago who doesn't feel obligated not to play. Surely, in planning how to feel, I can only go by the feelings I am prone to have in epistemically ideal conditions. The standards of Brandt's qualified attitude method, I am taking it, capture what sorts of conditions are epistemically ideal for moral judgment. If this is right, then my judgment that playing chicken-pull is wrong, even if no one disapproves, is warranted. I now voice my warranted judgment:

Playing chicken-pull is wrong even if no one disapproves.

Most philosophers who regard themselves as "moral realists" take this tempered position. Even if some people with no independently identifiable epistemic defect wouldn't agree, they say, that doesn't entail that we fail to know that playing the game is wrong. This position isn't consistent, though, with the extreme moral realist position that moral facts are factlike in every way that a nonmoral fact can be. In this regard, we might say that moral facts are "quasi-facts," and the correct metanormative view isn't a form of full realism but of quasi-realism.

There is such a thing as moral knowledge, I am maintaining, and it does rest on moral intuitions. It is different, though, from knowledge of such natural facts as that natural selection accounts for the genetic propensities of our species. This belief is warranted for anyone with our evidence: the layout of fossils, similarities of DNA, and the like. Not so for the belief that being cruel to animals for fun is wrong: this belief is warranted for those with our affective sensibilities but not for everyone who has our evidence. Communities whose affective sensibilities differ from ours may differ in which moral beliefs are warranted for them. We are warranted in our conviction that it was wrong for Hopi young men to play the chicken-pull game, even though they weren't prone to feeling obligated not to play it. The Hopi of a century ago would have been warranted in rejecting this conviction.

So can normative insights be sources of normative knowledge? Normative insights are affective responses, and when they meet certain conditions, I have concluded, what they give rise to is not exactly normative knowledge. It is what we might call normative "quasi-knowledge." Our affective responses can justify us in believing those responses warranted.

NOTES

1. Such a view is proposed by Ewing 1939.

2. Kahneman (2011) speaks of "Type one" and "Type two" processes.

3. Dworkin 1996; Scanlon 1998; Shafer-Landau 2003; Enoch 2011; Parfit 2011.

4. Another form of expressivism is developed by Simon Blackburn in *Spreading the Word* (1984), *Ruling Passions* (1998), and other writings.

5. Brandt discusses whether moral disagreement over cruelty to animals is fundamental: *Hopi Ethics* (1954). I discuss Brandt's finding in my "How Much Realism" (2011).

REFERENCES

Ayer, A. J. 1936. *Language, Truth and Logic.* London: Victor Gollancz. 2nd ed. 1946.

Bentham, Jeremy 1789. *An Introduction to the Principles of Morals and Legislation.* London: T. Payne.

Blackburn, Simon. 1984. *Spreading the Word: Groundings in the Philosophy of Language.* Oxford: Clarendon Press.

———. 1998. *Ruling Passions: A Theory of Practical Reason.* Oxford: Clarendon Press.

Brandt, Richard B. 1954. *Hopi Ethics: A Theoretical Analysis.* Chicago: University of Chicago Press.

———. 1959. *Ethical Theory.* Englewood Cliffs, NJ: Prentice Hall.

———. 1979. *A Theory of the Good and the Right.* Oxford: Clarendon Press.

Dworkin, Ronald. 1996. "Objectivity and Truth: You'd Better Believe It." *Philosophy and Public Affairs* 25 (2): 87–139.

Enoch, David. 2011. *Taking Morality Seriously: A Defense of Robust Realism.* New York: Oxford University Press.

Ewing, A. C. 1939. "A Suggested Non-Naturalistic Analysis of Good." *Mind* 48: 1–22.

Gibbard, Allan. 1990. *Wise Choices, Apt Feelings: A Theory of Normative Judgment.* Cambridge, MA: Harvard University Press.

———. 2003. *Thinking How to Live.* Cambridge, MA: Harvard University Press.

———. 2011. "How Much Realism? Evolved Thinkers and Normative Concepts." In *Oxford Studies in Metaethics* 6, ed. Russ Shafer-Landau, 33–51. Oxford: Oxford University Press.

Haidt, Jonathan. 2012. *The Righteous Mind: Why Good People Are Divided by Politics and Religion.* New York: Pantheon.

Joyce, Richard. 2001. *The Myth of Morality.* Cambridge: Cambridge University Press.

Kahneman, Daniel. 2011. *Thinking Fast and Slow.* New York: Farrar, Straus & Giroux.

Mackie, John L. 1977. *Ethics: Inventing Right and Wrong.* Harmondsworth: Penguin Books.

Mill, John Stuart. 1863. *Utilitarianism.* London: Parker, Son, & Bourn.

Moore, G. E. 1903. *Principia Ethica.* Cambridge: Cambridge University Press.

Parfit, Derek. 2011. *On What Matters.* 2 vols. Oxford: Oxford University Press.

Rawls, John. 1971. *A Theory of Justice.* Cambridge, MA: Harvard University Press.

Scanlon, T. M. 1998. *What We Owe to Each Other.* Cambridge, MA: Harvard University Press.

Shafer-Landau, Russ. 2003. *Moral Realism: A Defence.* Oxford: Clarendon Press.

Sidgwick, Henry. 1907. *The Methods of Ethics.* 7th ed. London: Macmillan. 1st ed. 1874.

Whewell, William. 1845. *Elements of Morality including Polity.* London: John W. Parker.

CHAPTER TEN

Truth and Knowledge in Literary Interpretation

————

CARSTEN DUTT

Sabine MacCormack, in memoriam

As the title of my essay indicates, I am not dealing here with interpretation in general—a far-reaching and highly complex matter[1]—but instead with a specific (and notoriously controversial) academic genre of it, which is—for better or worse—my genre: *literary interpretation*. My question is, What is the role and relevance of truth and knowledge in literary interpretation? In order to answer this question, I will argue that the pursuit of truth and of what Bernard Williams has called its virtues—accuracy, circumspection, intellectual integrity[2]—sustain literary interpretation as a knowledge-seeking and, when felicitous, knowledge-enhancing practice. Furthermore, caring about truth, not only in the sense of seeking to answer veridically each single question one may raise in interpreting a work of literature but also in the sense of subscribing to the ideal of a *comprehensive true account* of that very

216

work, could help us to counter and perhaps halt the ongoing tendency toward uncritical pluralism, parochialism, and mutual noncommunication between different schools—some observers have called them "tribes"[3]—of literary interpretation. Although, according to my view, truth is and should be acknowledged as the standard goal for forming beliefs and making assertions in interpreting literature, it is undeniable that some typical results of literary interpretation and criticism do not fall under this description and its cognitively normative force. For clearly some of the remarks that critics offer in lectures, books, or articles on works of literature have a different aim and scope from that of discovering and ascertaining what is true about these works in terms of genesis, structure, meaning, function, impact, or reception. I'm referring to remarks with which critics seek to flesh out what is only suggested or even left open in a literary work. For example, critical discourse quite often weaves together what as a story line is only loosely connected, noncausally juxtaposed, or even randomly scattered, and thus in certain respects undetermined. Also, critical discourse quite often rounds out characters by imaginatively supplementing motives for their thoughts or actions which are in fact not, either explicitly or implicitly, given in a literary work. The great Polish phenomenological philosopher and literary theorist Roman Ingarden has dubbed this type of interpretive activity *concretization*.[4] Now, obviously, within the framework of a realist conception of truth, to which—in spite of all antirealist and constructivist rhetoric—human beings in practice do and should adhere,[5] concretizations as complementing determinations of what in a literary work are places or zones of indeterminacy can be neither true nor false, for there is no fact of the matter that would allow for ascribing positive or negative truth values to them. So within certain limits of aptness different and even mutually exclusive concretizations of a literary work can be interpretively legitimate and fruitful, even though they are not acquisitions of truth and a fortiori not acquisitions of knowledge. I argue that a sufficiently nuanced account of literary interpretation has to take this into account. It has to observe that in addition to being a *cognitive process* of acquiring truths and knowledge, literary interpretation is also a *creative process* of adding to the aesthetic, philosophical, moral, or religious value of experiencing a work by pertinent and appropriate operations of concretization. In this respect literary interpretation fulfills a function quite similar to that fulfilled by performative interpretations of musical scores in the concert hall or of dramatic works on stage. It would be mistaken, however, to think of the cognitive and the creative functions of literary interpretation as neatly separable. In fact, interpretations that enhance the value of experiencing a literary work by showing it in the light of creative concretizations are cognitively dependent on that work's interpretation in terms of truths about its intrinsic and relational properties. In order appropriately and productively to complement a work's zones of indeterminacy, literary critics have first to identify these zones and second to discern how they are embedded in well-determined structures. Furthermore, quite differently from performative interpretations, which by their very choices (in playing a composition or staging a play, etc.) practically exclude each other, critical interpretations of literature can theoretically integrate different and even mutually exclusive concretizations on a higher level of understanding. And this is one of the many reasons why subscribing to the idea of a comprehensive and true account of a literary work is indispensable for good interpretive practice.

Let me start by summarizing some insights about interpretation as an endeavor of acquiring truth and knowledge.

1. Pace Nietzsche and Heidegger, not all perception or apprehension can aptly be viewed as interpretive; some is clearly non- or (as Richard Schusterman has put it) preinterpretive perception and apprehension.[6] And typically, preinterpretive states of perceiving and apprehending in which we acquire, process, and store a lot of information about the world around us serve as the points of departure for interpretive activities proper.

2. Interpretive activities proper involve the formation of questions and hypotheses about a given object, the *interpretandum*. They involve the exploration and weighing of possible classifications in terms of genesis, structure, meaning, purpose, or function regarding

the *interpretandum*. And therefore interpretation proper involves conscious thought, explicit reflection, inference, and reasoning.

3. Interpretation proper requires some form of nonobviousness: "the *nonobviousness* of what is being interpreted" to the interpreter.[7] If he or she securely knows that *x* is *F*, then forming and stating the belief that *x* is *F* for her are not acts of interpreting *x*.[8] Interpretation proper is a step or more commonly a series of steps toward knowledge one seeks to have about *x* but does not yet have.

4. However, interpretation proper also requires some knowledge pertaining to *x*, the object in question. Merely guessing that *x* is *F* is *not* an act of interpreting *x*. The concept of interpretation is undoubtedly more demanding: it is internally linked with the concepts of justification and reliability in the process of forming interpretive beliefs and coming up with the corresponding interpretive assertions about a given object.[9] When we interpret an object with regard to some question of the type, *is x F*? we standardly do not flip coins; for flipping coins is not a reliable and intellectually justifiable way of belief formation; it may lead us to a true belief and to a true assertion about *x*, but only accidentally, only by chance; and in the business of interpretation we don't want to be subjected to chance—at least not when we take that business seriously; we want to arrive at beliefs that are true or most likely to be true, and these beliefs are, of course, the well-grounded ones, beliefs supported by sound reasoning and sufficient evidence. In order to arrive at interpretive beliefs of such quality, we have to have relevant propositional knowledge and to know how to use it productively in the process of interpreting the object in question.[10] There is no interpretation from scratch. In other words: *felicitous interpretation adds to the knowledge we must have and make use of in order to get our interpretive business going.*

Let me flesh out what I have said with an example—not from literature, but from the visual arts. A rather marginal case of everyday interpretation, it will take us from the so-called lifeworld to scholarly contexts of interpretation. So let us suppose we take a stroll through the lovely Pinacoteca Communale di Faenza in Italy. Suppose that our attention is caught by a strikingly beautiful painting by the seventeenth-century artist Francesco Maffei (1605–60), representing a young woman with a sword in her left hand, who, with elegant support from her right hand, is holding on her left arm a platter with the decapitated head of a bearded man on it (fig. 10.1).[11]

According to the concept of interpretation I have just outlined, we do not interpret Maffei's painting when we perceive or describe the depicted figures in such a way. We do not interpret; we simply see and know according to our habits of seeing that this painting depicts a young woman with a sword in her left hand and in her right a platter with the decapitated head of a bearded man on it. And that is that. But now interpretive-minded gallery visitors among us may start asking themselves who exactly this young woman and her trophy are, and in doing so at least some of these visitors may not be restricted to purely guessing; instead they may embark on the business of interpretation by using pertinent knowledge, biblical and iconographic knowledge in this case. Some may hold that Maffei's painting shows Salome with the head of Saint John the Baptist on the platter, mentioned in the Gospel of Saint Matthew;[12] others may doubt this interpretation and point to the sword in the young woman's hand, which scarcely accords with the story of Salome. Rather it indicates that the depicted figure might be Judith with the head of Holofernes, whose sword the brave young lady took "and approached to his bed, and took hold of the hair of his head, and said, 'Strengthen me, O Lord God of Israel, this day.' And she smote twice upon his neck with all her might, and she took away his head from him." But what about the platter? As we all know, Judith "gave Holofernes' head to her maid; And she put it in her bag of meat."[13] There is no platter in the Book of Judith, but there is a platter in the Gospels story of Salome and the beheading of Saint John the Baptist.

Now, this is what we call *a conflict of possible interpretations*: it is a paradigmatic case of divergent evidence in forming interpretive belief. And note that this conflict about scriptural reference and iconographic content is not a purely positivist or antiquarian one; it is of deep import to the understanding and appreciation of the painting—its hermeneutic and aesthetic identity. For it is obvious that under the description of Judith with the head of Holofernes the visual salience of

Figure 10.1. Francesco Maffei (?), *Judith*, ca. 1640, oil on canvas, 26.7 x 35.4 in., Pinacoteca Comunale di Faenza, Italy

the depicted scene and especially of the depicted woman will differ strongly from its visual salience under the description of Salome with the head of Saint John the Baptist. Just look at these lascivious eyes . . . Now, some ludic minds may be fine with this situation and enjoy the back and forth of taking Maffei's painting now this way and then the other: Is it a duck, or is it a rabbit? Neither, of course, for it is Judith with the head of Holofernes, as Erwin Panofsky convincingly argued more than fifty years ago against older interpretations that identified the depicted lady as Salome.[14] Panofsky did so by providing evidence from what art historians call the history of types (*Typengeschichte*). The pertinent materials show that it was quite common in northern Italian art of the period to "transfer" something like Saint John's platter to depictions of Judith (evidenced as such by the presence of Judith's maid in some of these paintings), whereas there hasn't been found a single painting in which Salome would have been ennobled with a sword like that of Judith. Also, the features of the decapitated head have more in common with Holofernes heads than with Saint John the Baptist heads. Of course, Panofsky's comparative evidence, his argument from the history of types, is not a watertight proof for the truth of his iconographic claim. Positivistic art historians would surely expect more and different external evidence, ideally perhaps a contract between the painter and a noble commissioner.

I am convinced that Panofsky would have very much appreciated such further evidence, for he undoubtedly shared an intentionalist stance toward the iconographic interpretation of that painting in particular and the visual arts in general. According to an intentionalist framework of interpretation, an interpretive statement is true if it reports correctly the intentions an artist has realized by painting a certain picture—in this case Francesco Maffei's intention to paint a Judith with the head of Holofernes in close-up and upgraded with a platter. Needless to say that artists as well as writers form and realize their artistic or writerly intentions within the constraints of artistic or literary conventions—as we form and realize our semantic and communicative intentions as speakers of a natural language within the constraints of its grammar and certain communicative rules and conventions.[15]

The given example, I think, nicely illustrates how wonder and a fortiori the awareness of a certain lack of knowledge vis-à-vis an object initiate interpretation and how interpretation typically proceeds in order to reach and secure its results: some questions, at least one, come up; pertinent knowledge is activated and applied to form hypotheses and to explore interpretive possibilities; the evidence at hand is assessed but does not allow for a justified and reliable decision between interpretive possibilities; additional evidence is searched for, achieved, and weighed; the less plausible hypothesis is dropped in favor of a well-founded and therefore very likely true interpretation; the correct answer to the interpretive question (or questions) at stake. Note how a rather tentative and probing mode of interpretation—"It could be a depiction of Salome"; "It could also be a depiction of Judith"—develops into a determinative mode: "It is most likely a depiction of Judith, and not of Salome"; "It is a depiction of Judith."[16] Interpretation initiated by the awareness of a certain lack of knowledge aims at filling that very lack. It aims at acquiring and justifying relevant true beliefs about the object interpreted, and in that sense interpretation standardly aims at knowledge, for knowledge is, according to the standard analysis of the concept, justified true belief.[17]

In literary interpretation, to which I turn now, questions of knowledge-seeking and therefore truth-oriented interpretation come in various sizes or, to put it differently, on various levels of the object interpreted. Some of them apply to individual words, phrases, or sentences of literary works: "Are they ambiguous?" "Are they ironic?" "Should this verse be understood literally or metaphorically?" Other questions apply to larger parts of a given work and some to the work as a whole: "What is its thematic content?" "What is its overall outlook and aim?" "What is its communicative purpose and function?" And yet other questions apply to the work in relation to other works or to its social, cultural, philosophical, or biographical contexts, and so on. The web of interpretive issues in dealing with literature is chronically vast and full of repercussions: findings on the level of microinterpretation often affect our results on the level of macrointerpretation—and vice versa. A single ironic word in a seemingly full-blown happy ending of a novel can alter the work *as a whole,* and overlooking that single ironic word would result not in a local but in a total misinterpretation. Needless to underscore that answers to a certain interpretive question typically prompt a whole bunch of follow-up questions about the work and/or its contexts. That is why I am offering the metaphor of a web of interpretive questions, issues, and tasks. For example, we simply cannot discuss or answer questions about the communicative purpose and function of a certain work without discussing and answering questions about the relation between its formal and semantic features, and so on.

Now, what does the literary interpreter need to know in order to deal accurately and circumspectly with this web of questions? Clearly she has to master the concepts involved. She has to master genre concepts like "comedy," "sonnet," "novel," or "tragedy"; she has to master linguistic and stylistic concepts from general and apparently simple ones like "word" or "sentence" or "stanza" to more specialized ones like "ottave rime," "genus grande," or "mise en abyme"; she has to master aesthetic concepts like "the sublime" or "the beautiful" and historical concepts like "romanticism" or "classicism." The literary interpreter needs, to a certain degree, mastery of these concepts in order to find out whether and, if so, how they apply to the literary work she is interpreting. On the other hand, by making use of her conceptual mastery the interpreter will be enabled to refine it, for by accurately and circumspectly applying literary concepts in the business of interpretation, a critic will gain a more nuanced outlook on the intension and extension of the concepts she uses. Thus successful literary interpretation serves the enhancement not only of empirical but also of conceptual knowledge.

Let us now turn to some objections against the cognitivist account of literary interpretation for which I have argued. Sentences with which literary interpreters answer interpretive questions—sentences like "X is a tragicomedy"; "Y is a parable that advocates the value of forgiveness"; "Z is not as one might think a political proposal but a political satire"— are assertions by which critics present themselves as having knowledge, that is, appropriately justified true beliefs, about the works interpreted. But can they have such knowledge? Some theorists of literary interpretation, in the English-speaking world most notably the philosophers Joseph Margolis[18] and Robert J. Matthews,[19] have denied this. According to them there can be no such thing as veridical interpretive knowledge. Why not? Because, according to these theorists, there are no truths to be found in the process of interpretation. Interpretive statements in literary and art criticism, Matthews argues, are "typically neither true nor false"; they are "as a general rule epistemically weak . . . because they are radically *underdetermined* by the interpreted work."[20] In which sense should such statements be underdetermined? Here is Matthews's answer:

> Statements are true (or false), when they are, in virtue of certain facts about the world, but "the facts" typically fail to decide the truth or falsity of interpretive statements in art criticism. To maintain that these statements are nonetheless "either true or false" is in effect to deny the special relation that true (and false) statements bear to the world. . . . Clearly there is, as many have suggested, a similarity between the interpretations of the critic and those of the performing artist. . . . [I]n both cases the interpretation is underdetermined by the interpretandum. In neither case does the interpretandum determine a unique interpretation; rather it constrains them only loosely. And precisely because interpretation does involve "going beyond" the given, interpretations require the added contribution of the interpreter.[21]

Is Matthews right? I don't think so, for he unduly generalizes a special type of interpretive statement that in a sufficiently nuanced account of literary interpretation—let me call it a *differentialist account*—should be distinguished from interpretive statements whose truth or falsity *is* determined by the *interpretandum* they refer to.

Indeed, Hamlet's build and walk are not determined by Shakespeare's play; each actor has to add these and other features as part of his interpretation to "complete" the tragic prince of Denmark. And as we all know, from Laurence Olivier to Derek Jacobi and Simon Russell Beale, there is a wide and undoubtedly still extendable range of in many aspects radically different but equally outstanding performances of *Hamlet*. Not only would it be closed-minded caviling; it would be a misuse of the term *true* if one should allocate it exclusively to Olivier's or exclusively to Jacobi's interpretation of Hamlet. Great creative interpretations by performance are not "true," even though they are eye-opening in the sense that they show us moving, gripping, thought-provoking concretizations of Shakespeare's drama we were previously unable to imagine.

Analogously, critics quite often add *discursively* to a literary work by filling out what Roman Ingarden in his theory of the (partly) schematic character of the literary work of art has called "places of indeterminacy" (*Unbestimmtheitsstellen eines literarischen Werkes*).[22] Think for instance of a critic whose interpretation deals with the motives of a fictional character—or more likely a whole set of fictional characters. Typically, there are many places or zones of indeterminacy in a fictional work's representation of its characters. Why does Mme Chauchat leave *The Magic Mountain* after her passionate one-night love affair with Hans Castorp? Out of decadent tedium or in order to protect the vulnerable young German from the sufferings of infatuation? Though even this question might be suggested by the work itself, it contains no information, neither explicit nor implicit, that could answer it. Critics who nevertheless come up with an answer in their rendition of *The Magic Mountain*'s narrative or in their characterization of its first part's heroine (or antiheroine?), neither discover nor miss a hidden truth in the work; instead they transform an indeterminacy built into Mann's novel into a more determinate but comparatively *partial* account of the work. Interpretive statements of this kind—though they may more or less fit in the overall context and be more or less consistent with the "laid down" character traits of Mme Chauchat—are neither true nor false. For there are no facts, that is, neither stretches of discourse nor logical or pragmatic implications of pertinent stretches of discourse,[23] in Thomas Mann's *Magic Mountain* that would determine whether Mme Chauchat acted out of this or rather out of that motive.

Admittedly, there are typically many zones of indeterminacy within literary works.[24] But this does not warrant Matthews's and other theorists' exaggerated claim that literary interpretation is "epistemically weak" by just hinging on indeterminacy. On the contrary, it seems to me that carefully determining (and this tasks includes, of course, carefully explaining) the scope and forms of indeterminacy in a given work—syntactic indeterminacy is one form, narrative indeterminacy another—is and should be one of the primary tasks of literary interpretation in its truth- and knowledge-seeking mode.

Let me once again quote the suggestive but potentially distortive metaphor used by Matthews that literary interpretation does involve "going beyond" the given. In order to make sense of this job description, the ones on the job should be able to determine *where* they are "going beyond" what is given. If a (not local but total) principle of indeterminacy would rule out that possibility, going beyond would not be going beyond. And only if we have knowledge about a literary work's determined features will our creative efforts of going beyond these features and thereby adding to the value and significance of experiencing that very work have a good chance of being appropriate and productive.

Of course, in order to interpret a given literary work we do constantly "go beyond": beyond its given *text*. Granted that the original wording has been preserved or soundly reconstructed, we classify and explain a work's features and its overall status not just in terms of its text but also in terms of realized authorial intentions, effective literary conventions and aesthetic rules, historical circumstances, and so on. Let me therefore recall the utterly important distinction between a literary work and its text.[25] To ask and determine what is in a text is not the same as asking and determining what is in a work. A text has lexical, syntactic, and semantic features, identification of which determines the text's content. But this is linguistic, not yet literary, content, a product of linguistic conventions, of syntactic and semantic rules that bear on the language in question. A text that is not contextualized further is in many aspects not subject to interpretive constraints and can mean or rather be made to mean anything that the language for that stretch of written discourse permits. In contrast, a literary work is contextualized; not only is it written in a certain time and culture, but it is also typically written for a certain purpose or set of purposes and therefore typically invested with semantic, pragmatic, and aesthetic intentions its author has realized by writing that very work. Retrieving this investment by true and aptly justified statements about the work and thereby achieving an understanding of it as the product of the intentional activity of its historically situated author is and will be an indispensable step for knowledge-seeking literary interpretation—in spite of all the arguments the different schools of rigid anti-intentionalism have brought up.[26] Ignoring authorial intent is clearly unwise and in many cases a ticket to arbitrarily misusing a work and missing the attainable truth about it. Saying this, I do not at all deny that the meaning of a literary work and the meaning that its author intended in the process of writing it can and do often diverge. I do not at all deny that a literary work is often richer and more complex than its author himself would have thought. Furthermore, the idea that knowledge-seeking interpretation acquires and justifies true beliefs about a literary work is not restricted to the task of establishing which semantic, pragmatic, or aesthetic intentions have been successfully realized in a literary work. Not only bygone states of mind that have shaped a work's features and thereby left their imprint on them are "truth makers" for interpretive claims; also public semantic facts and in virtue of them a wide range of semantic properties can objectively be part of a literary work's meaning and therefore "truth makers" for interpretive claims about it. As Tom Stoppard wittily and insightfully suggested, the relation between an author and a critic resembles that between a traveler and a customs inspector: The inspector opening the traveler's suitcase finds a lot of things in it which the traveler has to acknowledge are in it, although he can truthfully protest that he has not consciously packed them.[27]

Let me conclude by getting back to the two main levels on which I see knowledge as a central goal and the pursuit of it as a central obligation for literary interpretation. As I said at the outset, the pursuit of knowledge applies not only to each single question one may have to deal with in interpreting a literary work. It also applies to the more demanding task of achieving a *comprehensive true account* of a literary work that weighs on and integrates the partial achievements of either complementary or conflicting interpretations of that very work. As a general rule, interpretations, even excellent ones, are partial and incomplete compared to the inexhaustible richness of great literary works of art. So the old-fashioned new critic does not capture everything, nor does the now-fashionable discourse analyst. But the scrappiness of first-order interpretations can be overcome on a higher level of interpretive integration, which, of course, cannot just be a container or some sort of dustbin into which everything goes. Integrative second-order interpretation should be a critical comparative assessment of extant readings. In order to arrive at such an assessment, one has, of course, first and foremost to care about truth. Provided that interpreter A and interpreter B haven't fallen into the pitfalls of conceptual vagueness when they talk about, say, pantheism, then A's claim that a certain poem, Goethe's "Ganymed" for instance, is pantheistic and B's claim that it is not cannot both be true. But of course, it could be that the poem in question shows signs both of embracing a pantheistic view of the world and of rejecting or subverting such an outlook. Then neither of the two interpretive claims would be *comprehensively true*, and truth-oriented interpretation would be obliged to acknowledge ambiguity in the poem and perhaps—if this follow-up question could be decided on the evidence available—indecision on the poet's side. There are undoubtedly cases in which no first-order interpretation can be established over its first-order rival. And that is exactly why a critically integrating second-order interpretation is the better interpretation—a step in the ascent to comprehensive truth and knowledge.

Notes

Many thanks are owed to Robert Audi and Mark Roche for helpful comments and excellent suggestions.

1. For thoughtful accounts, see Stuart Hampshire, "Types of Interpretation," in *Art and Philosophy*, ed. Sydney Hook (New York: New York University Press, 1966), 101–6; Göran Hermerén, "Interpretation. Types and Criteria," *Grazer Philosophische Studien* 18 (1982): 131–61; Ronald Dworkin, "Interpretation in General," in *Justice for Hedgehogs* (Cambridge, MA: Harvard University Press, 2011), 123–56.

2. Bernard Williams, *On Truth and Truthfulness: An Essay in Genealogy* (Princeton: Princeton University Press, 2002), passim.

3. Dworkin, *Justice for Hedgehogs*, 126. For a straightforward relativist account of tribal relativism in literary criticism, see Stanley Fish, *Is There a Text in This Class? The Authority of Interpretive Communities* (Cambridge, MA: Harvard University Press, 1982).

4. Roman Ingarden, *The Cognition of the Literary Work of Art*, trans. Ruth Ann Crowly and Kenneth R. Olson (Evanston, IL: Northwestern University Press, 1973).

5. For a vigorous defense of "alethic realism," see William P. Alston, *A Realist Conception of Truth* (Ithaca, NY: Cornell University Press, 1996).

6. Richard Schustermann, "Beneath Interpretation: Against Hermeneutic Holism," *The Monist* 73 (1990): 181–204.

7. See Jerrold Levinson, "Two Notions of Interpretation," in *Contemplating Art: Essays in Aesthetics* (Oxford: Oxford University Press, 2006), 275–87. For an illuminating typology of epistemic situations that call for interpretive efforts, see Annette Barnes, *On Interpretation: A Critical Analysis* (Oxford: Blackwell, 1988).

8. Though, of course, she might interpret x as F for others who are not yet in the know. Classroom interpretation is a striking example of this inward-outward asymmetry in interpretation.

9. Note that this does not only apply to scholarly contexts but also to everyday interpretation. Just think of interpreting a Japanese menu to a group of fellow travelers. In order to be able to interpret that menu, you have to know Japanese, or at least you have to know how to use a bidirectional English-Japanese dictionary, the use of which would in this case be a somewhat reliable way of forming interpretive beliefs and uttering corresponding assertions about what the menu features.

10. As a general rule, the requisite knowledge for interpreting a given object is of different kinds, overlapping the distinction between propositional and practical knowledge.

11. More recently, the painting has been attributed to Bernardo Strozzi (1581–1644) (see http://pinacotecafaenza.racine.ra.it/ita/opere/op_704.htm). However, in the present context we can ignore the controversy over the painting's authorship.

12. Matthew 14:8–12.

13. Judith 13:6–10.

14. See Erwin Panofsky, "Iconography and Iconology: An Introduction to the Study of Renaissance Art," in *Meaning in the Visual Arts: Papers in and on Art History* (Garden City, NY: Doubleday, 1955), 26–54.

15. For an enlightening discussion, see Robert Stecker, "The Role of Intention and Convention in Interpreting Artworks," *Southern Journal of Philosophy* 31 (1993): 471–89.

16. For a discussion of these two modes of interpretation, see Levinson, "Two Notions of Interpretation."

17. The problems that the standard analysis of knowledge has to face since Edmund Gettier came up with troublesome counterexamples are complex, but

as far as I can see, it has not been replaced by a more convincing account. See Jonathan Jenkins Ichikawa and Mathias Steup, *The Analysis of Knowledge* (http://plato.stanford.edu/archives/win2012/entries/knowledge-analysis/). Of course, a circumspect approach to the theory of knowledge has to go beyond justificationism. See William P. Alston, *Beyond "Justification": Dimensions of Epistemic Evaluation* (Ithaca, NY: Cornell University Press, 2005).

18. Joseph Margolis, *The Language of Art and Art Criticism: Analytic Questions in Aesthetics* (Detroit: Wayne State University Press, 1965). For a critique of Margolis's position, see Monroe C. Beardsley, "The Testability of an Interpretation," in *The Possibility of Criticism* (Detroit: Wayne State University Press, 1970), 38–61.

19. Robert Matthews, "Describing and Interpreting a Work of Art," *Journal of Aesthetics and Art Criticism* 36 (1977): 5–14.

20. Ibid., 5; original emphasis.

21. Ibid., 11–13.

22. Ingarden, *Cognition of the Literary Work*, 52.

23. For a general discussion, see Peter Lamarque, "Reasoning to What Is True in Fiction," *Argumentation* 4 (1990): 333–46.

24. Also, there are different kinds or types of zones of indeterminacy. It is clearly not sufficient to discuss them only in terms of fictional content. An important type is indeterminacy of illocutionary role or force. To give just one example: what kind of iussive subjunctive is uttered in the opening line of Goethe's poem "Das Göttliche" (The Divine)? "Edel sei der Mensch, / Hilfreich und gut" (Let man be noble / generous and good). Is it an iussive of admonition, or is it an iussive of encouragement? In literary interpretation, illocutionary details of this kind quite often have to be determined by sensible concretization. And it is not by chance that critics in order to substantiate and justify their concretizations of what is undetermined in a work refer to what is determined by it.

25. See Gregory Currie's seminal paper "Work and Text," *Mind* 100 (1991): S325–40.

26. See the contributions in Gary Iseminger, ed., *Interpretation and Intention* (Philadelphia: Temple University Press, 1992), esp. Jerrold Levinson, "Interpretation and Intention: A Last Look," 221–56.

27. Quoted after Barnes, *On Interpretation,* 121.

CHAPTER ELEVEN

Historical Truth

———

AVIEZER TUCKER

This essay explores the meaning of historical truth. It argues that much of historiography and the historical sciences are true in the sense of employing reliable methods for generating sufficiently probable representations of the past. How highly probable historiography must be to be considered historical truth is context dependent. I defend this probabilistic and epistemically contextual sense of historical truth as better than its alternatives and argue against the plausibility of arguments against the possibility of historical truth.

The historical sciences include textual criticism, comparative historical philology, historiography (of the human past), phylogeny, evolutionary biology, archaeology, natural history, and cosmology. I have argued that over the past couple of centuries the historical sciences have developed reliable methodologies for the inference of highly probable representations of the past that in most contexts are considered historical truth. The philosophy of historiography should aim to discover and describe these reliable, truth-conducive, methodologies. I have argued also that the methodologies of the sciences that generate historical truth, truth about the past, are similar. They use different information theories about the transmission of information in time via different media similarly to infer representations of the common sources, origins, of contemporary evidence that preserves information from that origin (Tucker 2004).

How can we know that historians possess the reliable, truth-conducive, methodologies that I claim they do? If they do, how can philosophers know what these reliable processes of inference may be? Historians do professionally many different things, and they sometimes disagree with each other on some of their ideas of best practice. Bevir (1999) argued that the philosophy of historiography cannot follow the philosophy of science in analyzing obvious "success stories" like those of the paradigms associated with Galileo, Newton, Einstein, or Darwin to discover what is science because such a methodology must presuppose criteria for choosing what philosophers consider successful science and there is no basis for justifying such criteria in the philosophy of historiography. Yet, even without stating explicitly their criteria and their tacitly assumed cognitive values, few historians would doubt the success of Burckhardt's discovery of the Renaissance in the late nineteenth century. This discovery in the history of ideas has been so successful that most people do not even realize that the Renaissance is a hypothesis of the historiography of ideas that was introduced by a Swiss student of Ranke a little more than a hundred years ago. Likewise, the discoveries of the Scientific and Industrial Revolutions (the concepts did not exist during the historical periods they refer to) and the documentary components of the Homeric sagas and the Old and New Testaments are recognized by practically all historians to have been successful. Historians do not spend much time contemplating these successes because their professional practice consists of debates with other historians rather than the philosophical analysis of what is assumed within the professional consensus and therefore is not controversial. Consequently, these success stories remain tacit in the sense of being accepted and recognized by those who know them but are not discussed explicitly exactly because they compose the received historiographic tradition. Similar success stories can be found in historical philology, the Indo-European hypothesis; phylogeny, its inferences of common ancestry from genomic analysis; natural history, the tectonic plates theory; and cosmology, in the inference of the Big Bang and the subsequent history of the universe. All these successes are in discovering truths that were entirely hidden, unknown, for almost all the history of the human race. The task of philosophy then is to articulate and explain, make sense of, the reliable institutional truth-conducive practices of these historiographic successes.

The self-consciousness of historians about their own practices is not useful for understanding historical truth and how historians infer it. Historians disagree among each other about what they think they are doing even when they clearly follow very similar practices. The reliable methodologies that historians use to infer historical truth are often tacit. Historiographic institutional practices display the hallmarks of what Collins (2010) called "collective tacit knowledge." Training transmits tacit knowledge through an apprenticeship that cannot be formalized and written down in a textbook. Tacit knowledge must be acquired directly, by hanging around people who possess it, such as teachers and peers. Collective tacit knowledge is acquired through social embedding. Explicit knowledge, by contrast, may be transmitted via intermediaries.

The tacit nature of historiographic veridical methodologies allows rationalizations. Rationalization of tacit knowledge means its explication in terms of contemporary fashionable epistemologies or ideologies that are simple, easy to understand, and offer an epistemic legitimizing facade. Rationalization explains the consecutive adoptions by historians of different generations of passing epistemic fads—nineteenth-century empirical inductivism, early-twentieth-century positivism, structuralism, and finally postmodernism—while practicing the same archival methodologies within the same paradigmatic framework that Ranke introduced to historiography almost two centuries ago.

Many of the classic textbooks on historiography present rationalizations as a professional ideology, a defense mechanism against external criticisms. The result is often conceptually messy: the conflations of explanation with causation, causation with conditionality, and all of them with necessity, necessity with determinism, and necessity and determinism with teleology and on and on.[1] Symbolically, on the cover of my Penguin paperback edition of E. H. Carr's *What Is History?* there is a reproduction of *Representatives of Foreign Powers Arriving to Hail the Republic as a Sign of Peace* by the nineteenth-century master of the naive style, Henri Rousseau. The relation between Carr's rationalization of historiography and historiography is not unlike the relation between Rousseau's painting and actual international diplomacy.

I have argued that the process of inference of representations of past events in all the historical sciences amounts to the inference of representations of information-generating origins from their present information-preserving effects. The inference often is of models of information transmission "trees" or "bushes" that connect past events to present evidence. The means of transmission of the information are different in human history (testimonies and texts), historical linguistics (languages), phylogeny (morphology and later DNA), and textual criticism (documents). The information transmission and mutation theories that these historical sciences use are different. But the stages of inference are identical: They first attempt to prove that the evidence is more likely given some common source of its shared preserved information than given separate sources by finding dysfunctional homologies that are unlikely given separate sources such as biological rudiments (such as the appendix or the wings of birds that cannot fly), infelicities in texts, and testimonies that are not in the interest of the witnesses. If they are successful, they try to infer the history of the transmission of information between the origin and its present effects. If they have sufficient evidence and theoretical background they can achieve a probable modeling of the transmission of information in time. Finally, they infer the properties of the origins that transmitted the common information, the origins of species and languages, historical events and processes, and the original forms of texts. The process of inference is Bayesian in the sense of producing a series of probabilistic inferences: first that the similarities in the units of evidence are more likely given preservation of information from a common origin than given separate sources; then that the modeling of the transmission of the information is probabilistic (explicitly quantitative in phylogeny and some branches of historical linguistics, and tacitly so in the other historical sciences). The ultimate inference of the state of the origin of the information transmission is of course probabilistic in nature as well (Tucker 2004, 92–140; 2011).

I want to argue here that the result of this typically historiographic inference is historical truth (I refrained from discussing historical truth in my book). When the result of this inference is probable enough in a context, it becomes historical truth. As in jurisprudence, contexts affect how high the probability must be to be considered the truth. I examine critically first alternative concepts of historical truth. Then, I reject claims that there is no historical truth. Finally, I return to say more about my probabilistic and epistemically contextual concept of historical truth.

I

The most primitive form of rationalization is naive "empirical" realism that considers historiographic knowledge empirical knowledge. This is a strategy for suppression of the epistemology of our knowledge of the past, against the examination of the tacit methods historians use to infer representations of the past. Suppression is not an argument. Historians do not and cannot possibly "see the past" and then report what they saw as the authors of travel books report on what they experienced in foreign lands, preferably by telling amusing anecdotes. Everything we know and can possibly know about the past is always inferred, mediated through the evidence. Epistemology is built into the historiographic enterprise, unavoidable and inevitable. Even in the case of cosmology where we can see the past but cannot see the present because of the time it takes light to reach us, the interpretation of the light as traveling from distant stars and the correction of its color for red or blue shifts and the use of telescopes are all information theory laden and inferential rather than immediate.

Suppressive "empiricism" results in skepticism. Since the past is inaccessible directly to any of our senses, a correspondence theory of truth leads to the conclusion that there is no historical truth. Without direct access to the past, there is nothing for the truth to correspond with.[2]

A more sophisticated strategy for resisting a philosophical examination of historical truth, while assuming it unreflectively, may be to suggest that epistemic questions are not raised in the *context* of ordinary historiographic inquiry because its results are probable enough for that context. As much as in ordinary everyday contexts we are not skeptical of the general reliability of our senses and the information they transmit to us, arguably, in ordinary contexts, knowledge of the past is sufficiently implicitly reliable and true. Contextualists like DeRose (2009) and Lewis (1996) argued that skeptical doubts about the possibility of knowledge do not arise in ordinary everyday contexts but only in specific philosophical contexts, and so can be ignored in most contexts. In ordinary contexts we can ignore those distant few possible worlds where we are brains in vats. A parallel argument may be invented for knowledge of the past. However, there are many more close and similar worlds where our knowledge of the past is different. Historically, what most people believe about the history of humanity, life, this planet, and the cosmos, has changed quite radically over the past couple of centuries. We know about the Big Bang for less than a hundred years. The theory of evolution revolutionized our concept of the history of life 150 years ago. The Rankean archival methods are just a little older. Textual criticism has changed the views of some people about the scriptures for only the past quarter millennia or so. Some parts of historiography are still contested or must work with difficulty to distinguish historical truth from popular myth. By contrast, with the exception of mystics, idealists, and some philosophers, people have always believed in the existence of the world and the general reliability of our senses, and even the idealists have behaved pretty much as if they have been realists. The reliable methods that historians use to infer representations of the past are almost always used in contexts where they need to be examined critically rather than just contextually assumed.[3]

II

Peter Kosso (2001) advocated the most empiricist version of historical realism that is not epistemically repressed and repressive. He followed Dretske (1969) in expanding the meaning of "observation" to include any transmission of information through the senses. If so, it may be possible to "observe" history through the evidence. Dretske distinguished in 1969 between primary and secondary ways of epistemic "seeing." Secondary ways of "seeing" are of objects through their effects on other objects that we perceive. Kosso loosened and broadened the ordinary meaning of "observation" to encompass what Dretske called a secondary epistemic way of seeing. Kosso suggested that an information-bearing signal is conveyed through a series of interactions beginning with historical events and concluding with the evidence. Similar information-bearing signals connect evidence with events in the natural sciences. Historiographic information-bearing signals are considerably slower and are composed often of words, rather than of photons, but arguably these properties do not distinguish epistemically between historiography and science. Scientists understand the transmission of light; historians analyze the fidelity of textual information. Data in history play an evidential role that is similar to data in science, images in microscopes, tracks in particle detectors, and so on. Both bear information from less accessible objects of interest.

Evidence need not be observed to be perceived. But if we consider historical events "observable" through the evidence, as Kosso proposed, it becomes difficult to distinguish historical truth from historical evidence. Kosso is right that all the "observations" in science are of the past. Trivially, photons that enter the retina begin their journey in the immediate past. The difference lies elsewhere: All scientific observations in the theoretical sciences can usually be replicated when scientists reproduce types of experiments or at least observations. All the historical sciences, by contrast, depend on particular information causal chains that cannot be replicated. If a particular information signal is lost, it cannot be regenerated. Another way of putting this difference is between sciences that are interested in information about a particular *token* of an event and those that are interested in a *type* of event. The latter sciences attempt to replicate or discover other tokens of the event type. In the sciences that examine particular token events, they are not replicable. For example, when scientists infer universal constants, they are not interested in any particular token of them but in the type. By contrast, historians are interested in particular token events like the French Revolution rather than revolution as a type (Tucker 2012; cf.

Cleland 2002). Kosso acknowledges as much but retorts that the natural sciences as well deal with unique events such as the Big Bang. The Big Bang is a token event that for all that we know is the only token of its type. I do not interpret the uniqueness of the Big Bang as a reductio ad absurdum of the attempt to distinguish the historical from the theoretical sciences but bite the bullet to argue that cosmology is a historical science.

III

Collingwood (1956), Murphey (1973, 1994, 2009), and Goldstein (1976, 1996) noted the obvious: Historiography makes no observations of historical events but presents descriptions or representations or constructions of such events in the presence of evidence. There are no given objectively true historical facts: Historiography "is a science whose business is to study events not accessible to our observation, and to study these events inferentially, arguing to them from something else which is accessible to our observation, and which the historian calls 'evidence' for the events in which he is interested" (Collingwood 1956, 251–52). The immediate, primary, subject matter of historiography is evidence and not events.

Murphey (1973, 16) likened George Washington to the electron: "an entity postulated for the purpose of giving coherence to our present experience. . . . [E]ach is unobservable by us." This *theoretical* concept of historiography considers historiographic truth a type of theoretical truth: "Historical Knowledge is a theoretical construct to account for presently observable data" (Murphey 2009, 6). If theories model aspects of nature, for example, the model of the atom in theoretical physics or the double helix model of DNA in biology, historiographic theories may model the past, for example, the model of George Washington's presidency. History is as invisible as scientific theoretical entities. Historiography can be as true as scientific theories. Murphey (2009, 11) proposed that the veracity of historiography can be evaluated using the criteria for choosing between theories: whether the theory is best at explaining all the relevant data about its subject, consistent with related theories, and explains new data as they are added, and, I may add, directs historians to discover new evidence. Murphey praises this kind of realism, which he calls *constructivism*, for articulating a concept of historical truth without having to resort to correspondence theories of truth.

However, there is a basic difference between the electron and feudal society on the one hand and George Washington and the formation of our solar system on the other. The electron and feudal society, as theoretical entities, are *types;* they have no space and time, and they do not require any particular set of token pieces of evidence to confirm them, as different laboratories can conjure different tokens of the same types of experiments to confirm them. By contrast, George Washington and the formation of the solar system are token events. They occurred once at particular spatiotemporal locations, and they had never happened before and will never happen again. George Washington and the formation of the solar system are not theoretical entities. This is the foundation for the difference between what I called the theoretical and historical sciences (Tucker 2011, 2012) and Cleland (2002, 2009, 2011) and Turner (2007) called the experimental and historical sciences.[4] Irrespective of labels, some sciences attempt to study types and others study tokens, and those two disparate goals dictate entirely different methodologies for discovering different types of truths.

Historiography is theoretical in the sense of using theories to infer representations of token historical events like George Washington's life and times from evidence in the present. These theories are typically information theories about the transmission of information in time via various media like documents, languages, DNA, artifacts, light from distant galaxies, and so on. These theories assist in tracing back the information signals we receive in the present from the past. Historiographic representations are theory laden in the sense that they are founded on information transmission theories. But the representations are expressed using tokens. Even when the representations of the birth of the solar system are influenced by astronomical theory and the representations of historical societies are influenced by social theories, they are still representations of tokens and not types. Their relation to the evidence is different from that of theories in the theoretical sciences which are not interested in tokens, in this or that particular experiment that can go wrong, but in types and their relations that compose theories.

Murphey (2009, 7) defended his application of "theory" to historiography, relying on a quotation from Quine who described theories as "the set of sentences about that thing one holds to be true."[5] Historiography shares with scientific theories the postulating of objects and events that are not observable and must be confirmed or inferred. Highly confirmed historical events for which there is overdetermining evidence are at least as well confirmed as the best scientific theories.

The weakness I find in Murphey's account is similar to the one I found in Kosso's use of "observation" above. He broadened the sense of the concept so much that it lost its potency (conceptual deflation by hyperinflation). A robust and philosophically useful sense of scientific theories must grant them broad scope and consilience: they must be applicable to many different kinds of cases. They must be confirmed by replication, if not of experiments, then at least of observations of different tokens of interesting types. To do that, theories must be composed of types. By contrast, historiography and the historical sciences are about token events that happened once, cannot be replicated, and can never be observed. Historians utilize scientific theories about the transmission of information in time. But what they infer from the token evidence in the present and these information theories are typically representations of events that are described using tokens and not types. The French Revolution is a token of a revolution, but general theories of revolutions do not infer it, nor can it refute them (Tucker 2012). It is inferred from countless documents and physical remains through the use of information theories about where to look for the evidence and how to analyze it. Likewise, phylogeny infers a token common ancestor of species, who lived at a particular place at a particular time.

Murphey (2009, 151) claimed that replication is as possible in historiography as in science. Different historians can reinspect the same document or material remains. Murphey explained that historians do not replicate such observations because journals would not publish accounts of visits to archives that confirm the previous evidential observations of other historians. However, Murphey failed to notice that replication is boring in the historical sciences because it is of the same tokens, while it is interesting in the theoretical sciences because it is of different tokens of the same types, necessary for confirming theories about types. In the historical sciences replication of observation of token evidence is interesting only if it challenges previous such observations, not if it agrees with them. By contrast, in the theoretical sciences, replications that agree are interesting in what they tell us about their types, while replications that fail can be discarded, explained away as "something went wrong with the experiment," unless replicated several times.

IV

David Carr (1986) considered historiography to have a narrative form. Yet Carr also thought that it is a true story because historiographic narratives are isomorphic to an independently existing historical narrative. He claimed that time and collective action, as they are experienced, have a narrative structure. *We* have an experience in common when *we* grasp a sequence of events as a temporal configuration. Its present phase derives its significance from its relation to a common past and future (Carr 1986, 127). Each community has a narrative that constitutes it. This narrative is the unity of story, storyteller, audience, and protagonist. Storytellers tell stories whose protagonist is the communal *we* of their audience, the community. A second-order, historiographic, narrative is told by historians. It might have, for cognitive or aesthetic reasons, a different content from a first-order narrative. But if both narratives share an identical subject, the narrative forms remain isomorphic, according to Carr.

Instead of correspondence, some kind of isomorphic communal self-consciousness becomes the essence of historical truth in Carr's narrative realism. But historians do not wish always to talk about communal subjects that were present in the consciousness of a historical community, nor do they always participate in a kind of collective entity where they can benefit from historical self-consciousness. Social historians may write legitimately about social categories whether or not the historical subjects of these categories were conscious of them. Carr's model of historiography does not fit most of historiography and all the other historical sciences that do not deal with the phenomenology of consciousness of historical communities through time. There can be and there are mutually inconsistent competing isomorphic second-order historiographic narratives that tell different stories that share their protagonists and plot structure. They cannot all be true.

V

A combination of realist empiricist elements and antirealist elements can be found in what I call "strudel and apples" philosophies of historiography. It is obvious that in order to bake a strudel pie we need apples. Some workers have to go to the apple orchard to pick the apples off the trees. They must choose which apples are ripe enough and which are rotten and should be discarded. The apple pickers are necessary, and their work is important. But they are not experts or geniuses. Their work does not require much expertise or experience. However, once the apples are brought to the kitchen, the genius of the chef is displayed in how she works with those apples, how she slices or cooks them, which ingredients are added (cinnamon, raisins, etc.), and how she makes the dough and bakes the strudel. If observers wish to understand why a particular strudel is good or bad or excellent, they usually study what happens in the kitchen and not what goes on in the orchard. Good apples are all the same, but each good strudel is different. Likewise, arguably, when historians walk into the orchard of the archive, they pick and choose the ripe "facts" and discard the forged or otherwise unreliable evidence. The facts are collected in a basket and brought to the kitchen of the historian, where the master historian conceptualizes, slices, and combines them to form explanations and pose causal links as well as structure them in the form of a narrative. Arguably, if philosophers of historiography are interested in understanding historiography they should not pay too much attention to the necessary but boring collection of facts but study the construction of concepts, explanations, and narratives. Historical facts then are true but boring. The historiographic narrative is interesting, and contains true ingredients, but on the whole is not true or false.

Hayden White (1987, 1–25) distinguished three levels of historiography, annals, chronicles, and narratives, that roughly correspond with the questions of what happened, why, and what it means. Each level, claimed White, requires extra conceptualization. According to White, the conceptualization comes from the narrative forms that are innate rather than historical, in the mind or in language rather than in the past. White suggested that the evidence-based chronicle can be true or false but not the narrative. Ankersmit (2001) as well considered historiography a combination of the scientific with the aesthetic. Historical truth makes historiographic narratives merely adequate, and can be shared by multiple narratives. The aesthetic dimension distinguishes historiographic narratives from one another and is the more interesting subject matter for the philosophy of historiography.

However, there are no ripe and ready "facts" in historiography that the historian can pick as an apple picker can pick ripe fruits off a tree. The archive does not resemble an orchard. It is not made of distinct atomic units that need to be selected and then put together, sliced, and cooked in the historian's narrative workshop. Historiographic "facts" are postulates that explain present evidence (Murphey 2009, 6). Since it is trivially true that the present is the effect of the past, the historian requires information theories to identify which present effects are likely to preserve which types of information about the past.

Narrative historiography should be compared with popular science or scientific textbooks, not with scientific research. As Kuhn noted, if we want to understand science, we need to look at what scientists have been doing, at the history and sociology of science, rather than at the textbooks that scientists write about their practices and the histories of their disciplines, which may resemble fairy tales. It is hardly surprising or even very interesting that historians with different interests, values, and group identities write different historiographic narratives. It is much more interesting and surprising that they are able to agree on so much about history and not just about "atomic facts" despite all their differences.

VI

The most famous antirealist philosopher of historiography is probably Michael Dummett, who argued (Dummett 1978) that sentences about the past are not assertoric, they do not assert anything, they are neither true nor false, because there are no clear truth conditions such as observations that would allow or disallow us to assert them. He claimed that since the past is inaccessible directly, all we have is what historians tell us; further ontological assumptions about the past are not warranted.

Dummett exaggerated the veridical difference between direct observation and what we infer from evidence that can be observed in the present. What we see with our own eyes can be less reliable than what we infer from multiple independent testimonies. The states of affairs that make historiographic propositions true do not have to correspond with them. They can be theory-laden descriptions of evidence, most notably multiple units of evidence such as testimonies, genomes, or languages, that are independent of each other and preserve the same information from their common sources or origins. Dummett seems to have reached his conclusion in a state of innocence of any of the historical sciences, their methodologies or practices.

Years later Dummett (2004) declared his earlier antirealist conclusions about historical truth "repugnant" and made the opposite argument, for the truth of our knowledge of the past. However, through this reversal, Dummett has maintained his innocence of the historical sciences and their philosophy. He seems to have had no idea how historians reach consensus on their conclusions and why so many people consider them true. Dummett's philosophy was "radically naive and inappropriate . . . for statements about the past, and especially ones at any significant historical remove. Goldstein's [1976] discussion has then the virtue of highlighting what sorts of inferential practices actually come into play in constituting the past. Better actual practices than philosophical fictions to the same effect" (Roth 2012, 322).[6]

Instead of examining historiographic inferences, for example, from multiple independent information-preserving testimonies and other units of evidence, Dummett maintained what he called a justificationist view that bases truth on a subjunctive: Historical truth is what someone present in the past *would have* observed. This justificationism is too narrow and too broad. Too narrow, because nobody would have observed the Industrial Revolution or the Renaissance. Contemporaries observed machines and paintings. Ideational changes within the minds of historical people such as humanism during the Renaissance could not have been observed while they happened. Events and processes are not necessarily concrete enough to be observed by a single observer in a limited time. As Roth (2012, 322) noted, most of what historians write about, including what Danto (1985) called narrative sentences that refer to two distinct times (e.g., "the First World War began with the assassination of Archduke Ferdinand in 1914"), was not and would not have been observable by contemporaries. Justificationism is too broad, because some subjunctives are difficult to substantiate and so are epistemically useless. Dummett's account misses a discussion of historical subjunctives, what observers would have seen in history had so-and-so been true, and, most significantly, how historians can know whether these observers would have seen what is imputed to them. Can a sentence about the conditions in the early universe that is not evidence based be true if somebody could have observed it under conditions where no human could have survived? What should be assumed about the information-extracting technologies of the hypothetical observer? If we allow any technology however science-fictional, then the whole procedure is redundant because we can apply the counterfactual to the present and talk about an ideal observer in the present with superior technology to extract much more information from present traces than is possible today. If not, then what level of technology is relevant? It seems that the later Dummett, just like his earlier self, did not understand what goes into justifying assertions about the past.

Dummett did not distinguish the probabilities of what multiple independent witnesses testify to from those of single observations. Observation in the past was for him like an observation in the present. It could be transmitted by memory, eyewitness reports, or through a chain of testimonies. Dummett (2004, 68) writes, "We are in as good a position to know by testimony that the past event was observed as if we were told by a living observer. Dying does not deprive anyone of the status either of an observer or an informant: the dead remain members of the community—the community I have been referring to as "we"—with whose collective and imperfectly shared knowledge I have been concerned." Murphey (2009, 16–17) chides Dummett for ignoring that observations by others are testimonies and their evaluation requires reference to reliability and competence. Murphey also noted correctly that the long dead are not members of our community and their testimonies are not the mythical observation sentences of the positivists; they require interpretation (17–18). This requires historical professional expertise. Historians, as Murphey noted, do not consider the testimonies they use to infer from historical truth observations. Testimonies are often mutually contradictory and false. Historians look for the best explanations of testimonies irrespective of the truth of their propositional content.

Dummett (2004, 44) argued in favor of his subjunctive justificationism: "If the account of meaning demanded that we allow as true only those statements about the past supported by present memories and present evidence, then large tracts of the past would continually vanish as all traces of them dissipate." True, information decays. In earlier stages in the history of the universe more of the universe would have been visible and information decayed about vast stretches in the history of the universe, the planet, life, and humanity. But those large stretches are indeed beyond the scope of historical knowledge. The opposite tendency of recovering nested information about large stretches of the past is the result of advances in historical science. True, memories fade, but little of our knowledge of the past is based on them. The other evidential sources of information have actually multiplied over the past couple of centuries with new methods for extracting information from existing evidence. We know many more truths about the past today than we did two centuries ago. So, while the tendency in cosmic time is for information to decay, the tendency in the much shorter modern era of historical science has been to discover more of the past by developing new methods for extracting existing nested information about the history of biological evolution from fossils and genomes, of human prehistory from genomes and languages, and of human history from documents. The significant result is that what we take to be true about the past is the balance between these two tendencies for information decay and scientific extraction (cf. Cleland 2002, 2011; Turner 2007; Tucker 2011).

Dummett concluded, "We should be committed to a metaphysical conception according to which nothing exists but the present: the past would be a mere construct out of whatever in the present we treat as being traces of it. We could not so much as think of a statement about the past as having once been true, though now devoid of truth-value, save in terms of present evidence that evidence for its truth once existed. This conception, though not incoherent, is repugnant: we cannot lightly shake off the conviction that what makes a statement about the past true, if it is true, is independent of whether there is *now* any ground that we have or could discover for asserting it" (2004, 44). Constructing the past "out of whatever in the present we treat as being traces of it" is what the historical sciences have been doing to great effect. The historical sciences have been called many things over the history of philosophy; "repugnant" is new, even if Dummett did not realize that he was addressing them rather than a metaphysics he disapproved of. Sentences about the past that have no evidence for or against can still be meaningful, but then Dummett would have had to have a different theory of meaning with a weaker or no connection between meaning and truth, and that is probably what he found so repugnant. The very claim of the historical sciences for truth, for generating true propositions about the past, is evidence based. Without evidence there can be no truth in the historical sciences.

In his discussion of the reality of the past and the future, Dummett noted the basic metaphysical asymmetry between the past and the future: "We assign to the past those events capable of having a causal influence upon events near us, so that we can receive information from them and of them, but have no means of affecting them; and we assign to the future those events that we can affect, but from which we can receive no information" (2004, 86). However, he did not draw the obvious conclusion from this basic metaphysical insight, namely, that historical truth is founded on the information we receive from the past, not on observations of the past, real, or subjunctive.

McCullagh (1998) also attempted to explicate a concept of "truth" appropriate for historiography. He elaborated a "correlation" theory of truth to replace the untenable correspondence relation between historiography and history. Historiographic descriptions can be true in his opinion in the sense that a description of the world is true if it is part of a coherent account of the world, and if the observation statements implied by that account would have been confirmed by people of the appropriate culture and with the appropriate interests. This shows how the truth of a description depends upon the way the world is while allowing that it also depends upon the rules of the language of the description, and upon the concepts of the world which those rules refer to. McCullagh acknowledged that it is impossible to prove that historiographic descriptions are true in this sense, but historians want to get as near to the truth as they can. So, like Dummett, he explicated a sense of truth that is applicable to history but is not useful epistemically to answer whether a proposition about the past is true or not. The subjunctive about what contemporary observers would have observed and conceptualized brings McCullagh's correlation theory of truth close to Dummett's account. It is both too narrow, because information from the past can be preserved without contemporary observations, and too broad, because in many cases there is insufficient evidence to confirm the subjunctive.

VII

Murphey (2009, 12–13) suggested that historical skepticism is motivated by naive realism. If philosophers of historiography consider correspondence to be the only theory of truth, they must conclude with the early Dummett and the postmodernists that there is no historiographic truth; they must retreat to what Murphey called "some form of linguistic idealism according to which all that we know we can know is our own language" (12). The main challenge to historiographic antirealism is to explain a series of "miracles." First, the miracle of consensus: If historiography is not true in some sense, what can explain the broad agreement among historians about historiography? There are two candidate explanations, politics and methodology.

The political explanation claims that the consensus among historians can be explained by factors external to historiography such as politics, economic interests, social background, and so on. This externalist explanation is less convincing in the history and philosophy of historiography than in the philosophy of science because of the greater heterogeneity of historians in comparison to scientists. The economic and social barriers to entrance to the historical profession are lower than those for entering science. Being a historian does not require long and expensive education and access to laboratories and specialized instruments. Consequently, the backgrounds of historians are more diverse and heterogeneous than those of scientists. Indeed, many historians belong to opposing political, social, and religious camps. It is difficult to imagine how these diverse and even contentious backgrounds can cause so much agreement among historians, unless it reflects common knowledge of historical truth!

Alternatively, internal factors can account for the consensus, yet not imply truth. Leon Goldstein (1976, 1996) suggested that historiography has established a consistent family of methods for the interpretation of evidence. Consistent application of these methods yields determined interpretation of evidence according to strict professional norms. A methodological consensus, however, does not imply the truth of their results. Goldstein denies that determined historiography is a true representation of the past or anything more than the most plausible interpretation of the evidence. This antirealism is ontologically more parsimonious than historical realism; it makes fewer assumptions. Yet it pushes the miraculous a step further. It eliminates the antirealist mystery of consensus on historiography at the cost of a new miraculous mystery, a concensus on methodology that is not necessarily truth conducive: Why has a uniquely heterogeneous and uncoerced large group of historians come to agree on the information theories and methods that define the historiographic community since the emergence of the Rankean paradigm at the beginning of the nineteenth century? Goldstein failed to offer a convincing explanation of the historiographic consensus on theories and methods.

If historiography is the best explanation of the historical evidence, it does not imply that it is a representation of the past; it could be wrong, it is fallible. Yet the theories and methods of historiography are shared by a large heterogeneous and uncoerced community of historians, as well as by biblical and classical scholars, philologists, detectives, and judges. When historians reach an uncoerced, uniquely heterogeneous and large consensus on historiography, the best explanation is that they possess knowledge of the past (Tucker 2004, 25–45).

The case for the truth of historiography and the historical sciences is stronger than that for the theoretical sciences like physics. One of the strongest arguments against the truth of scientific theories is the pessimistic induction: The refutation of many of the scientific theories that dominated science up to a century or so ago may imply that all scientific theories that have not been proven false yet will be proven false in the future (Laudan 1981). Even apparently highly well confirmed theories like Newtonian physics were proven wrong. Scientific paradigms succeed each other, and whether or not this succession is progressive in some sense, it may not indicate increasing approximation to the truth. Realist attempts to salvage some truth-value in scientific theories that were proven unsuccessful have concentrated on finding elements that are preserved after the collapse of a paradigm and the refutation of its theories and are salvaged and carried over for the next paradigm and its theories (Park 2011). In the historical sciences, by contrast, there is every reason to believe in an optimistic induction, that much of our present knowledge and theories about the past will continue to withstand the test of time. All the historical sciences have had one and only one founding revolution that transformed them into sciences, usually through the introduction of new theories about the transmission of information in time. The documentary hypothesis in biblical studies, the Indo-European hypothesis in historical comparative linguistics, Rankean archival-based scientific historiography, Lyell's paradigm in geology, Darwinian biology and the hypotheses about the origins of species, genetic phylogeny, and so on, have not been proven false, nor have we had to revise any of their main conclusions or assumptions. To be sure, they have expanded. We know today much more about the history of life than Darwin did or about social and cultural history than Ranke did. But the founding texts, assumptions, and information theory–based methodologies have preserved their truth for two hundred years. It seems hard to believe that we will come to reject one day the hypothesis that men and apes have a common origin or the theory of evolution upon which it is based, or that the author of the *Iliad* could not be the author of the *Odyssey* or the philological theory upon which it is based. A positive induction may at the very least argue for a probabilistic gap between the historical and theoretical sciences that makes the first more likely to be true.

VIII

The common scientific theoretical background that allows historians to reach uncoerced consensus concerns the transmission of information in time, not the evolution of society. This point has often been confused because in textual criticism, comparative linguistics, and evolutionary biology the *evolution* of the studied system, texts, languages, and species *is the transmission of information in time* and its selection, whereas in historiography and archaeology the *evolution of society* and the *transmission of information* from and about past events are *independent of each other*. The theoretical background allows scientists who examine possible common origins to prove first that the similarity between effects is more likely given a common information source than given separate sources and then to prove which origin hypothesis increases the likelihood of the evidence more than others. These hypotheses put together compose our probable knowledge of the past, historical truth. Such hypotheses may have all levels of generality or concreteness; they may be descriptive or explanatory.

Our knowledge of history is limited by the information-preserving evidence that survived the ravages of time in the historical process that connects history with historiography. Much of historical truth is overdetermined: Much of the evidence we possess at the moment for World War II or for the genetic history of mammals or for the common origins of Czech and Polish is redundant. Historians could discover the same historical truths even if much of the evidence disappeared. However, in other cases, the evidence provides weaker support for historiographic hypotheses or even underdetermines it. For example, Murphey

(2009) examined the hypothesis that the Gospel of John was written in response to the gnostic Gospel of Thomas. This hypothesis is coherent with everything else that is accepted as historically true about the history of Christianity. The linguistic and thematic-theological similarities between the two texts are explained by the writing of John as a response to the earlier contemporary appearance and circulation of Thomas. However, the probability of this hypothesis is clearly lower than that of the Anti-Federalist Papers being written as a response to the Federalist Papers, or of Marx's theses on Feuerbach being written as a response to Feuerbach and the young Hegelians.

Murphey analyzed this lower probability in terms of the absence of direct evidence. Nowhere in John is there any direct reference to Thomas, nor is there a third contemporary source that attests to the influence of Thomas on John. However, there is no such direct evidence for the relation between Sanskrit and Greek or for the importation of the potato to Polynesia from South America prior to European exploration. Yet these hypotheses have considerably higher probability; they are historically true. The reason is that there is no probable separate sources hypothesis that can possibly explain the similarities between Sanskrit and Greek and the genetic identity between the South American and Polynesian potatoes. Sanskrit and Greek must have had a common origin, and the originally Andean potato must have somehow been transported to Polynesia. By contrast, there is some small probability that the themes and ideas of John could have been developed independently of Thomas, given the various theological and doctrinal debates of early Christianity.

The question is whether the probability of the hypothesis about the relation of John to Thomas is sufficiently high to be considered historical truth. The answer in my opinion depends on the context of inquiry. Epistemic contextualism suggests that what we consider truth, the determination of truth-value, depends on context. For example (DeRose 2009), it depends on context whether we consider true a proposition that a certain bank branch is open on Saturday because somebody remembers so. If the stakes are low, we consider it true. If the stakes are high, if going to the bank on Saturday rather than Friday to deposit a check may result in missing a payment on a house and initiating foreclosure, memory is an insufficient foundation for truth. If much is at stake, we apply a more exacting standard of truth, and we would not say we know the bank is open on Saturday until we call there or check the web page of the bank. In common law, there are different standards of evidence for criminal law (guilt beyond reasonable doubt), civil law (the preponderance of evidence), and licensing cases (presumption of guilt). The standards of evidence correlate with the severity of the consequence to the accused. In criminal cases that may result in incarceration or worse, it is very high. In civil cases, where the worst outcome for the accused is substantial financial loss, it is lower. In cases of licensing, where the worse outcome is a moderate fine, the standards of proof are low (Ho 2008). For example, in the recent "celebrity" murder cases of O. J. Simpson and Robert Blake, the defendants were acquitted of killing their wives in a criminal court but were held responsible for the deaths in civil courts. Without epistemic contextualism, it would seem that they were at once guilty and not guilty of killing their wives. However, the juries found the probability of their committing these crimes lower than beyond reasonable doubt but sufficiently high to be justified by the preponderance of the evidence. My impression is that in most historiographic cases, the standard of proof is comparable to that in civil cases, following the preponderance of evidence. But when the effect of the historiographic account may be sufficiently significant in the present, it may require a more stringent criterion of truth, comparable to "beyond reasonable doubt." When living people are affected by what is accepted as historical truth, the stakes and standard are higher. It is one thing to infer from a document that somebody was a spy for the Habsburg monarchy in the nineteenth century; it is quite another to prove that a living person was an informer for the Communist regime a few decades ago on a comparable evidential basis. In the case of the influence of Thomas on John above, the textual evidence may suffice for a person who considers John a text from the Roman era. But a person for whom the correct interpretation of John may be of utmost theological significance may find the probability of the influence of Thomas on John insufficient for considering it truthful.[7]

In some cases there is insufficient evidence for preferring one historiographic hypothesis as more probable than all others. To achieve a preponderance of evidence, one hypothesis has to be clearly more probable than any of its alternatives. But when there is a limited body of evidence, there may be multiple possible hypotheses. For example, the Neolithic figurines of buxom women that are found all over Europe may be images of the political rulers of matriarchal societies, or fertility goddesses, or Stone Age pornography. Hitler surely had some kind of mental illness or personality disorder, but was he a psychopath, a hysteric, a bipolar, or a combination of the above? Such hypotheses are underdetermined by the evidence. The social manifestation of underdetermined historiography is the absence of the kind of uncoerced uniquely heterogeneous consensus we find in determined parts of historiography (Tucker 2004, 140–84). Underdetermined historiography does not justify a skeptical interpretation that "anything goes" in historiography and the belief that historiography has the same veridical status as fiction. The evidence that underdetermines some hypotheses in some parts of historiography may still suffice to refute most hypotheses, leaving only a handful of alternatives. Still, multiple similarly probable, yet mutually inconsistent historiographic hypotheses cannot receive a realist interpretation, cannot claim to be true at the same time.

NOTES

1. Even worse than rationalization is resistance, fighting off any discussion of historiographic epistemology and methodology by using academic political and economic powers. Methodological angst has led to the elimination of classes in historiographic methodology, theory, and philosophy and the exclusion of theoreticians or philosophers and other metalevel thinkers about history from academic employment if they are young, and their marginalization if they are already part of the profession, while pressuring them to avoid raising foundational questions in public. History departments rarely offer postgraduate seminars in theory. They teach methodology tacitly through practice. This may explain a self-reinforcing mechanism by which trained historians are not conscious of the reliable processes of reasoning and belief formation about the past that they actually wield as they learn unreflectively tacit methodology through practice. Consequently, they are anxious about its reliability and resist

discussions of the epistemology of our knowledge of the past. They then educate another generation tacitly, and so on.

2. Unless we assume some sort of idealist ontology and believe we can somehow commune with the ideas of dead historical figures and then see if they correspond with their historiographic representations (see Murphey 2009, 5).

3. The archival contexts of documents are significant, but they are nowhere as complex and heterogeneous as those of human action. The possible variations and forms of explanations of documents are far less numerous than those of human action. Consequently, making explicit the tacit assumptions and processes historians use to explain their evidence is much easier than explicating human action (cf. Collins and Kusch 1999). For example, the best explanation for the independent diaries of soldiers that state that on a certain date their unit came under heavy bombardment and therefore panicked and retreated is that indeed they came under heavy bombardment and therefore panicked and retreated. There is no need for further knowledge of the psychology of human action under fire. Had this explanation of the retreat depended on psychological theories, it would have been indeterminate, since under fire soldiers are known to retreat out of fear, become paralyzed with fear and stay put, or become emboldened with rage and charge on, and these are the exhaustive and mutually exclusive three possible responses. The mere description of the stimulus together with background conditions and contemporary psychology would be insufficient for explaining the actual retreat. But psychology is redundant here. The preservation of information on panic and retreat is the best explanation of the independent evidence for it. The relevant background theory is not psychological but informational: the reliability of independent witnesses who witnessed and participated in the events and wrote down their experiences immediately after the events took place for no external purpose, in diaries.

4. For my reasons for preferring the terminology of theoretical to experimental sciences, see Tucker 2009.

5. Murphey (2009, 75–102) distinguished four types of historiographic theories: narratives, hypotheses for which there is indirect evidence, social science theories about the past like Turner's Frontier Theory, and philosophies of history (which some call substantial or speculative).

Narratives and theories can, but do not have to, coincide. Hypotheses about the past are indeed part of historiography, but they use tokens rather than types. Social science theories are theories but are parts of the social sciences and not historiography (Tucker 2012). Philosophies of history are neither science not historiography (Tucker 2004, 14–17).

6. Unfortunately, Roth (2012) did not practice what he preached in his own "irrealist" account, an excessively mechanical application of Ian Hack-

ing's theory of historical ontology to the philosophy of historiography. Indeed, historiographic conceptualizations of the past are fluid. But to understand the conceptual choices historians and their communities have made, it is necessary to study them, e.g., how and why concepts like the Renaissance or the Industrial Revolution became accepted. To do that, Roth would have had to conduct research in the history of historiography. He would have found then the extent to which historiographic conceptual choices depended on information theories that connected a broad scope of evidence to new fruitful concepts.

7. Obviously, the discovery of more evidence would be the elegant way to decide whether the influence of Thomas on John is true or not, even according to an exacting "beyond reasonable doubt" criterion. Unfortunately, in many cases history has not preserved information about the past, and historians must make do with a fixed and limited scope of evidence. In such cases standards of truth that vary with context can explain what historians accept and reject as true and why. In the context of debates about epistemic contextualism, this explains why epistemic contextualism cannot be reduced to certain epistemic attitudes to evidence. Unlike Nagel's (2012) claim, some contexts where the stakes are high cannot be transformed into attitudes that require action for pursuing more evidence. Sometimes this is impossible and the truth of propositions depends on their contexts.

REFERENCES

Ankersmit, Frank. 2001. *Historical Representation*. Palo Alto, CA: Stanford University Press.

Bevir, Mark. 1999. *The Logic of the History of Ideas.* Cambridge: Cambridge University Press.

Carr, David. 1986. *Time, Narrative, and History*. Bloomington: Indiana University Press.

Cleland, Carol E. 2002. "Methodological and Epistemic Differences between Historical Science and Experimental Science." *Philosophy of Science* 69: 474–96.

———. 2009. "Philosophical Issues in Natural History and Its Historiography." In *A Companion to the Philosophy of History and Historiography*, ed. A. Tucker, 44–62. Malden, MA: Wiley-Blackwell,

———. 2011. "Prediction and Explanation in Historical Natural Science." *British Journal for the Philosophy of Science* 62: 551–82.

Collingwood, R. G. 1956. *The Idea of History*. Oxford: Oxford University Press.

Collins, H. M. 2010. *Tacit and Explicit Knowledge*. Chicago: University of Chicago Press.

Collins, Harry, and Martin Kusch. 1999. *The Shape of Actions: What Humans and Machines Can Do*. Cambridge, MA: MIT Press.

Danto, Arthur. 1985. *Narration and Knowledge (including the integral text of Analytical Philosophy of History)*. New York: Columbia University Press.

DeRose, Keith. 2009. *The Case for Contextualism: Knowledge, Skepticism, and Context*. Vol. 1. Oxford: Oxford University Press.

Dretske, Fred I. 1969. *Seeing and Knowing*. Chicago: University of Chicago Press.

———. 1981. *Knowledge and the Flow of Information*. Cambridge, MA: MIT Press.

Dummett, Michael. 1978. *Truth and Other Enigmas*. Cambridge, MA: Harvard University Press.

———. 2004. *Truth and the Past*. New York: Columbia University Press.

Goldstein, Leon J. 1976. *Historical Knowing*. Austin: University of Texas Press.

———. 1996. *The What and the Why of History: Philosophical Essays*. Leiden: Brill.

Ho, H. L. 2008. *The Philosophy of Evidence Law: Justice in the Search for Truth*. Oxford: Oxford University Press.

Kosso, Peter. 2001. *Knowing the Past: Philosophical Issues of History and Archaeology*. Amherst, NY: Humanity Books.

Laudan, Larry. 1981. "A Confutation of Convergent Realism." *Philosophy of Science* 49: 19–49.

Lewis, David. 1996. "Elusive Knowledge." *Australasian Journal of Philosophy* 74 (4): 549–67.

McCullagh, C. Behan. 1998. *The Truth of History*. London: Routledge.

Murphey, Murray G. 1973. *Our Knowledge of the Historical Past*. Indianapolis: Bobbs-Merrill.

———. 1994. *Philosophical Foundations of Historical Knowledge*. Albany: State University of New York Press.

———. 2009. *Truth and History*. Albany: State University of New York Press.

Nagel, Jennifer. 2012. "The Attitude of Knowledge." *Philosophy and Phenomenological Research* 84: 678–85.

Park, Seungbae. 2011. "A Confutation of the Pessimistic Induction." *Journal of General Philosophy of Science* 42: 75–84.

Roth, Paul A. 2012. "The Pasts." *History and Theory* 51: 313–39.

Tucker, Aviezer. 2004. *Our Knowledge of the Past: A Philosophy of Historiography*. Cambridge: Cambridge University Press.

———. 2009. "The Philosophy of Natural History and Historiography, review of Derek Turner, *Making Prehistory: Historical Science and the Sci-*

entific Realism Debate (Cambridge: Cambridge University Press, 2007), and Rob Inkpen, *Science, Philosophy and Physical Geography* (London: Routledge, 2005)." *Journal of the Philosophy of History* 3: 385–94.

———. 2011. "Historical Science, Over- and Under-determined: A Study of Darwin's Inference of Origins." *British Journal for the Philosophy of Science* 62: 825–49.

———. 2012. "Sciences of Tokens and Types: The Difference between History and the Social Sciences." In *The Oxford Handbook of Philosophy of the Social Sciences*, ed. Harold Kincaid, 274–97. Oxford: Oxford University Press.

Turner, Derek. 2007. *Making Prehistory: Historical Science and the Scientific Realism Debate*. Cambridge: Cambridge University Press.

White, Hayden. 1987. *The Content of the Form*. Baltimore, MD: Johns Hopkins University Press.

CHAPTER TWELVE

Truth and Unity in Chinese Traditional Historiography

Nicola Di Cosmo

Let's imagine Chinese historiography as an immensely long, apparently seamless piece of cloth woven in broadly similar patterns but with shifting shades and subtle differences, extending over twenty-six centuries. If we take that bolt of cloth and unfurl it to its starting point, it would take us to a long, frayed, multistrand beginning with weak and loosely connected threads. No matter how tattered and frail, those strands produced what is arguably the foundation of China as a unified cultural entity. During the Han dynasty (221 BC–AD 220), scattered annalistic traditions were pulled together and woven into a much stronger historical fabric by the founders of imperial historiography, Sima Qian (ca. 145 BC–86 BC) and Ban Gu (AD 32–92), respectively, the authors of the first comprehensive history of China, the *Shiji* (Memoirs of the Grand Historian), and of the first dynastic history, the *Hanshu* (Nienhauser 2011; Durrant 2005).

The warp and weft of human events were placed on the historical loom by Sima Qian and, ostensibly, his father, Sima Tan, with a clear sense that what was conceived of as history resulted (almost alchemically) from the fusion of two types of knowledge. On one plane were events that unfolded in diachronic sequence, and therefore could be arranged chronologically according to the annalistic model. On another plane were thematic narratives, such as biographical accounts, treatises on matters of concern to government and society (astronomy and economics, for instance), stories about certain categories of people, essays on foreign peoples and geography, or, in other words, valuable knowledge that would guide, instruct, and admonish.

Underlying both categories—events and accounts—were philosophical questions on the function of history. The inherited Confucian tradition assumed that historical knowledge was to be selected on the basis of moral standards and deployed in the form of exemplars and parables for the edification of present and future generations. On the other hand, annals and records were also a storehouse of accumulated experience for the instruction of rulers and officials in the management of public affairs (Balazs 1961). Sima Qian's revolutionary construction of a unified frame of historical knowledge posed the foundations for dynastic as well as comprehensive histories and established the classic model of official and private historiography, representing a watershed between an ensemble of scattered and loose collections of records that conveyed (in the general interpretation) mostly moral judgments in the form of annalistic notations and historical knowledge as an organized practice, intellectual endeavor, and cultural patrimony. We could say, without fear of exaggeration, that the *Shiji* is responsible for the creation of the largest repository of historical knowledge in human civilization, to state a fact that was once defined, with good reason, as a "truism" (Pulleyblank 1961, 135).

Historical documents of an annalistic nature had been produced for centuries before the Han dynasty, but in order to preserve and correctly transmit both the information about the actual events they contained and the lessons to be gleaned from it, the "facts" had to be collected, organized, evaluated, and understood with regard to their multiple implications for the explication of the causes and effects of human actions and how these actions and events fit into a larger philosophical matrix. Moreover, one of the most important innovations we find in the *Shiji*, the monographic treatises (*shu*), as well as some single or collective biographies (*liezhuan*), transcended the single event and allowed history to become comprehensive of various types of knowledge, from economic policy to astronomy, state ritual, geography, and foreign peoples (Hulsewé 1961).

Shortly after its composition, the structure established by Sima Qian was modified to fit the model of the dynastic history by Ban Gu, and ever since scholars debated the nature of the correct matrix to which historical knowledge should conform. These debates generated not just a vast amount of historical literature but also, by the eighth century, penetrating studies of historical criticism. At the same time, the high political and intellectual stakes of historical production led to the imposition of ideological orthodoxy and state censorship. But there was always an internal dialectical relationship between historical ideals and the methods of historical writing. Subordination of history to philosophy can be seen in its most unalloyed form with the triumph of Neo-confucian thought in the Song dynasty, while the philological turn of the Qing period provided new avenues to expand the range and tools of historical research. The vein of historical criticism that runs through the full spectrum of Chinese traditional historiography indicates a precocious and heightened awareness of what it meant to control the past. The creation of the History Office under the Tang dynasty led to a growing bureaucratization of historical research, and from the seventh century AD on the state never relinquished its prerogative (or shirked its duty) to produce the history of the previous dynasty. This became an unchallengeable cultural and political responsibility fully intertwined with the politics of legitimate succession and proper rule.

The dynastic history tradition continues to cast a powerful shadow even on contemporary historiography, as can be seen in the government-sponsored project to produce an official history of the Qing dynasty. The historian Dai Yi, the doyen of Qing history, who was appointed editor in chief of this massive project about ten years ago, recently said, "It seems that the traditional quadruple structure [of the dynastic histories], containing basic annals, biographies, tables, and treatises, should not be followed to the letter, nor should it be disposed of in its entirety. Our job is to decide what to discard and what to keep" (Dai, 11). Surprisingly, the new dynastic history commissioned by the Chinese state harkens back to a bygone model that seemed to have been completely condemned and buried after decades of Marxist historiography (Weigelin-Schwiedrizik 2005). What appears to be an act of extreme anachronism is witness of the continuity of a discussion about the shape and content of history that has been an integral part of the Chinese cultural tradition from the very beginning.

Seen from the point of view of "truth" and "unity," historical knowledge can arguably be structured as a series of dichotomies, or binary combinations, that, through their internal dialectical dynamism, contributed to the growth of historical ideals as well as to the "craft" of the historical profession. The dichotomies that can be singled out, without any ambition to be exhaustive, are as follows. First, we have the tension between private and public historiography, which includes a subset of other questions, in particular, the responsibility of the historian to "tell truth to power" and the equally weighty responsibility of each dynasty to compile a dynastic history of the previous dynasty. A subset of this question, which has proven extremely important for the development of historical criticism, is the opposition between the slavishness of official historiography and the creativity of individual works. A second binary set, which at times intersects the first, is about the fundamental purpose of history, and in particular the tension between the moral and philosophical foundations of its enterprise and the need to produce an objective record of the past. A third source of tension, which emerges almost from the beginning of a reflexive and self-conscious attitude toward historical writings, rests on the division between the "dynastic" and the "comprehensive" models, which are rooted in nearly opposite views of what historical knowledge should accomplish. An additional contrast can be drawn in reference to the internal organization of historical knowledge between the annalistic (the barebones records) and the narrative elements. Finally, a longstanding issue is the relationship between history as a self-standing category of knowledge and the canonical Confucian Classics, of which the two most salient aspects are the separation of history from the classics and the "historicist" turn in which attempts were made to reinterpret the Classics as products of a specific historical context, as propounded by the eminent Qing historian Zhang Xuecheng (see below).

Among the many complex aspects that characterize the evolution of historical writing in China, truth and unity can be taken as continuous and central concerns. However, they both need to be qualified. If a notion of "truth" can be applied to philosophical discussions in early China by looking for a specialized lexicon that may indicate semantic analogues, we face difficulties discussing historical knowledge that ought to be addressed in a less straightforward manner (Schmidt-Glintzer 2005, 116). On the one hand, historians surely wondered about the trustworthiness of their sources, and one way to address "truth" is by asking how historians strove to provide a truthful representation of facts and to assess the reliability of documents. At another level, historians questioned their sources about the true meaning of an event, often by seeking to establish correlations of a metaphysical nature or by assigning moral values. The question of unity, on the other hand, is somewhat less difficult to address, as it turns on how best to represent historical change once China defined itself and was recognized as a culturally (if not always politically and territorially) coherent entity. Whether compressed in the dynastic model or stretched across eras, the notion of change (represented most typically in a cyclical fashion) is inextricably linked to China's avowed historical unity.

Truth

In history writing "truth" primarily concerns the reliability of sources, that is, whether a certain piece of information is something that can be taken as having really occurred in the manner described. It also refers to the "true value" of a given piece of information, that is, the interpretation of its meaning once inscribed in a ritual or moral context, including its religious and political aspects. Truth and truth claims can only be dated to a time in the development of Chinese historiography when the activity of recording events and royal utterances was accompanied by a narrative exposition in which the author, whoever that may have been (authorship is a contested question in early Chinese texts, and the *Shiji* itself, while attributed to Sima Qian, was initiated by his father, Sima Tan), specifically doubted the reliability of a specific fact or judgment. Sima Qian famously dismissed several claims that he found in ancient texts, such as the *Shanhaijing*, a literary compilation that contains plenty of supernatural elements or fantastic stories, as simply fanciful—as unreliable historical sources.

In preimperial times, the earliest instance of an inquisitive attitude emerges in the wake of the commentarial tradition, in response to the *Springs and Autumns.* In the *Zuozhuan* (Commentary of Master Zuo), for instance, the annalistic structure incorporates an expanded narrative description of events, cause-and-effect relations are established, and moral lessons are made explicit with the inclusion of dialogues and speeches. Most important, the historian's own voice, in phrases such as "the master says . . . ," makes its appearance (Schaberg 2005). The explicit addition of the author's own opinion in works such as the *Shiji* and the *Hanshu* thus functions as a rhetorical device charged with the task of consciously separating "subjective" statements from the general narrative, which then acquires, by contrast, the semblance of "objective" and unadulterated history. The notion that historical accounts contain truthful statements in early Chinese historiography, meaning that it is possible to identify passages that show greater or lesser factual adherence to actual events, has been challenged by interpretations emphasizing how literary or stylistic aspects shape and inflect whatever sense of historicity a given account may carry (Li 2011, 431).

The question of "truth," however, should not be addressed by searching for a correspondence between a text and an actual historical event—a volatile concept under any circumstances—but rather to see whether "truth" or a notion akin to it, such as the reliability or accuracy of reports and documents, can be observed in the construction of the narrative as part of the author's declared or assumed intent. Did ancient historians care about transmitting true or false records? Scholars have assumed for a long time that in the early dawn of Chinese historiography the term later translated as "historian" (*shi*) indicated a class of court scribes required to record all the actions and utterances of the kings.

Yet not a single annalistic compilation for a given state has been preserved for either the Spring and Autumn or the Warring States periods, with the exception of the *Chunqiu* and its commentaries, none of which were the product of court scribes, according to the tradition. Given the number of states that came into existence over the course of half a millennium, one would assume that records were produced in large numbers, but to my knowledge no such compilations have been recovered even though over several decades archaeological research has unearthed a large variety of texts. It is indeed possible that each state had its own genealogies and some form of recording, and an argument has been made that these compilations were "dictated" by the political situation (Lewis 2011, 450). Without actual evidence, however, how they were produced and what they looked like remain open questions, since it is equally unclear what the *shi* (the "scribe" as a court official) was actually in charge of: annals, chronicles, genealogies, daily records, or all of the above. The absence from the extant record of annalistic compilations and chronicles—with the exception of the *Chunqiu* (Spring and Autumn Annals of Lu, attributed to Confucius) and its commentaries—that can be attributed to court scribes suggests caution when we are called to define the manner in which annals were redacted and the historical values that inspired them. It is therefore a matter of conjecture if, and in what manner, a faithful, "true to the facts," if slavish chronicle of all events was ever compiled by specialized, court-employed personnel. Recently some scholars have pointed out that the primary concern of early historiographers was not the factual reality of an event but rather its "ritual reality" (Gentz 2005, 235). What this notion entails is that adherence to reality was subordinated to adherence to certain principles such as devising the intention of the historical actor, placing him or her in a social hierarchy, examining the event in relation to established codes of conduct, and other elements that effectively discriminated between what ought to be recorded and the "nonrecordable," therefore presenting a picture of the unfolding of events entirely controlled by a ritual matrix.

If the chief example of this type of historiography is the *Chunqiu*, its commentaries somewhat paradoxically include more historical material by aiming to instruct the reader on the reasons why a given event was included or expunged from the record. In particular, the need to provide an interpretation and an explanation of why a certain record was missing in Confucius's work implicitly points to the fact that such an event nonetheless took place and was purged by Confucius because of specific concerns. Known in Chinese historiography as "appropriate concealment" (Ng and Wang, 38; Li 2011), this technique was understood as a form of moral chastisement.

The *Zuozhuan* (the *Chunqiu*'s chief commentary) often "reveals" information that does not appear in the *Chunqiu* as facts that had been concealed. In this act of revelation we can arguably see the implicit imperative, on the side of the historian, to be "true" to the event no matter how unpalatable and condemnable. The same work shows also concerns about causality, since the occurrence of an event is often explained in a given political and social context or chain of events. The circumstances of an event may also include elements that one may regard as irrational or fantastic, such as dreams and the appearance of ghosts. The reporting of "paranormal" events was part and parcel with the explicatory structure, and it would certainly be erroneous to expect a fully rationalistic attitude in parsing plausible from fanciful. Could one lend credence to an event that defied normal sensorial experience but was all the same related by otherwise trustworthy (i.e., neither deranged nor self-serving) people? The historian often chose to report without making a judgment. Truth, if we understand it as fidelity of the text to the representation of events, in preimperial historiography resides also in reporting accurately what is known about an event, no matter how fanciful. The "context" in which an event was immersed is supposed to provide accurate information and moral relevance to the narrative of a single event but not necessarily a rationalistic explanation or internal coherence. Whether such a goal was eventually achieved in the *Zuozhuan* is at any rate immaterial because the text that has reached us was certainly a composite product, in which layers of accretions can be recognized (probably composed in the late fourth century; Li 2011), and to seek a definite authorial intention would be misdirected. What matters, rather, is the introduction of a context that elaborates on the event by explaining its meaning as well as its genesis and by doing so establishes a higher degree of persuasiveness and plausibility even in the presence of different, and sometimes outlandish, explanations. This may not be a truth claim as we understand it, but it is nonetheless a step that takes us closer to Sima Qian's implicit faithfulness to contradictory sources by reporting multiple versions of the same event, which is a consistent feature of his historical method.

The transition from the Warring States to a unified empire in 221 BC in historiographical terms means above all the transition, fully conscious in Sima Qian's own programmatic statements, from the *Zuozhuan* (as the most important product of the *Chunqiu* tradition) to the *Shiji*. These two texts are on different evolutionary planes, each of which defined a different historical conception, sensibility, and methodology. Stephen Durrant, in discussing the question of truth in *Shiji*, takes a pragmatic approach. He looks at truth in history in terms of accuracy but also in terms of the greater truth that is supposed to be embedded in historical knowledge. The authority of the Classics, the *Shangshu* (Book of Documents), the *Shijing* (Book of Odes), and the *Chunqiu* (Spring and Autumn Annals), was not questioned, at least not directly, and the information they provided was accepted as foundational to China's intellectual tradition. The intent of sorting out what was reliable and authoritative on one side and what was fanciful and deceptive on the other carries with it a determination of truthful representation of the material that the historian had at his disposal, and therefore of the shape and substance of "history" as it was handed down, and as we have it today. The challenge for Sima Qian was to bring together in a coherent fashion all the different "traditions" while at the same time determining which documents and traditions were "true"(or simply more reliable) whenever he had to make a choice. In this he chose to side with the texts that carried the greatest authority.

At the same time, since much of the *Shiji* covers the period when Sima Qian and his father were alive (the first half of the Former Han dynasty), for those contemporary or near-contemporary events the standard for truth or accuracy involved directly the work of the historian as a witness and collector of facts, not just as interpreter and transmitter of ancient texts. This double epistemology indicates the opening of an important gap in Chinese historiography, which will be in evidence from Sima Qian on and especially in relation to the compilation of dynastic histories, between the usage and interpretation of inherited documents and the production of current records. Both operations were open to multiple theories and vulnerable to a variety of fallacious practices, not to mention political pressures, personal interpolations, and intellectual agendas.

By joining these two planes of historical production into a single overarching framework, Sima Qian's *Records* created a holistic view of Chinese history and laid the foundations on which later historians could build. The model of the dynastic history that established itself with the Han dynasty was therefore conceived from the beginning as a modular (or segmental) addition to Sima Qian's magnum opus but should not be seen as a simple imitation. The *Hanshu*, while conceptually indebted to the structure of the *Shiji*, introduced changes in the overall organization of the source materials, of which there were a greater number than had been available to Sima Qian due to the expansion of the state bureaucracy and which were also more easily accessible because of the official status accorded to historians.

The styles of narrative history, moreover, varied considerably from historian to historian, and the dynastic histories, while outwardly similar in structure, did not approach the question of "truthfulness" or reliability in the same manner. Fan Ye (398–446), author of the *History of the Later Han Dynasty* (*Hou Hanshu*), introduced significant stylistic innovations, and while his work has been praised for objectivity, it has also been charged with reporting speeches that are either highly dubious or fully invented by the historian (Bielenstein 1954, 52–61). The quality of the history that was produced was often judged by later historians on the basis of the documents that were marshaled and of the narrative style. As a "transmitter" of knowledge, the historian could choose simply to report what he had learned and then let the reader decide, and questions about the plausibility or reliability of a certain piece of information, speech, or account were not always posed.

One category of historical records that has attracted particular interest is that of portents and omens, which were often charged with political significance. The *History of the Later Han* has a dedicated treatise on portents and abounds with mentions of solar eclipses and natural disasters (Mansvelt Beck 1990, 156 ff.), but Fan Ye was certainly not the first to pay special attention to portents. Sima Qian was ambivalent about omens (Durrant 2011). As a Han astronomer, one of the critical aspects of his intellectual formation concerned a belief in the interconnectedness of human and heavenly realms, and therefore of special linkages between, for instance, atmospheric and planetary phenomena and human events. In this order of ideas, anomalies were seen as carrying some meaning on the human level. If inexplicable things could occur in the heavens as well as in the earthly world, the boundary between the expected and the unexpected in human events could not be defined in any rigorous manner either. The expectation of natural portents and anomalies, which could be charged with an array of different meanings from political prognostications to after-the-fact rationalizations, required that even strange events be duly noted. Truth was preserved by reporting all that seemed to be relevant, no matter how improbable. Ultimately, it was the sensitivity of the historian that remained the final measure, and as far as I can tell there is no argument in early Chinese historiography that did not take the historian to be the gatekeeper of historical truth.

A fundamental turn took place with the bureaucratization of official historiography under the Tang dynasty (618–907). The replacement of an individual's labors with the complex and cumbersome activity of clerks and officials working in various departments under the purview of the History Office (a branch of the state administration) made a much greater volume of documents available to various committees of historians. The goal of these various offices was the compilation of the Veritable Annals (*shilu*), which constituted the essential chronicle of all events of an emperor's reign period and would be used by the succeeding dynasty to prepare the full dynastic history of the previous one. The annals were a distillation of various types of records, which included the *Diaries of Activity and Repose* and the *Records of Current Government*, compiled respectively by the court diarists and the Great Minister, which were submitted to the History Office. In turn, this office produced the Daily Records (Twitchett 1992). All these materials, as well as reports and documents generated by other branches of the government, flowed through a process of selection and compression into the compilation of the Veritable Annals, to which biographies of eminent people who had died during the period treated by each section of the Annals were then appended (Twitchett 1961). The different phases of production and redaction were supposed to ensure not just a complete set of records but also a type of history that reduced the historical fact to a straightforward historical notation and thus limited as much as possible moralistic judgment and political manipulation. The word *shi* in *shilu*, translated as "veritable" in the sense of true and honest, indicates that there was an explicit concern for an account that would not betray the truthfulness of the historical record. This entailed whittling the record down to its basic essence, compressing it into what one could call the "naked truth" of the event (Vogelsang 2005, 161–62). The compilation of the *shilu* will remain a central feature of official historiography down to the Qing dynasty.

While making record-keeping activities grow to industrial proportions, the Tang dynasty also produced the first systematic critique of historical writing, of which truthfulness and adherence to a historical ideal that valued independent thought were central aspects. In his *Shi Tong* (General Principles of History), Liu Zhiji (661–721) attacked official historiography on several grounds (Ng and Wang 2005, 121–28; Pulleyblank 1961). First, he critiqued historiography as a collective enterprise. The main target of Liu Zhiji's criticism was the "committee work," as every phrase had to be approved at various levels of scrutiny before it could be inserted in the final version. Second, Liu protested the fact that private historians had limited access to official documents. Third, he denounced the intervention of powerful people who tried to influence the historiographical work. Another point of criticism was that official historians were not free to develop their own methods or apply their own standards and were instead forced to follow the guidelines set by their supervisors, who were mere civil servants, and thus incompetent as historians. He argued that while the various categories in which historical knowledge was organized (in particular, annals, treatises, and biographies) were acceptable as a general structure, each era required additions that could accommodate new knowledge. According to Liu, historical writing should be concise, dry, and synthetic and refrain from an overly ornate literary quality, as style might interfere with a transparent exposition and obscure the facts.

If we try to extrapolate a sense of "truth" from Liu's "principles," we would find it in his efforts to safeguard historiography from being polluted by the bureaucratic apparatus and his focus on the essential. While Liu called into question the reliability of received texts, including some Confucian Classics, he emphasized the rectitude and passion of historians as individuals devoted to their craft and how this would protect the truthfulness of the historical narrative from mistakes and interpolations. The sophisticated methods of analysis that the philological school of the Qing period developed to investigate textual authenticity were still to come (see below), but the fact that historical criticism developed at this early stage testifies to the advances of Tang historiography, not just in terms of the institutions and "bureaucratic technology" involved in the production of official histories, but also in the lucid awareness that at least some historians showed about the dangers to which this gargantuan organization exposed historical knowledge.

Later historians often voiced Liu's complaints, such as the inability of collective official enterprises to produce high-quality historical works, the lack of due attention to the intrinsic value of each document and source, the inadequate, careless treatment of these sources, and the absence of a critical opinion and judgment of the historical event, to which a moral content should be assigned, so that it would not just be a mere record of the past. The Ming scholar Wang Shizhen (1526–90) about eight years later, in his "Critical Treatise on Historical Errors" (*Shisheng kaowu*), made a vigorous critique of Ming official historiography that was reminiscent of Liu's positions (Ng and Wang 2005, 213–14). He appreciated the fact that the History Office was able to gather official documents, which a single historian could not do, but he found that the highest standards of critical interpretation and philological accuracy could only be found among private historians working independently. At the same time he acknowledged that several privately produced history works contained subjective personal views, often the product of disgruntled literati venting their anger and frustration.

The aforementioned dichotomy between private and official historiography therefore presents dangers to the rendition of "truthful" accounts on either side of the divide. If officially produced histories were open to general incompetence, political pressures, and the absence of a critical mind that could organize and give meaning to the various records, private works suffered from limited access to documents, an often biased interpretation of events, and the historian's own limitations as a creative scholar.

One of the most acclaimed historians of all ages, Ouyang Xiu, who directed for a period of time the compilation of the *New Tang History* and authored private works of historical scholarship, such as the *New History of the Five Dynasties* (*Xin Wudai shi* or *Wudai shiji*), was the most prominent Confucian intellectual of the eleventh century (Lee 2002). The intellectual agenda introduced in historical writing led to both a greater attention to the language of historical writing and an impoverishment of the overall historical record. Ouyang Xiu tried to imitate the original Confucian method of implicit judgment and privileged terse and essential usage of an allusive language as a means to summon historical lessons for philosophical purposes. However, Ouyang deleted from the record a large portion of documents preserved in the *Old Tang History* because they did not meet his high standards for philosophical and historical worthiness. The elimination of a large part of the available historical documentation makes his history a less valuable source than the *Old Tang History,* but the standards he adopted set an example that would be praised and imitated by later scholars (Ng and Wang 2005, 136–41). Ouyang's commitment to accuracy and reliability in the selection of documents does not mean that he saw history simply as a catalog of events to be transmitted in an objective and detached manner. The author's voice is preserved, and his sense of moral outrage and philosophical leanings are openly expressed in the sections in which he exposes his own opinion, which begin with the phrase "I lament . . ." (Hartman and DeBlasi 2012). If until then historical production had been a bureaucratic enterprise that served the government as a whole and preserved a cultural record that was shared by scholars, officials, and politicians as a common heritage, with Ouyang Xiu it was appropriated by the Confucian literati to impose their sense of what history ought to be, teach, and transmit. In regard to the question of truthful representation, Ouyang deeply believed in an objective recording of events and did not support the theory of legitimate succession (*zhengtong*) to determine the proper sequence of dynasties. The debates about the legitimate transmission of imperial rule that flourished under the Song and also during the Jin dynasty (Chan 1984) necessarily hinged on historical questions, since the very legitimacy of a given dynasty depended on its moral foundations, and these moral foundations rested on the interpretation of historical events. Given that the authority of the emperor was theoretically universal and indivisible and that there could only be a single legitimate "Son of Heaven," the political importance of a historiography that upheld the correctness of the succession was self-evident. It is not an accident, however, that issues of *zhengtong* were downplayed in Song historiography. The territorial unity that China had achieved during the Tang had not been reconstituted, and the Song partial reunification occurred after about sixty years of division during which various short-lived dynasties succeeded each other and fought for legitimacy. The Song lived in a period of multiple rulerships, and while they never doubted that their dynasty was the legitimate successor to the Tang, some practical accommodation was required (Wang 1983).

Both Sima Guang (see below) and Ouyang Xiu (1007–72) championed what was undoubtedly seen as History, with a capital *H*: a type of History that was as reliable as possible and at the same time animated by a moral purpose. Historical analogy and the "exemplary lives" included in the biographical sections were vehicles of moral teaching used not only for the edification of the emperor and state officials but also, and more importantly, for the recruitment of civil servants through the examinations system. Officials were expected to be knowledgeable in history and used historical allusions, quotations, and references, in a variety of contexts: memorials to the throne, debates, policy decisions, and even military operations.

The triumph of Neoconfucian historiography is nowhere more evident than in the writings of the preeminent philosopher of his age, Zhu Xi (1130–1200). His work, the *Tongjian gangmu* (Outline and Details of the Comprehensive Mirror), based on Sima Guang's encyclopedic opus, became part of state orthodoxy toward the end of the Southern Song and continued under the Mongols when recruitment of official bureaucrats by means of state exams was reinstated (1313). This work is the most celebrated expression of the notion that history should serve a greater "truth," namely, a philosophical ideal to guide society and government according to Confucian codes and norms. Historical precedents drawn from Sima Guang's *Zizhi Tongjian* (Comprehensive Mirror for Guide in Government) were extracted and reworked using the "praise and blame" coded language of the *Chunqiu* (Hartman 2012,

50; Ng and Wang 2005, 159–64). Truth was to be found by penetrating the perennial, unrelativized moral essence of universal principles revealed in the seamless continuum of recorded events, sieved through the sensitivity of the historian and their relevance to one's own age.

Qing scholarship by and large rejected the Neoconfucian orthodoxy that set in during the Song dynasty. For Qing historians, especially of the eighteenth century, the issue of truthfulness in history rested primarily with the philological precision and source criticism that became the hallmark of the school of "evidential research." Documents were checked carefully for errors and contradictions and subjected to a search for authenticity that in turn led to the development of various ancillary disciplines, such as archaeology and historical geography. Qing emperors themselves took a keen and direct interest in historical production. The philological turn made the didactic aspects of history far less relevant and raised the standards of professionalism in the historian's craft. The analytical tools developed by Qing scholars allowed them to correct errors present in the standard histories through a meticulous comparative examination of extant documents. The treatises, biographies, and annals that were utilized in the compilation of standard histories and other works, because of the convoluted, hasty, or simply incompetent handling of the documents, had produced internal inconsistencies and contradictions that detracted from the value of the work. Evidential scholarship went about restoring "truth to history" in an especially rigorous manner (Ng and Wang 2005, 244), and several products of official historiography that were regarded as especially poor, such as the Song and Yuan dynastic histories, were targeted for emendations and corrections. The view of scholars such as Qian Daxin (1728–1804) was that the historical accounts had to be checked against all extant documents and relevant works. The expansion of the range of historical sources led to what one might call a "dense history," in which research in various areas was brought together in order to elucidate the actual historical facts.

Together with high-quality textual exegesis, the Qing period is notable for the emergence of influential works of historical criticism. Zhang Xuecheng (1738–1801), arguably the most important historian of the Qing dynasty short of the reformists of the end of the nineteenth century, in his work "General Principles of Literature and History"

(*Wenshi tongyi*) combines a notion of historical cyclicality, whereby permanent universal principles manifest themselves over and over again, expressing a notion of change and evolution. Institutions, governments, laws, and political forms evolve but are still subject to failure or success depending on how they may fit those universal principles (*dao*) that harmonize nature, cosmos, and humankind. Without the knowledge of how society, institutions, laws, and the human condition in general have evolved, it would be impossible to perceive what action, solutions, and measures a certain era requires. In this he remained a fairly orthodox Confucian while rejecting a notion of history fully subordinated to the philosophical tenets and didactic purposes of the Neoconfucian school (*daoxue*). Besides this fundamental work of historical criticism, Zhang's most important contribution as a historian was in local history, focusing on the collection of local documents, inscriptions, and manuscripts as an integral part of the historical patrimony. It has been noted that Zhang's historiographical ideal was one in which the historian was able to convey a sense of empathy toward the past as a moral mission and as a way of making historical knowledge relevant to the present (Mittag 2005, 392). One scholar has compared Zhang to Giambattista Vico for the attention paid by both (who lived one generation apart) to the philosophical foundation of history and to its moral purpose. Demiéville saw in Zhang Xuecheng's work something analogous to Vico's aim "to break the bulkhead between philology and philosophy, to fecundate them mutually, to convert the 'certainty' of historical *facts*, as established by philology, into *truths* of reason which were the object of philosophy (*verum ipsum factum*)" (Demiéville 1961, 185; original emphasis).

UNITY

There are various ways to approach the question of "unity," but a possible starting point is the distinction between dynastic and comprehensive history, which is one of the great dichotomies that traverse the full spectrum of Chinese historiography. The unity of historical knowledge was predicated for the first time by Sima Qian. In the celebrated letter to his friend Ren An, the historian candidly exposed the reasons that he had embarked on an enterprise that was so uniquely consuming, and which proved so dangerous.

> I too have ventured not to be modest but have entrusted myself to my useless writings. I have gathered up and brought together all the old traditions of the world that were scattered and lost. I have examined the events of the past and investigated the principles behind their success and failure, their rise and decay, in 130 chapters. I wished to examine all that concerns heaven and humankind, to penetrate the changes of the past and present, putting forth my views as one school of interpretation. (Watson 1993, 236)

The quest for patterns and laws in human events belongs to the same intellectual milieu as the work of the astrologer who explores the heavens in search of regularities that might reveal a transcendent truth. To bear fruit, the examination has to be constant and the records accurate, detailed, and comprehensive over a long period. Therefore the accuracy of the event has to be matched by a unity of the whole record that allows the historian (and astronomer) to spot regularities and establish cyclicalities. The "cycle" is a notoriously complicated concept in Chinese history and philosophy. On the one hand, it may simply refer to a dynastic cycle, but in fact it stems from metaphysical notions, such as the *dao* or universal principle, that go back to the very roots of Chinese historical thought (Huang 1995). However, regardless of how these "cycles" were understood, they implied the existence of transcendent laws that determined the serial occurrence of phenomena in the natural world and in human affairs.

In particular, change was inscribed by Sima Qian in an imperial vision, and the motives for his historical revolution were closely linked to the unification of the empire achieved by the Qin dynasty and consolidated by the long-lasting Han dynasty. The empire, now politically and culturally coherent, found in the *Shiji* its perfect historical expression. The historian deliberately gathered the scattered records from the various preimperial kingdoms in a single composite architecture that transmitted a holistic vision of history both in chronological scope (from the remotest origins to the present) and in political and territorial terms. The concept of *tianxia* (All under Heaven) expressed both the universalistic claims of the emperor and the actual spatial and cultural extension of the empire, whose frontiers were marked by foreign, often hostile independent peoples. Sima Qian had indeed a clear sense of the limits of the empire, marked as they were by the inclusion of foreign peoples and of far-flung regions which were also essential to the definition of China as a bounded community. No area or period of recorded human activity was regarded as laying outside the scope of historical investigation. The model of this universal, comprehensive view is reflected also in the compilation of histories of foreign peoples, such as the attempt to establish a genealogy of the Xiongnu (a nomadic people who established a powerful empire hostile to the Han dynasty) from a mythical beginning that was traced back to a time more or less consistent with the beginning of China's antiquity. Sima Qian's views on the history of his own times and representation of events drew criticism from his immediate successors mainly for political reasons, given that the historian's unorthodox and independent views were often understood as a direct challenge to the emperor's authority. His model of comprehensive history was then abandoned in favor of the dynastic form, but the unsurpassed beauty of the grand civilizational vision that inspired it remained culturally influential.

This model was to be revived, over a thousand years later, by the celebrated work by Sima Guang (1019–86), the *Zizhi Tongjian* (Comprehensive Mirror for the Practice of Government) (completed in 1084), which covers the period from the Warring States to the year before the founding of the Song dynasty (403 BC to AD 959). As a universal history, rather than a dynastic history, it aimed to present a detailed year-by-year annalistic record from the Golden Age of Confucius to the present. As a "mirror," the *Zizhi Tongjian* maintained the vital function of history as an aid to the present in all political and administrative matters, or, in other words, as essential knowledge to assist anyone involved with government functions (Hartman 2012). The unity of the narrative and the inherent patterns and cycles that one may draw by comparing various periods could instruct statesmen and emperors as to the best course of action, or at any rate to be less blind to the potential consequences of a certain course of action.

What is especially remarkable in Sima Guang's method is the fusion of a highly moralistic approach with equally high standards of accuracy in vetting, organizing, and cross-checking documents in a process aimed to eliminate contradictions (by favoring the most reliable sources) or filling out lacunae (by looking for additional secondary sources). Those sources that were suspected of political or personal bias were simply eliminated. The thirty fascicles comprising the "Examination of Discrepancies" show a remarkable effort to wrestle with problems of source analysis and critical interpretation. The discussion of what version of an event "seems to be closest to the truth" (Pulleyblank 1961, 157; cited in Ng and Wang 2005, 149) indicates the ongoing concern with the reliability of the source and the production of a record that was as consistent as possible with all available information, in order to transmit what could be regarded as the "real event." At the heart, Sima Guang aimed to report faithfully those human achievements that needed to be taken into account, and he did so in an annalistic form that included every year of Chinese history from the age of Confucius on without overtly grafting overarching philosophical or moral principles onto the flow of events. According to Thomas Lee (2002, 70), the greatest achievement of Sima Guang's historiography is to be found in textual criticism and the rejection of supernatural forces or other fanciful explanations.

A long-running question in Chinese historiography consists of the evaluation of change. "Change," understood often, as mentioned above, in terms of cyclical recurrence, tended to oscillate between pure philosophical speculation, in which historical eras were identified with dominant "agents" and "forces," each of which carried certain qualifications, and the search for "laws" and patterns of change inherent to human institutions and principles of governance. The circularity inherent in these schemes was supposed to both explain the past and present and predict the future. But already in the Tang and during the Northern Song the issue of change was approached historically by searching for discontinuities and transformations within the flow of human activities and the development of institutions. Zheng Qiao (1104–62), the Southern Song author of the *Tongzhi* (Comprehensive Treatises) assembled pieces of former histories to create a long narrative not constrained by the dynastic model that would reveal causal nexuses as well as fractures and continuities in a number of areas relevant to society, politics, and government: rituals, music, laws, civil service, and economy (Ng and Wang

2005, 156–58). Ma Duanlin (1254–1324/5), a Yuan historian, in his *Wen-xian tongbao* (Comprehensive Investigation of the Literary Traditions), documented the evolution of government institutions from the dawn of history to the end of the Song. He propounded a rational evolutionary view of history by uncovering the reasons for changes in the historical process through a periodization based on distinctive developments of government institutions (Chan 1982, 69–72). The focus on institutions, examined systematically in twenty-four sections and ranging from land taxation and population to court rituals, music, and the military, allowed him to show history not just as a series of events, but as organic development within which continuity and change had to be evaluated on a grander scale than was allowed by the dynastic history (Ng and Wang 2005, 185–86). Following Zheng Qiao, he questioned the applicability of the Five Agents theory and the moralistic principles of the *Chunqiu* to history. In terms of Confucian values, he espoused the promotion of welfare, the suppression of private interest, and a commitment to a higher moral order.

An encyclopedic approach to history was one of the defining features of Song and post-Song historiography and is responsible for the en masse rearrangement of the historical patrimony into different configurations, introducing a comprehensive vision that gave a different sense and direction to historical knowledge. Although such a deconstructive operation had didactic and moralistic purposes, it also led to major advances in historical criticism and in a general dismissal of the supernatural or metaphysical in favor of an anthropocentric view of human events. It has been noted that the widespread use of the word *tong* in Song historiography links semantically the notion of comprehensive (in the sense of complete or encyclopedic) and the idea of comprehension (in the sense of penetrating and understanding) already present in Liu Zhiji's *Shitong*, that is, "comprehending history" (Lee 2002, 75).

Finally, a few words should be said on the relationship between the Classics and History as this is one of the major themes in Chinese historiography, and is directly relevant to a conception of historical knowledge as an independent branch of intellectual inquiry. In a nutshell, one could say that History was part of Classical learning from the very beginning, given the status accorded to the *Shangshu* and the *Chunqiu*, but it also broke free of that tradition by being accorded a separate section in the early classifications of books that we find in the dynastic history of the Sui dynasty, compiled under the supervision of Wei Zheng (580–643). If during the Han and the Tang dynasties historical practice and ideals had moved away from Classical learning and had become independent forms of intellectual production, the literati of the *daoxue* school of the Southern Song and Ming strongly reaffirmed the subordination of human affairs to an ethical hermeneutic that used the Confucian Classics as its control system. Only during the Qing dynasty, with evidential research and "exegetical criticism" (to borrow the term coined by D. W. Robinson), did historical research become an intellectual activity that was able not just to gain meaning from the reconstruction of a much more accurate and error-free historical record, but to generate its own theories of knowledge. The most important exponent of Qing historical criticism, the aforementioned Zhang Xuecheng, famously said that even the Six Classics are historical writing. This dictum has been understood in different ways, but in general we can say that with it Zhang Xuecheng placed the Classics in their own historical context, and in doing so relativized their universal meaning, dislocating the usual perception according to which the Classics had eternal significance while the works of history dealt with an ever-changing reality whose underlying patterns and laws, when they could be devised, were only valid for the period in question. For Zhang, the Classics were produced by the sages of antiquity because here was a contingent necessity to manage the state and to nurture the people (Mittag 2005, 390), and therefore the creation of the Classics should be seen as the product of specific historical circumstances (Elman 2002, 135). During the Qing, too, however, the Confucian canon remained central to Qing scholars' learning and continued to embody the ideals, with respect to social order, moral conduct, and proper governance, that had inspired literati for centuries. What changed was the intensity with which the past was scrutinized, not just to gain moral lessons, but to establish the best version of it.

We can say that truth and unity, in the manner defined above, have been critical ingredients in the development of Chinese historiography. The foundations of the organization of historical knowledge were laid at the very beginning of imperial China, in the particular intellectual milieu that followed the imperial unification due to the efforts of individuals who understood history as a fundamental branch of knowledge, and indeed, in Sima Qian's view, the type of knowledge that could unify all knowledge. The key principles that guided historical writing from the beginning, and especially the standard histories, show a large degree of continuity, yet were never static. The institutionalization of history writing led to the preservation of a large mass of documents and elevated history to a government enterprise, a societal value, and an object of study, but from a very early stage also encouraged experimentation, innovation, criticism, and much rewriting. A factor of change was the tension between the production of historical works as records of the past, their political implications, and the moral teachings that the historical narratives were supposed to convey. Each of these realms had its own standards of "truth." The philosophical underpinnings of history writing, with their emphasis on "praise and blame," the didactic value of history, and its subordination to a philosophically and politically correct interpretation of events, continued to clash with the need to organize, gather, select, and evaluate historical documents with objectivity and trustworthiness. Finally, the bureaucratization of historical writing to a certain degree stymied historical production but did not prevent private historians from voicing criticisms and striving for a better type of history. The contrasts and dialogue between the two stimulated the growth of historical ideals and alternative modes of history writing, and continue to do so to this very day.

REFERENCES

Balazs, E. 1961. "L'Histoire comme guide de la pratique bureaucratique (les monographies, les encyclopédies, les recueils des statuts)." In *Historians of China and Japan*, ed. W. G. Beasley and E. G. Pulleyblank, 78–94. London: Oxford University Press.

Beasley, W. G., and E. G. Pulleyblank, eds. 1961. *Historians of China and Japan*. London: Oxford University Press.

Bielenstein, Hans. 1954. "The Restoration of the Han Entry, with Prolegomena on teh Historiography of the *Hou Han Shu*." *Bulletin of the Museum of Far Eastern Antiquities* 26:1–81.

Chan, Hok-lam. 1982. "'Comprehensiveness' (t'ung) and 'Change' (pien) in Ma Tuan-lin's Historical Thought." In *Yuan Thought: Chinese Thought and Religion under the Mongols*, ed. Hok-lam Chan and W. Theodore de Bary, 27–87. New York: Columbia University Press.

———. 1984. *Legitimation in Imperial China: Discussions under the Jurchen-Chin Dynasty (1115–1234)*. Seattle: University of Washington Press.

Dai, Yi. 2009–10. "The Origin of the Qingshi (Qing History) and Its Initial Planning." *Chinese Studies in History* 43 (2): 6–14.

Davis, Richard L. 2004. Introduction to *Historical Records of the Five Dynasties*, by Ouyang Xiu, lxiii–lxxix. Trans. Richard L. Davis. New York: Columbia University Press.

Demiéville, P. 1961. "Chang Hsüeh-ch'eng and His Historiography." In *Historians of China and Japan*, ed. W. G. Beasley and E. G. Pulleyblank, 167–85. London: Oxford University Press.

Durrant, Stephen. 2005. "Truth Claims in the Shiji." In *Historical Truth, Historical Criticism and Ideology: Chinese Historiography and Historical Culture from a Comparative Perspective*, ed. Helwig Schmidt-Glintzer, Achim Mittag, and Jörn Rüsen, 93–114. Leiden: Brill.

———. 2011. "The Han Histories." In *The Oxford History of Historical Writing*, vol. 1: *Beginnings to AD 600*, ed. Andrew Feldherr and Grant Hardy, 485–508. Oxford: Oxford University Press.

Elman, Benjamin A. 2002. "The Historicization of Classical Learning in Ming-Ch'ing China." In *Turning Points in Historiography: A Cross-Cultural Perspective*, ed. Q. Edward Wang and Georg G. Iggers, 101–44. Rochester, NY: University of Rochester Press.

Feldherr, Andrew, and Grant Hardy, eds. 2011. *The Oxford History of Historical Writing*, vol. 1: *Beginnings to AD 600*. Oxford: Oxford University Press.

Foot, Sarah, and Andrew Robinson, eds. 2012. *The Oxford History of Historical Writing*, vol. 2: *400–1400*. Oxford: Oxford University Press.

Gentz, Joachim. 2005. "The Past as a Messianic Vision: Historical Thought and Strategies of Sacralization in the Early Gongyang Tradition." In *Historical Truth, Historical Criticism and Ideology: Chinese Historiography and Historical Culture from a Comparative Perspective*, ed. Helwig Schmidt-Glintzer, Achim Mittag, and Jörn Rüsen, 227–54. Leiden: Brill.

Hartman, Charles. 2012. "Chinese Historiography in the Age of Maturity, 960–1368." In *The Oxford History of Historical Writing*, vol. 2: *400–1400*, ed. Sarah Foot and Andrew Robinson, 37–57. Oxford: Oxford University Press.

Hartman, Charles, and Anthony DeBlasi. 2012. "The Growth of Historical Method in Tang China." In *The Oxford History of Historical Writing*, vol. 2: *400–1400*, ed. Sarah Foot and Andrew Robinson, 17–36. Oxford: Oxford University Press.

Huang, Chun-chieh. 1995. "Historical Thinking in Classical Confucianism—Historical Argumentation from the Three Dynasties." In *Time and Space in Chinese Culture*, ed. Chun-chieh Huang and Eric Zürcher, 72–88. Leiden: Brill.

———. 2004. "The Philosophical Argumentation by Historical Narration in Sung China: The Case of Chi Hsi." In *The New and the Multiple: Sung Senses of the Past*, ed. Thomas H. C. Lee, 107–20. Hong Kong: Chinese University Press.

Hulsewé, A. F. P. 1961. "Notes on the Historiography of the Han Period." In *Historians of China and Japan*, ed. W. G. Beasley and E. G. Pulleyblank, 31–43. London: Oxford University Press.

Lee, Thomas H. C. 2002. "New Directions in Northern Sung Historical Writing." In *Turning Points in Historiography: A Cross-Cultural Perspective*, ed. Q. Edward Wang and Georg G. Iggers, 59–88. Rochester, NY: University of Rochester Press.

Lewis, Mark. 2011. "Historiography and Empire." In *The Oxford History of Historical Writing*, vol. 1: *Beginnings to AD 600*, ed. Andrew Feldherr and Grant Hardy, 440–62. Oxford: Oxford University Press.

Li, Wai-yee. 2011. "Pre-Qin Annals." In *The Oxford History of Historical Writing*, vol. 1: *Beginnings to AD 600*, ed. Andrew Feldherr and Grant Hardy, 415–39. Oxford: Oxford University Press.

Mansvelt Beck, B. J. 1990. *The Treatises of the Later Han: Their Author, Sources, Content, and Place in Chinese Historiography*. Leiden: Brill.

Mittag, Achim. 2005. "What Makes a Good Historian: Zhang Xuecheng's Postulate of 'Moral Identity' (*shi de*) Revisited." In *Historical Truth, Historical Criticism and Ideology: Chinese Historiography and Historical Culture from a Comparative Perspective*, ed. Helwig Schmidt-Glintzer, Achim Mittag, and Jörn Rüsen, 365–405. Leiden: Brill.

Ng, On Cho, and Q. Edward Wang. 2005. *Mirroring the Past: The Writing and Use of History in Imperial China*. Honolulu: University of Hawai'i Press.

Nienhauser, William H., Jr. 2011. "Sima Qian and the Shiji." In *The Oxford History of Historical Writing*, vol. 1: *Beginnings to AD 600*, ed. Andrew Feldherr and Grant Hardy, 463–84. Oxford: Oxford University Press.

Pulleyblank, E. G. 1961. "Chinese Historical Criticism: Liu Chih-chi and Ssu-ma K'uang." In *Historians of China and Japan*, ed. W. G. Beasley and E. G. Pulleyblank, 135–66. London: Oxford University Press.

Schaberg, David. 2005. "Platitude and Persona: Junzi Comments in Zuozhuan and Beyond." In *Historical Truth, Historical Criticism and Ideology: Chinese Historiography and Historical Culture from a Comparative Perspective*, ed. Helwig Schmidt-Glintzer, Achim Mittag, and Jörn Rüsen, 177–96. Leiden: Brill.

Schmidt-Glintzer, Helwig. 2005. "Why Has the Question of Truth Remained an Open Question Throughout Chinese History?" In *Historical Truth, Historical Criticism and Ideology: Chinese Historiography and Historical Culture from a Comparative Perspective*, ed. Helwig Schmidt-Glintzer, Achim Mittag, and Jörn Rüsen, 115–30. Leiden: Brill.

Schmidt-Glintzer, Helwig, Achim Mittag, and Jörn Rüsen, eds. 2005. *Historical Truth, Historical Criticism and Ideology: Chinese Historiography and Historical Culture from a Comparative Perspective*. Leiden: Brill.

Twitchett, D. C. 1961. "Chinese Biographical Writing." In *Historians of China and Japan*, ed. W. G. Beasley and E. G. Pulleyblank, 95–114. London: Oxford University Press.

———. 1992. *The Writing of Official History under the T'ang*. Cambridge: Cambridge University Press.

Vogelsang, Kai. 2005. "Some Notions of Historical Judgment in China and the West." In *Historical Truth, Historical Criticism and Ideology: Chinese Historiography and Historical Culture from a Comparative Perspective*, ed. Helwig Schmidt-Glintzer, Achim Mittag, and Jörn Rüsen, 143–75. Leiden: Brill.

Wang, Gungwu. 1983. "The Rhetoric of a Lesser Empire: Early Sung Relations with Its Neighbors." In *China among Equals: The Middle Kingdom and Its Neighbors, 10th–14th Centuries*, ed. Morris Rossabi, 46–65. Berkeley: University of California Press.

Wang, Q. Edward, and Georg G. Iggers, eds. 2002. *Turning Points in Historiography: A Cross-Cultural Perspective*. Rochester, NY: University of Rochester Press.

Watson, Burton. 1993. *The Records of the Grand Historian: Qin Dynasty*. New York: Columbia University Press.

Weigelin-Schwiedrizik, Susanne. 2005. "History and Truth in Chinese Marxist Historiography." In *Historical Truth, Historical Criticism and Ideology: Chinese Historiography and Historical Culture from a Comparative Perspective*, ed. Helwig Schmidt-Glintzer, Achim Mittag, and Jörn Rüsen, 421–64. Leiden: Brill.

PART V

Art and Religion

CHAPTER THIRTEEN

The Architecture School within the University

———

MICHAEL LYKOUDIS

Traditionally, the city is where we have gathered to find shelter, security, and economy. The city serves our nature, our individual needs, and our common purposes. It is where we come to find truth. The idea of the city historically has embodied and brought together all of the aspects of culture from a multitude of professions and vocations: politics, law, commerce, agriculture, and worship. For traditional and classical architects and urbanists of today, the city and its architecture represent the physical manifestation of the unity of knowledge.

In this essay I first outline how architects engage at varying levels virtually all the disciplines found at the modern university. To be architects, we do not need to be, nor can we be, scholars in many of these disciplines, but within the confines of the needs of the art of building, we must master many of them and apply them to the creative process and execution of our craft. Second, I outline how the traditional city and its architecture represent the unity of knowledge as it mediates between nature and the man-made and the universal and the specific through the monumental and the vernacular.

With respect to the sciences, the architect needs to have an understanding of mathematics. On the most pedestrian level, area and volume calculations, proportions, and geometry are essential to the design process as well as to meeting the need for increasingly complex computations with respect to building codes, zoning ordinances, and environmental sustainability requirements. For understanding the complex structural, mechanical, and electrical loads on a building and community, the architect is trained to use algebra, trigonometry, and calculus and apply these to his or her work. Truth be told, we generally like to let our friends the engineers actually be the ones on the record for the calculations, but that is a liability issue more than a professional necessity. In fact, some architects, such as Santiago Calatrava, insist on designing their own structural systems. A foundation in engineering itself is also essential. An understanding of and ability to perform the mechanical, structural, electrical, and civil engineering on a project is required of the architect if he or she is to speak knowledgeably with the engineer. Physics is another area in which architects must have a solid grounding. An understanding of the materials and properties that keep buildings standing, liquids moving, sounds isolated, and air managed requires a fairly substantial background in physics. Biology is probably an unexpected area in which architects must be knowledgeable. From biology, architects have learned analytical methodologies such as the transect as they try to better understand the city as an ecosystem. As we try to also better appreciate the city and the countryside and the distinction between the two for reasons of environmental sustainability, we need to be educated about a region's fauna and flora as well as the effect of microorganisms on buildings and their interiors. Chemistry is an essential ingredient in the education of the architect. For example, galvanic action and other chemical reactions can play a critical role in the performance and durability of a building.

In the traditional architect's mind, architecture and the city are more about a sense of place than they are about a sense of time. Thus anthropology links some of the concerns of the biologist, examining the natural resources in a given locale and how the local culture uses and adapts the local geology and patterns of circulation through local conventions. In addition, psychology and organizational behavior are needed to better understand how communities interact, the dynamics within one's own office, and, of course, the mind-set of the all-important client.

The architect must also know the law: from zoning and building codes and limits to professional liability and contracts. Architecture is ultimately a business. Successful architects must become entrepreneurs and adept at marketing, finance, accounting, and business ethics.

Most important, architecture is an art. In antiquity, the architect managed the sculpture, painting, and iconographic program of the building. The building itself is an artistic object, subject to principles of composition, such as solid-void relationships, as are the other arts.

The architect places all these disciplines in the service of resolving competing needs and forces. Dissimilar things can coexist within a given structure as long as there is mediation among them. Architects, and particularly classical architects, mediate among these to achieve balance, harmony, and order.

The relationship of solid to void is a good place to begin to examine how we are able to describe our physical world and, by extension, the solar system, galaxy, and universe. Principally, in the visible universe, we have solids (matter) and voids (space). In a sculpture or a building, the voids are equally as important as the solids. The pattern of the openings or voids in a wall creates rhythms that make up the composition. The changing size of these openings adds to the grammar and syntax of architectural compositions, much like notes on a piece of music, which was once considered the allied art to architecture. Each bar has a measure that has a beat: quarter notes, half notes, and the like, tone and melody. The rhythm of the building can be seen in the regular cadence of openings and the melody in the punctuating changes in size and proportion of the openings. We can think of a layered facade as the many instruments of an ensemble playing their own part in the composition; each would be lessened without the company of the others.

What the solid-void relationships in architecture actually represent is the very basic nature of the visible universe. This leads us to the principle that dissimilar things can coexist within the same structure, and they are defined by what they are as much as by what they are not. A colonnade, for instance, is as much about the space between the columns and the columns themselves. The character of a colonnade changes significantly as one adjusts the distance between the columns.

Take what is often referred to as human nature. Our nature is not uniquely human; we are part of the cosmos and are hardwired to comprehend, analyze, appreciate, and create within its structure. We are also made to stand upright and look forward. We privilege what we see as a front, face, or facade. We organize our built environment around a Cartesian plane or mathematical model that not only describes how we perceive the physical world in three dimensions, but how we can also rationally organize our cities, towns, and villages into streets, squares, and blocks, place one stone on top of another to build our shelters, and create what is often described as "the city as a second nature."

The Roman castrum, or military encampments, were expediently organized in two dimensions with a north-south axis called the Cardo and the east-west axis called the Decumanus. The Roman city followed that principle, and hundreds of cities, towns, and villages in Europe were arranged along those lines. We see this around the world as well: Teotihuacán in Mexico, the diagram for the ideal Chinese city, or Marseille.

The other human natures that the city facilitates and expresses are those of the public and the private. We are social creatures and find knowledge, economy, inspiration, comfort, and joy in the company of others. The opposite of our social nature is the need for privacy. We gain security, inspiration, and comfort in the privacy of our homes. We cannot be isolated for long periods, and we need to return to our public realm after being recharged by our isolation. Another part of the private realm has traditionally been commerce, which until the twentieth century was largely the domain of individuals. The need for identity, to compete and vie for excellence, is as much a part of the human condition as the need for collaboration and cooperation. The city with its public and private spaces facilitates this dual and dissimilar nature. The private realm is represented by two types of buildings in the idea of the city: the residential fabric that offers privacy and shelter and the commercial entities that offer the competitive and individual enterprises making up the vitality of a culture. On the opposite side, the public realm is made up of capital buildings, town halls, libraries, schools, and other public institutions that both celebrate the accomplishments of a culture and facilitate its governance, education, and broader cultural aspirations.

With respect to buildings, walls give us privacy and identity and openings modulate the relationship of a space to the outside world.

Thus, on one end of the spectrum, bathrooms and kitchens have small windows, and on the other, living rooms and libraries can have large ones. Colonnades and arcades, which can be seen as walls—with as much of the material removed as possible—make the most porous connection between the public domain, such as streets, and the private or semipublic spaces behind them. Together, at the scales of both urbanism and architecture, the city, with its streets, squares and blocks, walls, openings, and roofs, facilitates the delicate balance between our public and private natures—the need for individual aspirations and the community that fulfills our common purposes.

The principles represented by the traditional city and its architecture are present through time and place in the history of the world. In architecture we call those elements types. In the traditional city, types are categorized according to the scales of urbanism, architecture, and construction. At the urban scale the types are streets, squares, and blocks; at the architectural scale the types are sacred buildings, public buildings, and private buildings; and at the scale of construction the types consist of walls, openings, and roofs. It should be noted that there are cultures that are outside these typological categories and that there are cultures that do not use all of the types.

Consider the building types illustrated and discussed by Carroll William Westfall in the book coauthored with Robert Jan van Pelt, *Architectural Principles in the Age of Historicism*.[1] The types are organized into the three categories: sacred, identified by the Temple and the Tholos; public, identified by the Theater and the Reggia or Palace; and private, represented by the Domus and Taberna. Westfall bases these types not on specific architectural forms or functions but, more broadly, around the religious, civic, and individual purposes found in most cultures around the world.

We are accustomed to think of history as a series of episodic ruptures, mostly disconnected, except for explanations of how one period led to another due to a series of specific and particular events. Thus we conceive of the Classical, the Gothic, the Renaissance, the Baroque, and the Neoclassical as unique and separate. That there are cultural and historical exigencies that separate these times may be true, but what is more important is the continuities that thread them together.

The general Cartesian organization of a city or town is there, whether or not the city is a grid at the local scale. Each intersection of streets is a visible Cartesian condition that comes together in a T or X connection. Since early antiquity, the urban tissue has been made up of streets, squares, and blocks. There is a clear distinction between public, private, and sacred buildings irrespective of time, and each is recognizable as such.

Similarly we consider African, European, Asian, and American cultures as separate and distinct. This may be the case, but it is also possible to see the continuities between them as well. I mentioned before the relationship between the Chinese and Roman cities. Both are arranged as idealized grids with major and minor axes. The fabric of both is made up of streets and blocks. How these are composed changes according to local custom and the conventions of the times, but that is a secondary issue when considering the formal continuities.

With respect to architecture we see the presence of certain building types in both the Chinese and Greco-Roman traditions. We also can see that the use of building elements such as walls, openings, and roofs are common to most cultures. Notions of sacred, public, and private realms identify buildings in most cultures with monumental architecture. We can also look at a parallelism between cultures and recognize several common building types. While we do not want to make false attributions of one culture's influence on another, the formal continuities suggest that there is something universal that is present and visible in all cultures.

"Character" has to do with the quality of urban, architectural, and structural norms that are specific to time and place. Thus the architectural character of the Gothic differs from the Renaissance; the Greco-Roman differs from the Chinese; and so on. In an age of globalization, when we are trying to fit all cultures to one industrial model, we can see how the world is unified on the one hand by typology and, on the other, how each culture and time differs according to character.

The political philosopher Peter Murphy defined beauty as follows: "Beauty is the sense that no force can ultimately overwhelm another force. Beauty is the line that keeps the contending forces apart and it is the shape that keeps those forces together. The ugly lacks both shape and line. It is 'formless.'"[2] I would add to that statement that, in general, balance is associated with beauty, while imbalance is not. Classical architecture relies on the idea that the natural materials used in its making (usually stone or wood) and the resulting architectural elements are in static equilibrium. Stone tends to be best in compression and not in tension, making it ideal for durable bearings. Wood has some tensile properties, so it is used in making the rafters or trusses of the roof. Together the stone and wooden assembly of the classical composition represents a body at rest. Thus balance and durability are harmonized; as a building weathers and erodes it stays in structural balance for a long time. In structures that use materials in tension, once their structural members have corroded, they fail quickly.

So while we can appreciate and see many works of art or architecture as beautiful that do not fall into the classical or traditional camps, the issue of imbalance related to sustainability requires a critique of our current attitudes toward the city and its architecture.

The Industrial Revolution brought humanity a renewed ability to feed, clothe, and shelter itself. In no small way this was due to the relatively inexpensive sources of energy, especially oil and other fossil fuels. According to the U.S. Department of Energy, nearly 70 percent of our energy goes to the built environment and the transportation network required to serve suburban sprawl and our cities.[3] We have consumed approximately half of the earth's proven oil reserves, and with the fast-growing economies of China and other populous countries, we are increasing our thirst for fossil fuels. This represents an imbalance, and it is not sustainable. With the passage of time, this problem will become more acute. Compounded with the effects of climate change, the impending confluence of these two crises threatens our civilizations.

It has been declared by the distinguished architect Demetri Porphyrios that "classicism is not a style. . . . [I]t is the philosophy of free will nurtured by tradition."[4] More specifically, classicism, in addition to being the idealization and representation of nature, is a philosophy of cultural conservation and sustainability. In the classical mind, the future and the past are part of a continuum. The ever-changing character of classical and traditional architecture reflects the changes in conventions over time. With each new generation, the classical architectural and urban elements of continuity remind us of our debt to the past as a conscious act of conservation rather than consumption. We could think of tradition as the projection of society's highest aspirations into the future, thus ensuring that the best, and perhaps the most sustainable, aspects of a culture endure. Tradition is therefore not duplication but rather a process that is always inventing itself. It is the inventive quality of tradition that allows each generation to shape the future in its own manner, and it is tradition's projection of the past that provides the sense of stewardship that is required for sustainability.

Tradition is largely based on the artistic principle of imitation. Imitation in this case is not the servile copy but rather a continuous reinterpretation of a thing or an idea. Consider two monasteries: Mount Saint Michael in England and Mont Saint Michel in Normandy. The English version is an imitation of the French one. Imitation is how we learn and how we invent. It is a process based on our nature and in nature.

The same is true of seemingly dissimilar objects in nature. Changes in nature are continuous but are always based on some precedent. Something is always becoming something else. Nature imitates itself as we as part of nature develop our cultures and civilizations through the process of imitation.

In the concept of imitation lies the role of myth as truth. We know something is not true, such as the Aesop's fable in which a grasshopper is speaking with an ant. We know ants and grasshoppers cannot speak, but the parable contains a truth within the fiction. We call this the fictive distance that art possesses that elevates representation to the level of art. In architecture it is the mythic origins of classicism and how they are represented that concern us.

The traditional city as a work of art contains many such truths, myths, and fictive representations. We can imagine in Paris the origins of its streets in the animal trails of the primordial forests that preceded them and the origin of the squares as clearings in that forest. Of course we know that is not true specifically for any particular city, but the mythic beginnings of the city are not far off. With respect to buildings, we can imagine the interiors of the Bibliothèque Nationale in Paris as an imitation of the canopy of trees in a forest.

In the city of Epidauros in Greece, the cavea is shaped by the valley that contains it, almost improving upon nature, and by the need for humans to gather around a performance that allows our aspirations to take flight. Architectural form here imitates both physical nature and human nature.

Nature informs our construction, our knowledge and wisdom, elevates shelter to craft, while myth elevates building to architecture. Consider the relationship of the rustic hut to the vernacular building and then to the classical. We see how the materials in the rustic hut are used raw, without refinement, to make shelter. We see the vernacular materials, more processed and refined, and in the classical condition the craft being transformed into a language.

For example, the mythic origins of classical architecture can be seen as the representation of the building's making. The column flutes are actually bundled tree trunks, the triglyphs are the ends of beams, the metopes are the spaces between those beams, and the moldings are ropes and other fasteners that mediate and connect the column shafts and entablatures. Looking at a Corinthian base, we see the allusion to ropes tied together to keep the stresses of the building from pulling the column apart. We also see how classicism expresses principles of physics, deforming the material after pressure is exerted on it and creating the molding known as a taurus. Similarly, the wall and its openings, once examples of a simple vernacular construction, are elevated to a classical language through idealization, representation, and imitation. Roofs give protection to the building and depending on the culture contain their own narrative or myths.

Recently America marked the hundredth anniversary of the sinking of the *Titanic*. That event is a parable of the collapse of a culture that did not heed the warnings that were visible before the fall. We have built such a system; its momentum cannot be changed easily. The principles of the traditional city and its architecture can help restore the balance in how we live together and inhabit our planet. There are other disciplines that have to play their role in this effort, but how we live together and how we build—urbanism and architecture—should help account for much of the solution in the coming age of austerity and energy limits.

If the traditional city and its architecture embody the idea of the unity of knowledge, what then about the modern city? It is clear that we are better off today than we were in 1350 for all sorts of reasons, but we have also built more buildings since 1950 than in the entire history of humanity. Why then are the cities and buildings we have built over the past sixty years so much poorer than those of the past? Before World War II, one had to travel far to find a bad building. Now one has to travel far to find a good one. On the one hand, the great modern masters make impressive buildings, sometimes very beautiful buildings, but in an age when we are trying to find ways of living today without sacrificing the opportunity for future generations to reach their potential, it seems a pity to waste resources on something that is a consumable object of entertainment rather than an investment in an economy of conservation.

As the world needs to accommodate a population of nine billion or more in the coming decades or centuries, it will be impossible to live like we did in antiquity or even close to modern times. Much as we might like to, we cannot replicate the eighteenth century or any other earlier period in history. But if we see history as a continuum, we can learn from the accumulated knowledge of the traditional city: regional and local economies and methods of building; buildings and cities built in accordance with the limits of their respective climates, geology, flora, and fauna; denser, more compact cities with mixed use that enable most of life's needs to be accommodated on a pedestrian scale; more durable buildings that can be adapted successfully to new uses; and buildings built of local materials that have low embodied energy and are durable for centuries.

So now we come full circle to examine the city as the place where the human search for truth takes place and the unity of knowledge is there for all to see. While the modern experiment, with its promise of limitless and cheap energy, is showing signs of weathering, its contributions are not lost but folded back into a culture of tradition. Because of it, we managed to make better institutions and political economies. Because of it, we see the world as a whole made up of many parts, and within each part we see a piece of ourselves. We are unified as a planet but celebrate our individual cultural identities. While this utopia may seem far off, we may be closer to at least part of it than we think.

NOTES

1. Robert Jan van Pelt and Carroll William Westfall, *Architectural Principles in the Age of Historicism* (New Haven: Yale University Press, 1991).

2. Peter Murphy, "The City of Justice," in *Building Cities*, ed. Norman Crowe, Richard Economakis, and Michael Lykoudis (London: Artmedia Press, 1999), 24.

3. U.S. Department of Energy, *Buildings Energy Data Book*, 1:1.3. 2011. http://buildingsdatabook.eren.doe.gov/TableView.aspx?table=1.1.3.

4. Demetri Porphyrios, Foreword to Crowe, Economakis, and Lykoudis, *Building Cities*, 7.

CHAPTER FOURTEEN

How Is Theology Inspired by the Sciences?

CELIA DEANE-DRUMMOND

This essay aims to set out a tentative map of some of the different ways in which theology might be inspired by the sciences. I am going to limit my discussion to the biological sciences, having once been a practicing biologist. I am also going to limit the range of theological ideas to those that I consider most relevant in relation to the explicit scientific examples and practices. The idea that theology might have something to say in relation to the sciences is certainly not new, and Thomas Aquinas's position on theology as "queen of the sciences" should be seen in relation to the perceived unity of knowledge in the premodern era.[1]

In a post-Enlightenment world, it becomes necessary for theology to be rather more self-conscious in its engagement with the sciences, in that while theology draws on philosophical traditions, those traditions are distinct from those that inform the sciences, with theology committed to metaphysical theism as a starting point, while science generally eschews theism in favor of methodological naturalism. Aquinas recognized that, compared to other sciences, theology was of a different kind, but evidence or principles taken from revelation by faith were not as problematic then as a basis for an argument. However, the kind of accommodation between theology and science that Aquinas managed to achieve still places science *in the service of* theology, so that natural reason serves to inform knowledge achieved through revelation. This is not so much "natural theology" understood as science serving a theistic apologetics; instead, he argues that a mind *trained* by the natural and theoretical sciences is better able to perceive revealed knowledge. In the first book of *Summa Theologiae*, Q.1.5, for example, Aquinas considers whether theology is superior to other sciences in light of the criticism that theology should be *less certain* as it is based on faith rather than on other sciences "the premises of which are indubitable." This is just the kind of argument that contemporary new atheists make in claiming the superiority of scientific knowledge, a topic that I return to below. But instead Aquinas argues that theology is superior in terms of certitude because the other sciences are able to make mistakes, since they are based on human reason, while theology is held in the light of divine knowledge. He also argues that the worth of theology's subject matter is superior since "it leads to heights that reason cannot climb." Theology, therefore, for Aquinas, does not so much *rely* on other sciences as use their guidance in order to help weakness of understanding in matters considered *above* reason by being mediated "through the world of natural reason from which the other sciences take their course."² This is, therefore, an argument that theology, even in matters of revealed knowledge, is actually enabled to perform its task better as a result of engagement with natural sciences. He also believed that such a view applies to both theoretical and practical issues; that is, theology is relevant to practical considerations of ethics.

The post-Enlightenment fracturing of the sciences and their dislocation from a sense of historical rootedness in Christian tradition, which permitted the burgeoning of experimental science, makes such an approach harder to sustain in a contemporary context but, I argue, not necessarily impossible, given certain qualifications. Certainly, we need to be wary of claims that are made by either science or theology without proper analysis of their presuppositions and methodological starting points. Alasdair MacIntyre, for example, in his *Three Rival Methods of Moral Inquiry*, points to the different styles of authority in the medieval writers who assumed the authority of texts, and whose interpretations were tested through disputation, through to the nineteenth-century encyclopedic positions, where authority lies in the individual, through to deconstruction in the wake of the critique of Nietzsche, whose search for the "truth" finally led him to resign his university post.[3] Nietzsche believed that an unrecognized motivation and unacknowledged purpose led to blindness about the multiplicity of possible perspectives in a manner that led MacIntyre to characterize his position as "genealogical." Nietzsche's claim that "truths are illusions that we have forgotten are illusions, worn out metaphors now impotent to stir the senses, coins which have lost their faces and are considered now as metal rather than currency," was highly controversial at the time but, arguably, left a profound mark on the intellectual landscape, particularly in the humanities.[4]

In light of the above, I suggest that as a prolegomena to any discussion of unity of knowledge there needs to be an analysis of tensions in the contemporary debate over what might be called alternative "truth claims" in theology and science. Such an analysis comes before laying out a map of common elements. I suggest that these tensions in themselves are not fruitless for the discussion but serve to inspire further research in theology and arguably the sciences as well. My premise is that, notwithstanding MacIntyre's helpful typology of the different ways of knowing and inquiry, it is possible to seek common understanding while acknowledging different presuppositions and starting points. It therefore remains a self-conscious search and aspiration for unity of knowledge rather than the bolder claim that such unity can easily be achieved. My argument in this essay is that a shared search for commonality between what seem to be highly disparate traditions is best grounded in practical considerations of the practices of science and the practices of religion, or their practical concrete focus recognized as specific social goals.

If an attempt to search for a unity of knowledge comes through *human experiences* of the practice of science and religion, then wonder experienced through science or scientific discoveries may border on an implicit religious experience, pointing to a common language. This notion informs the second section of this essay. If searching for unity of knowledge is mediated in shared practical concerns through common challenges to the global community, then it follows that both theology and science may be able to contribute to a shared goal. For example, ecological sensitivity has provoked many theologians to express their ideas in ways that make interrelationships between the natural world and theology much more explicit. "Ecotheology" has grown and developed into a field in its own right, and those adhering to this view range from the most conservative to the most liberal from a theological perspective. In the context of the ethical challenges arising out of the theory and practice of science, particularly the biosciences, theology is inspired to engage with specific scientific aspects of human societies. Sustainability is perhaps a good example of a nexus of highly complex problems where the ethical task must be multidisciplinary, and the search for common understanding should not be abandoned because it seems too difficult or complex. Finally, if the search for a unity of knowledge is practiced in an educational setting, then theology can be provoked by the natural and social sciences to find its place in university education more broadly, so that the particular agenda of any one of the sciences does not take hold of the student imagination. I want to suggest that the language of wisdom provides one way in which theology and the sciences can be thought of as having mutual but distinct roles to play in relation to building up their mutually enriching conceptions of truth. These conceptions are not illusions, as Nietzsche claimed, but they are situated in particular traditions built up through particular practices.

FINDING THEOLOGY BETWEEN TWO CULTURES

C. P. Snow imagined two cultures, humanities and science, where the gap between them poses a huge problem for communication between different disciplines.[5] After years of dialogue between science and religion, what has become of the two cultures? Has Snow's thesis been forgotten in the haste to find common ground and build bridges between various disciplines? Historically, this was posed as the tension between Jewish and Hellenistic traditions in Christianity; as the early church historian Tertullian notoriously asked, "What can Athens have to do with Jerusalem?"[6] The evolutionary biologist Stephen Jay Gould certainly imagined science and religion as two nonoverlapping Magisteria, but in his final works he seemed to point toward some common ground.[7] I think we need to take this gap seriously even as we seek to build dialogue and find forms of unity of knowledge that are still *meaningful* for scientists and for those in the humanities.

Evolutionary biologists, for example, have a *particular kind* of questioning that seeks explanations according to Darwinian concepts of evolution by natural selection. When it comes to a discussion of the origins and practices of religion, an evolutionary biologist will most commonly try to "explain" religion (or, ironically, perhaps, its opposite, atheism) in evolutionary terms.[8] Such explanations *presuppose* the Darwinian model, and religion presents a human behavioral puzzle to be "explained" in evolutionary terms.[9] Perhaps on the one hand religion is carried along by other traits that have selective advantages now but were not particularly beneficial in the past, known as *exaptation*.[10] On the other hand, religion may appear as a *spandrel* that lacks selective advantage both historically and in the present.[11] For the biologist Nikolaas Tinbergen, the "four causes"—ultimate, proximate, developmental and phylogenetic—of evolutionary explanation may be more or less dominant, but the "ultimate" is the evolutionary one assumed to be lurking in the background of other explanations.[12] However, in such discussions speech about "ultimate" explanations in evolutionary terms is surprising for theologians, who consider, following Dietrich Bonhoeffer's categorization that echoes to some extent Aquinas's views discussed above, that all explanations based on natural science are *penultimate* rather than *ultimate*, since ultimate explanations are about God rather than human reasoning.[13]

This example illustrates that evolutionary biologists draw on key narratives in order to express meaning, so when they use "ultimate language," this creates in their listeners a symbolic world, but that is not necessarily what biologists are attempting to claim. Some scientists are beginning to object to the use of ultimate language as it seems to not only promise more than it can deliver but also, perhaps, detract from important issues that are in danger of being ignored.[14] An evolutionary biologist's reply may be that language about God has *itself* evolved for specific purposes, hence the use of the "supernatural punishment" device and other tools to study religion.[15] One of the difficulties with this language is that what many evolutionary biologists are trying to do is to find a way to *operationalize* and test religious belief in a particular way according to particular *traits* that can then be studied from the perspective of evolutionary biology. Yet such a position tends to miss the other ways in which a phenomenon as complex as religion might be analyzed even *within* the sciences, including, for example, neuroscience and cognitive psychology, as well as "softer" sciences such as linguistics, social science, anthropology, and so on. Further, as I have hinted at already, even evolutionary biological science is grounded in its own cultural world, a world that biologists often seem not to recognize as important, both in terms of informing its explanations of reality and in terms of the cultural factors that make up human experience. In other words, in isolating biological factors as a means of analysis and explanation, other possible sources of variation tend to be pushed to one side or dismissed.

What are the philosophical assumptions in making claims about religious beliefs understood through scientific methods? *Naturalism* is the term sometimes used to capture the presupposition that particular human behaviors can be "explained" (some might say "reduced") to categories based on scientific methodology. This includes Darwinian or other evolutionary explanations such as genetic drift. Those theologians who are rather more forthcoming about their philosophical presuppositions recognize that metaphysical claims about God do not "fit into" scientific patterns of explanation that presuppose naturalistic interpretations. So can theological "God language" ever be analyzed according to the methodologies of natural science if, by definition, it is about *second-order* metaphysical claims about God that cannot be tested? Is it ever meaningful to say such second-order claims have "evolved," or does "evolution" mean something very different from Darwinian forms of evolution by natural selection? Could scientists simply "adopt" evolutionary language about God for their purposes, as a heuristic tool? If they do so, what does this do to *public perception* about science, or theology for that matter? And what might be the ethical implications of making such a shift?

Once specific issues are discussed around a common theme, such as that of evolution and human nature, for example, gaps open up that relate to the specifically theological claims about what it is to be human:

talk of soul, image of God, and so on. If theologians start to use scientific language in their more constructive theologizing, is this for the purpose of new theological reflections? In other words, does it matter that the starting point (gap) is there? Above all, I suggest we need to be completely honest about what we are doing and recognize the presuppositions in our decisions about *which* science and *which* theology to use in speaking about the relationship between them. Hence if theology is to be inspired by the sciences, then we need to question *which* particular science we are drawing on and *why*. Just as MacIntyre asked, Whose justice? Which rationality?,[16] we can add, Which science? Whose theory? Whose theology? What fragments remain after what might be termed "the univocal" language of some sciences, or theologies for that matter? Or, to put this in much more general terms, who has authority, and whose voice do we listen to and why?

Scientists, like theologians, in their theoretical reflections often seek unifying frameworks on the premise that there is an underlying truth about reality that can be discovered. In the evolutionary world this often boils down to evolution by natural selection as a foundational stance. But such a "unifying" framework echoes some of the dangers that Karl Rahner picks up in his discussion of theology and natural science.[17] For him, theology has a better chance than another branch of science of acting as mediator between disciplines, as it is itself a conglomerate of ideas, drawing on history, philosophy, and so on. Of course, there may be sciences that Rahner acknowledged, such as anthropology, but where he too readily assumed that secular anthropology was a disguised form of theology.[18] In the case of anthropology, given its plural disciplinary basis, there is arguably rather less tendency to take over other disciplines or subsume them under a particular dominating discipline in the way Rahner feared, but forcing one type of explanation into another is a view that emerges in E. O. Wilson's *Consilience*, for example.[19]

But there are also dangers in Rahner's elevation of a specific form of Christian theology, in his case, Roman Catholic theology, dangers that may be equally problematic compared to the elevation (reification) of, for example, evolution by natural selection in the biological realm. How can we navigate the boundary and allow theology to be inspired by the sciences without absorbing one framework into another? But the challenge remains: in transdisciplinary conversations how can we be true to our own disciplines (whatever they might be) without taking over others? In light of the above I suggest three possible strategies. First, find common ground in the *experience* of doing science and the *experience* of practicing faith through metareflection on "wonder." Second, find a common *task* to which theology and science might contribute. As an example, I refer here to global questions of sustainability, where theological and scientific insights are relevant. Finally, theology and science can come together and energize one another in formulation of *strategies for higher education*, where both theology and science need to be given a place at the table in developing *wisdom* for the twenty-first century.

JOURNEY INTO WONDER

That science might be inspired by religious or theological insights is well known in the history of science. We can consider, for example, the natural theology of the early thirteenth century, which moved from merely a contemplative activity to one that was imbued with an effort to understand how and why creation worked the way it did. Such natural theologies persisted to the eighteenth century, so that in the botanical realm William Paley's *Natural Theology* or John Ray's *The Wisdom of God* was intent on finding evidence of how God thought in the workings of the natural world.[20] Charles Darwin was apparently inspired by such natural theologies while a student at Cambridge, but his growing confidence in the explanatory powers of the scientific account left any theistic underpinning somewhat fragile.[21] In the secular climate today, the question becomes inverted, so that it now asks how theology might be inspired by the sciences, instead of how can science be inspired by theology. Indeed, some might consider that this question can no longer be asked, as the motivated quest for pure scientific discoveries as representing truth *about* the world tends to give way to pragmatic technological solutions to problems *within* the world. But if we hold onto the ideal of science as a search for truth about the world for a moment, then a common desire underlying such a search is one motivated by wonder at the complexity, beauty, and diversity of the world in which we live. Richard Dawkins, well known for his hostile representation of theism, acknowledges, in his book *Unweaving the Rainbow*, the wonder that arises from scientific discovery. He claims:

> The impulses to awe, reverence and wonder which led Blake to mysticism (and lesser figures to paranormal superstition, as we shall see) are precisely those that lead others to science. Our interpretation is different but what excites us is the same. The mystic is content to bask in the wonder and revel in the mystery that we were not "meant" to understand. The scientist feels the same wonder, but is restless, not content, recognizes the mystery as profound, then adds, "But we are working on it."[22]

Of course, he is quite wrong here to suppose that such a religious view, which he represents as stereotypical mysticism, is the only religious view possible in relation to a natural phenomenon. A scientist can just as easily be motivated to explore reasons why the mystery is there for explicitly religious reasons as for reasons of pure curiosity. Here we can think of wonder as a kind of preliminary elative experience that joins with intellectual curiosity to drive the search for the truth behind particular natural phenomena.

Is such an experience of wonder in the scientific quest at all analogous to specific *religious* experiences? The answer to this question is somewhat ambiguous and depends to a large extent on how far and to what extent natural theology is acceptable as a way of thinking theologically. By way of clarification, natural theology is most often understood as a methodological approach, a way of moving toward an understanding of God from close observation of the natural world. There are present-day examples of this position, such as Paul Davis's reflection on modern, contemporary cosmology, where, for him, the precise laws of our own universe point to the Mind of God.[23] This is a good example, as it shows up the limitations of such a method, for am I really inclined to believe in or be in a relationship with a God who is represented simply by such mathematical laws?

Those who hesitate to attach themselves to natural theology are also aware of the difficulties of bringing together belief in a good God with the apparently cruel and wasteful processes found in the natural world. This is particularly true for biologists, which may be one reason that theism is less common among prominent contemporary biologists compared to physicists. There seems no need for the God hypothesis, and, if anything, religious views are thought of as evolved capacities, selected either directly during the process of hominid evolution or indirectly as a result of other evolutionary advantages such as agent detection capabilities that were then conveniently transferred to belief in gods. More hostile elements associated with biology simmer here as well, not least by philosophers of biology, such as Christopher Hitchens, Sam Harris, Richard Dawkins, and Daniel Dennett, who advance rather more aggressive versions of atheism along with their biological explanations.[24]

Given this trend, it is hardly surprising that, following Karl Barth's famous "Nein" to his fellow theologian Emil Brunner, many Protestant theologians, at least, are wary of most forms of natural theology.[25] Such a skeptical view becomes reinforced by historical, cultural, and racial problems associated with linking belief in a given nature with religious perfection, such as in the blood and soil mentality of Nazi Germany. Accordingly, the *revealed* theology that puts the most emphasis on the revelation of God in the Bible, and more specifically in Jesus Christ, takes precedent. But then another problem arises, namely, how and in what sense might there be *any* relationship between revealed theology and the sciences? Can "natural theology" be dispensed with so easily?[26]

In order to address this question, it is a good idea to consider the way in which early theologians developed forms of natural theology rather than take examples simply from contemporary science or distorted versions of natural theology in cultural history. A good place to start is with the Franciscan writers who developed a tradition of natural philosophy. Saint Bonaventure, a Franciscan writing in 1259, claimed:

> The supreme power, wisdom and goodness of the Creator shine forth in created things in so far as the bodily senses inform the

interior senses. . . . In the first way of seeing, the observer considers things in themselves. . . . [T]he observer can rise, as from a vestige, to the knowledge of the immense power, wisdom and goodness of the Creator. In the second way of seeing, the way of faith[,] . . . we understand that the world was fashioned by the Word of God.[27]

Although Bonaventure believed that the Word of God as revealed in Jesus Christ is "superior" compared to the vestiges of God found in the natural world, for him, God as Creator was a cosmic presence, since God is the Creator of all that is.

It would be a mistake, therefore, to think that this form of natural theology was a way of finding God in the natural world somehow *independent* of faith in God, or that those who were habitual sinners could somehow just "see" God in the natural order of things without prior experience of God in prayer. Bonaventure also seems to go further than this in suggesting that *only* those who are acting out their faith through *actions of justice* and *only* those who already have some knowledge of God through *intense meditation* can begin the journey and see with a pure heart those vestiges of the wisdom of God in the creaturely world. Given that the believer could reach such heights of contemplative grace, it is hardly surprising that such a view, at first sight, appears antithetical to experimental science. But it is significant that Bonaventure *also* claimed we need to move *beyond* mere vestiges, for in creatures "He is present in them by his essence, His power and His presence."[28]

Bonaventure, heavily influenced by Augustine in his Platonic descriptions of creatures as "shadows" of that perfect wisdom found in God, also encouraged careful understanding of the truth, including the truth that could come from scientific activity. Such scientific activity is in his case put to a particular goal, namely, the goal of mystical union with God. He believed that the contemplation of the insights of the various sciences takes place in charity. In other words, all knowledge and human endeavor is instilled with the spirit of love. He links various aspects of human endeavor together: reading with fervor, speculation with devotion, investigation with admiration, observation with exultation, industry with piety, knowledge with love, understanding with humility, study with grace, and, finally, the mirror with wisdom.[29]

ECOLOGICAL PRAXIS

If, as Bonaventure suggests, wonder is a common language through which believing scientists express a kind of implicit religious experience, filled out by closer attention to natural theology, then a more direct inspiration of theology from natural science comes from practical concerns about environmental issues and ecology. Ecology as science can be distinguished from ecology as a social and political movement, and ecotheology draws inspiration from all elements associated with ecology, not just the scientific ones. Nonetheless, scientific accounts about the natural world and close, detailed attention to the behavior of other species act as sources of inspiration and motivation. Different theologians will focus on different aspects of the problem and draw on different elements of the sciences involved, ranging from climate science to discussions about animal suffering, biodiversity loss, and so on. The inspiration for such a reflection has as much to do with the *wonder* in that biodiversity as a need to address important ethical issues that science on its own does not seem able to solve. Ecotheology forces theological reflection away from the temptation to be narrowly anthropocentric, that is, focusing on humanity in a way that excludes consideration of other creatures and ecological contexts. The variety of forms that ecotheology might take are far too extensive to discuss in any detail here, but it is significant inasmuch as it embraces a huge range of methodological starting points, from traditional Eastern Orthodoxy to ecofeminism. Eastern Orthodox engagement with ecology retains a strong focus on the Logos (Word) as revealed in *logoi* (words) of the natural world and the place of human beings as microcosm and mediator between heaven and earth. By putting emphasis on asceticism and liturgical practices, it seeks to address the fundamental problems associated with a lack of sustainability, namely, the human tendency to take more than is required for a flourishing life and to define that flourishing in material rather than in spiritual terms.

The ecumenical patriarchate of Constantinople, Bartholomew II, also known in the media as the "Green Patriarch," has been active in promoting environmental responsibility throughout the world. While the extent of environmental damage as shown in scientific study inspires such activism, the underlying motivation is one that seeks to turn human beings away from selfish desires to live more responsibly in communion with God and other creatures. Symposia and conferences repeat the need for changes in practice and human responsibility, as the opening summit of the June 2012 conference in Halki indicated.

> Permit us to propose that perhaps the reason for this hesitation and hindrance may lie in the fact that we are unwilling to accept personal responsibility and demonstrate personal sacrifice. In the Orthodox Christian tradition, we refer to this "missing dimension" as *ascesis*, which could be translated as abstinence and moderation, or—better still—simplicity and frugality. The truth is that we resist any demand for self-restraint and self-control. However, dear friends, if we do not live more simply, we cannot learn to share. And if we do not learn to share, then how can we expect to survive? This may be a fundamental religious and spiritual value. Yet it is also a fundamental ethical and existential principle.[30]

Bartholemew claims, then, that a weakened sense of social responsibility stems from a lost ascetic spirituality. Roman Catholic social teaching also issues a similar call to environmental responsibility; in the writings of Pope John Paul II, we find a modification of the term *human ecology* used in social science to describe, as in the Orthodox Church, a way of emphasizing the importance of recognizing humanity's place within a wider ecological network of relationships.[31] The pope also used the term *ecological conversion*, referring to an understanding that all of creation is in one sense linked into a cosmic Christology.[32] While the idea of a cosmic liturgy goes back to the early church, for example, Maximus the Confessor, recovering this thread in contemporary discussion gives ecological language a significant place: an association with what is arguably the heart of faith in Jesus Christ. The Word made flesh becomes echoed in the *logoi* of creation. My own preference is to use the language of wisdom here: Christ as the Wisdom of God is found as in a mirror in the wisdom of the creaturely world.

My preference for *wisdom* relates to one aspect that ecological study consistently shows, namely, the suffering, predation, and death of myriad creatures, both in present ecological systems and recorded throughout evolutionary history. Some theologians have argued that we need a new kind of theodicy as a result of such insights.[33] Such limitations are important to recognize in order to remind ourselves that the temptation to hubris is always present, not least in the manner in which we might presume to be able to solve the difficult global problems of sustainability and what this might mean in terms of balancing different pressures in a truly human ecology, one that aims for what Pope Benedict XVI and his predecessors have called authentic or integral human development.[34]

Sustainability, therefore, in its complex demand on human societies, reaches beyond what might be termed a "univocal" response shaped by specific branches of modern science, if that science is thought of as cutting out aspects of human experience. Here, not just theology is inspired by the sciences, but different sciences come together with other social and human disciplines in order to seek real solutions to practical problems. *Sustainability*, therefore, when it is defined as inclusive of creatures other than human beings, represents what might be termed ecological praxis directed toward a particular end or goal, namely, the flourishing of the earth as such. Although science usually tries to avoid teleological language, it is clear that the agenda of sustainability is directed toward future generations as well as present ones. Part of the difficulty is knowing how to balance different demands, and in this context theology contributes to the discussion alongside science. I am convinced that the fruit of such interdisciplinary practices goes beyond that of respective disciplines and is generative of questions and their possible resolution in ways that would not be the case if we just kept to our comfortable watertight areas of specialization.

We need that aspect of prudence that Thomas Aquinas termed "*docilitas*": the openness to learn, not simply in relation to our own boundary of unknowing, but in relation to other scholars who join with us to explore this important complex of boundaries.[35] Prudence, or practical wisdom, is also, significantly, an intellectual virtue of *practical reason*, one that insists on right action following deliberation and judgment. But other elements of prudence are important as well. In the cognitive area, not only teachability but also *memoria* and *solertia* are important.[36] Part of the difficulty of ecological restoration, for example, is in knowing which particular historical period to go back to in order to construct a new landscape when its predecessor no longer exists as a result of human activities.[37] Memory that is "true to being" will consider the social and historical aspects of ecological restoration in sustainable projects and not simply an arbitrary historical baseline. Biologists can try to discern what an ecological system may have been like in the past, but they are not in a position to adjudicate which historical period is the one that should be aimed at today. This is an ethical question that requires prudential judgment. *Solertia,* or the ability to act right in the face of the unexpected, is also a skill that is not necessarily commensurate with scientific prowess. Given the number of environmental disasters that are also profoundly human tragedies highlighted on a repeated basis in the news media, I will name just a few: Hurricane Katrina on August 29, 2005; the earthquake in Haiti on January 12, 2010; or Hurricane Sandy on October 29, 2012. All these events involved a scientific account of what happened, but knowing how to respond quickly and decisively requires *solertia*.

I could also go on to name the other aspects of imperative prudence that arguably connect with practices of sustainability, including, for example, caution, insight, reason, foresight, and circumspection, which basically means taking account of what is known, in other words, the insights portrayed in science. Foresight is interesting in this respect: if we could have accurate foresight about, for example, climate change, perhaps there would be less intense debate about the level of scientific uncertainty in climate change models. For Aquinas, foresight is linked with God's Providence, and therefore it underlies one important difficulty faced by the modern believer and scientist. Do the changes that we are experiencing undermine our faith in divine Providence? Or does Providence give us confidence that, in spite of human sinfulness, or what might be called in this case anthropogenic sin, Earth will still somehow be under divine protection? This is too large an issue to address here; my intention is to show how theological reflection might be inspired by the uncertainties evident in modern science as much as their discoveries.

WISDOM IN THE UNIVERSITY

My concluding discussion reflects, perhaps, a wider sense that theological reflection should not just be seen as inspired by the sciences but as actively making a contribution to the way truth is not only perceived but also realized in practical ways.[38] MacIntyre famously described the normative principles of justice and rationality as culturally laden.[39] Much the same could be said about conceptions of truth but in this case drawing on distinct epistemological bases. The fragmentation and specialization of that knowledge in the modern university has tended to silence theological or religious discussion as not relevant or pertinent to university education. The University of Notre Dame is an important exception to that trend, by naming but not shaming its theological values as central to its mission as a center of excellence in university education. In such a context, we can recover, perhaps, a role for theology that recenters the human enterprise in the search for truth on the moral and religious claims that prioritize some fields of research over others. It would be appropriate to name this an exercise in seeking wisdom rather than simply knowledge, where wisdom is that classical sense of rediscovering the relationship between fields of study and, in theological terms, inclusive of a relationship with God. What might that wisdom look like in practice?

In the first place, theological wisdom in the university draws on education that students have already received in the context of family and community. In the Hebrew scriptures this way of learning was *practical* and *contextual* long before personified wisdom came to the fore and prior to contemporary uses of wisdom literature in theological discourse. This *praxis* understood as theory informed by practices is very different from utilitarian methods, which emphasize usefulness for its own sake and attempt to control knowledge, detached from other forms of knowing and contemplation. In the university setting itself, the context of students' community life is just as important to learning as the content of their courses.

Second, theological wisdom is expressed in the Hebrew Bible in feminine categories. I am confining my discussion of wisdom to Christian theology, but this should not be taken to imply that I think that other religions have little to offer to the debates on wisdom. I focus on arguably the most dominant religious tradition in the Western world in order to show what insights this tradition might lend to the university as an institution for higher education. Christian theology has been dogged in its history by interpretations of theology that are influenced by patriarchal societies and assumptions. Such influences also creep into a university setting in a way that is subliminal if not carefully examined. Catherine Keller, a leading feminist theologian, has drawn on the idea of *emancipatory wisdom* as that which best describes the future of theology in the university.[40] It is wisdom that can straddle the world of the academic and ecclesial communities to which theology must give an account of itself. For Keller, wisdom, "at least as practised in the indigenous and biblical traditions, is irredeemably implicated in the sensuous, the communal, the experiential, the metanoic, the unpredictable, the imaginal, the practical."[41] Her use here of "metanioic," from *metanoia,* meaning "change of heart," is significant as it implies transformation. This differs significantly from the coercive control of matter by the mind, which is the dominant agenda of modernity; rather it takes time to "let things become" and includes the social as well as the cosmological. Theological wisdom, therefore, is not individualistic but highly relational, operating from within the social context and reaching out to the natural world as well. It has the capacity, therefore, to enlarge a student's horizons to consider issues that are important not just to the human community, but to the community of other creatures. Indeed, based on Proverbs 8, God could be said to create the world in love but through wisdom.[42] Hence wisdom is a fundamental characteristic of the way God is perceived to create and sustain the world, perceived as a child at play, ever present with God at the dawn of existence. Yet such a theological interpretation of creation in wisdom, although grounded in a different metaphysics, does not need to be at loggerheads with cosmological and evolutionary accounts of the origin of the Earth inasmuch as they remain material accounts of origins.[43] Rather, it adds to such an account a dimension that fills out an interpretation of human origins in a way that complements the voice of science. Even many evolutionary biologists are now claiming that being religious is part of what makes human beings human.

Third, a theological voice is one that needs to be heard, for without it more extreme voices start to force their way into higher education's agenda. Such a worrying trend is only too apparent in those who wish to promote creationism, the belief that the story of Genesis is literally true and an alternative to the evolutionary account of science. While creationist science's voice has become rather more sophisticated through the notion of intelligent design, it still seeks to provide through ideology an alternative to neo-Darwinian notions of evolutionary science. Even if many biologists believe that neo-Darwinian theory is insufficient on its own to explain all aspects of evolution, thus including now more sophisticated accounts of epigenetics, behavioral inheritance, or symbolic learning, it is still accepted as a key working paradigm. It is hardly surprising that given this trend virtually all secular universities in the United States wish to keep theology out of their agendas. Yet perhaps it is for this reason that such counterreactions have found their force. For if people are inculcated into utilitarian methods of learning and thinking at universities, then a culture that is generally religious will sense some disorientation and so be more inclined to an equally narrow reaction to that utilitarianism. In other words, a narrowing of epistemology through a secularist agenda such as that expressed in university education all too easily leads to a counterreaction that is ironically a very reflection of such narrowness but now expressed in religious terms. The narrowing of epistemology and counteraction in creationist accounts highlights the importance of a rich understanding of theological wisdom that will discourage such retreats into what seem to be apparently safe havens.

Fourth, and more radical perhaps, New Testament theological wisdom finds expression through the paradox of suffering, rather than a celebration of human wisdom, in the wisdom of the cross.[44] While not doing away with the wisdom of the sages, the wisdom of the cross points to another way of being that makes most sense in the context of the Christian community. Yet could the wisdom of the cross have wider relevance as well? Certainly, it shows that a Christian image of God is one that is on the side of those who are suffering and in pain. One of the important tasks of the university is pastoral; students do not achieve in a vacuum but are enabled through their lived experiences. If such experiences are too traumatic, learning may suffer, at least temporarily. It is here that a university needs to include not just a curriculum but also provision for the pastoral needs of its students through adequate counseling and chaplaincy. Discussions of the wisdom of the cross in the Epistle to the Corinthians are also set in the context of an early Christian community in which different groups vied for authority according to different perceptions of wisdom. Instead of such rhetorical game playing, the author of the epistle encourages reflection on the wisdom of the cross. Such wisdom speaks of the need for humility rather than jockeying for positions of power through clever forms of speech. Is such a goal realistic in a university context? What would the shape of university management be like if such an approach were adopted by university presidents?

Let me end this essay with a citation from Thomas Aquinas, who viewed theology as the *scientia* of sacred doctrine.

> In man different objects of knowledge imply different kinds of knowledge: in knowing principles he is said to have "understanding," in knowing conclusions "science," in knowing highest cause "wisdom," in knowing human actions "counsel" or "prudence." But all these things God knows by one simple knowledge. . . . Hence God's simple knowledge may be called by all these names, provided that in using any of them of God we exclude from their meaning all that implies imperfection, and retain only what implies perfection.[45]

NOTES

This is an expanded version of a paper first presented to the Notre Dame Institute for Advanced Study conference, "Conceptions of Truth and Unity of Knowledge," held at the University of Notre Dame, April 12–14, 2012. I would like to thank the organizers for inviting me to participate and my research assistant, Rebecca Artinian Kaiser, for careful assistance in the final preparation stages.

1. Aquinas thought of theology as a science in a manner similar to the way some sciences work from premises established in light of a higher science, such as optics following from principles established in geometry. For Aquinas, theology followed from God-given principles. Hence, "Christian theology should be pronounced to be a science . . . for it flows from founts recognized in the light of higher science, namely God's very own which he shares with the blessed. Hence as harmony credits its principles which are taken from arithmetic, so Christian theology takes on faith its principles revealed by God." Thomas Aquinas, *Summa Theologiae*, vol. 1, *Christian Theology*, trans. Thomas Gilby (Cambridge: Blackfriars, 1963), 1a Q.1.2.

2. Aquinas, *Summa Theologiae*, 1a Q. 1.5.

3. Alasdair MacIntyre, *Three Rival Versions of Moral Inquiry: Encyclopedia, Genealogy and Tradition* (Notre Dame: University of Notre Dame Press, 1990).

4. MacIntyre, *Three Rival Versions of Moral Inquiry,* 35.

5. C. P. Snow, *The Two Cultures* (Cambridge: Cambridge University Press, 1998).

6. This was Tertullian's famous question regarding the Hellenization of Christianity which has served as an inspiration for scholars ever since. What indeed does Athens have to do with Jerusalem? What concord is there between the Academy and the Church? Between heretics and Christians? Tertullian, *De praescriptione*, Chapter VII; Tertullian, *Prescription against Heretics* (Kesinger Publishing, 2004). English translation also available on-line, *Prescription against Heretics*, New Advent Translation, www.newadvent.org/fathers/0311.htm.

7. See S. J. Gould: "Nonoverlapping Magisteria," *Natural History* 106, no. 2 (March 1997): 16–22; *Rocks of Ages: Science and Religion in the Fullness of Life* (New York: Ballantine, 2002); *The Hedgehog, the Fox and the Magister's Pox: Mending the Gap between Science and the Humanities* (New York: Three Rivers Press, 2003).

8. See, e.g., Dominic Johnson, "What Are Atheists For? Hypotheses on the Function of Non-Belief in the Evolution of Religion," *Religion, Brain and Behavior* 2, no. 1 (2012): 48–59.

9. C. S. Alcorta and R. Sosis, "Ritual, Emotion, and Sacred Symbols: The Evolution of Religion as an Adaptive Complex," *Human Nature* 16 (2005): 323–59; P. Boyer, *Religion Explained: The Evolutionary Origins of Religious Thought* (New York: Basic Books, 2001); S. Atran, *In Gods We Trust: The Evolutionary Landscape of Religion* (Oxford: Oxford University Press, 2004); J. Bulbulia, "Meme Infection or Religious Niche Construction? An Adaptationist Alternative to the Cultural Maladaptationist Hypothesis," *Method and Theory in the Study of Religion* 20 (2008): 1–42; J. M. Bering, *The God Instinct: The Psychology of Souls, Destiny and the Meaning of Life* (London:

Nicolas Brealey, 2010); R. Sosis, "The Adaptationist-Byproduct Debate on the Evolution of Religion: Five Misunderstandings of the Adaptationist Program," *Journal of Cognition and Culture* 9 (2009): 315–32.

10. Stephen Jay Gould introduced the term *exaptation* to explain that traits may evolve without any particular advantage but then become co-opted later in a way that enhances evolutionary fitness. S. J. Gould and E. Vrba, "Exaptation: A Missing Term in the Science of Form," *Paleobiology* 8, no. 1 (1982): 4–15.

11. There is an intellectual difficulty with the spandrel concept, which assumes that characteristics have evolved through natural selection and therefore must have attached to something else that is advantageous. This leads biologists to be more cautious about pressing adaptation too far. For discussion, see M. Pigliucci and J. M. Kaplan, "The Fall and Rise of Dr Pangloss: Adaptationism and the Spandrels Paper 20 Years Later," *Trends in Ecology and Evolution* 15, no. 2 (2000): 66–70.

12. N. Tinbergen, "On Aims and Methods of Ethology," *Zeitschrift für Tierpsychologie* 20, no. 4 (1963): 410–33.

13. See "Ultimate and Penultimate Things," in Dietrich Bonhoeffer, *Ethics*, ed. C. Green, trans. R. Krauss, C. West, and D. Stott, Dietrich Bonhoeffer Works 6 (Minneapolis: Fortress Press, 2005), 146–70.

14. In 1961 Ernst Mayr was the first to use the terms *ultimate* and *proximate* in biology, an idea he continued to develop until 1993. E. Mayr, "Cause and Effect in Biology," *Science* 131 (1961): 1501–6; and "Proximate and Ultimate Causation," *Biology and Philosophy* 8 (1993): 93–94. By "ultimate," he meant evolutionary in a historical sense. See, e.g., Kevin Laland, John Odling-Smee, William Hoppitt, and Tobias Uller, "More on How and Why: Cause and Effect in Biology Revisited," *Biology and Philosophy* (August 7, 2012), http://lalandlab.st-andrews.ac.uk/documents/Publication185.pdf.

15. The language of "supernatural punishment" appears in evolutionary accounts of religious belief, where such tendencies, however they are derived, are treated as modular psychological "objects" that can be analyzed by natural selection. See Dominic Johnson, "Why God Is the Best Punisher," *Religion, Brain and Behavior* 1, no. 1 (2011): 77–84.

16. Alasdair MacIntyre, *Whose Justice? Which Rationality?* (Notre Dame, IN: University of Notre Dame Press, 1988).

17. Karl Rahner, *Theological Investigations*, vol. 13, *Theology, Anthropology, Christology*, trans. David Bourke (New York: Crossroad, 1983), 80–102. Rahner also acknowledges Aquinas, but what is interesting is that he considers him the pioneer of a basically anthropocentric approach to theology. But he also acknowledged Thomas's ongoing relevance as one who could think in

a broad way, who was self-critical, who listened to the views of others and paid attention to points that might at first seem insignificant (5–7), all of which might be termed the "virtues" required of a theologian, or of any scholar for that matter.

18. Karl Rahner, *Theological Investigations,* vol. 17, *Jesus, Man and the Church,* trans. M. Kohl (New York: Crossroad, 1981), 64. So for him, what are apparently secular anthropologies are "secretly theological assertions," and theological statements are "the radical form of secular anthropological statements."

19. E. O. Wilson, *Consilience: The Unity of Knowledge* (London: Abacus, 2003).

20. William Paley, *Natural Theology, or, Evidences of the Existence and Attributes of the Deity Collected from the Appearances of Nature* (Oxford: Oxford University Press, [1802] 2006); John Ray, *The Wisdom of God Manifested in the Works of Creation* (1691), www.jri.org.uk/ray/wisdom/.

21. Arguably his growing confidence in the scientific explanation was not the direct cause of his eventual loss of faith, but other personal factors such as the death of his child and his own received theological views that interpreted different forms as a result of God's direct creative activity were hard to reconcile with his understanding of evolution by natural selection.

22. Richard Dawkins, *Unweaving the Rainbow: Science, Delusion and the Appetite for Wonder* (London: Faber and Faber, 1998), 17.

23. Paul Davis, *The Mind of God: The Scientific Basis for a Rational World* (New York: Simon & Schuster, 1992).

24. Daniel Dennett, *Breaking the Spell* (New York: Viking, 2006). In 2007, Daniel Dennett, Richard Dawkins, Sam Harris, and Christopher Hitchens created a video titled *Four Horsemen of the Apocalypse,* deliberately setting out to discredit the credibility of religious belief and the religious attacks on their science. See www.youtube.com/watch?v=MuyUz2XLp1E.

25. Karl Barth, *Nein! Antwort an Emil Brunner* (Munich: C. Kaiser, 1934).

26. A question also raised by Sarah Coakley in her recent Gifford Lectures, *Sacrifice Regained: Evolution, Cooperation and God,* www.abdn.ac.uk/gifford/. There is a difference in Coakley's approach, however, since she seems to argue for an *apologetic* version of natural theology based on a particular interpretation of the fifth of Aquinas's *Five Ways to God.* Coakley rejects, correctly in my view, pitching theistic teleological arguments *against* evolutionary theories, since this smacks of a dualistic competition between God and scientific interpretations and argues, further, that to portray evolution as simply "random" is far too oversimplified. But she seems to want to not just permit but also *highlight* an interpretation of the fifth teleological way as an explicit argument for God's existence (alongside other possible interpretations, such as

to bolster existing revelatory faith or bring to consciousness in a believer what may be hidden from view). But in finding the fifth way lacking in light of the possibility of a purely naturalistic, evolutionary interpretation, she then proposes an argument for God's existence through the ecstatic or excessive altruism of the saints, which, she argues, is necessarily and always outside the realm of possible scientific explanations and therefore not in competition with it. See Sarah Coakley, Lecture 5, "Teleology Reviewed: A New 'Ethico-Teleological' Argument for God's Existence," in *Sacrifice Regained,* 17–19. I am arguing for something rather more modest, and more in line with Aquinas's discussion in the *Summa* of the relationship between theology and the sciences, namely, a form of "natural" theologizing that is useful in order to clarify the theological task but presupposes faith in God. I am not attempting, in other words, to convince the nonbeliever or return to supposed arguments for God's existence, but, like Coakley, I also believe that theology needs to be given a place in the public sphere.

27. Bonaventure, *The Journey of the Mind to God,* ed. S. F. Brown, trans. P. Boehner (Indianapolis: Hackett Publishing, 1993), chap. 1, § 10–12, p. 8. For further discussion of Bonaventure, see Celia Deane-Drummond, *Wonder and Wisdom: Conversations in Science, Spirituality and Theology* (London: Darton, Longman and Todd, 2006), 56–58.

28. Bonaventure, *The Journey of the Mind to God,* chap. 2, § 1, p. 11.

29. Ibid., Prologue, § 4, p. 2. See also pp. 70–71 for commentary.

30. "Keynote Address of His Holiness Ecumenical Patriarch Bartholomew at the Opening Ceremony of the Halki Summit." Halki Theological School, June 18, 2012. www.patriarchate.org/documents/2012halkisummit.

31. For a full discussion of this topic, see Celia Deane-Drummond, "Joining the Dance: Ecology and Catholic Social Teaching," *New Blackfriars* 93, no. 1044 (March 2012): 193–212.

32. John Paul II, "General Audience Address," January 17, 2001. www .vatican.va/holy_father/john_paul_ii/audiences/2001/documents/hf_jp-ii_ aud_20010117_en.html.

33. See, e.g., Christopher Southgate, *The Groaning of Creation: God, Evolution, and the Problem of Evil* (Louisville, KY: Westminster John Knox Press, 2008).

34. Pope Benedict XVI, *Caritas in Veritate,* www.vatican.va/holy_father /benedict_xvi/encyclicals/documents/hf_ben-xvi_enc_20090629_caritas-in -veritate_en.html.

35. Aquinas, *Summa Theologiae,* vol. 36, *Prudence,* trans. Thomas Gilby (Cambridge: Blackfriars, 1973), 2a2ae Q. 49.3.

36. For more detailed discussion of the different facets of prudence, see Celia Deane-Drummond, *The Ethics of Nature* (Oxford: Blackwell, 2004), 9–15.

37. For more on the practical and historical limitations of ecological restoration, see Stephen T. Jackson and Richard J. Hobbs, "Ecological Restoration in the Light of Ecological History," *Science* 325, no. 5940 (2009): 567; Stuart Allison, "What Do We Mean When We Talk about Ecological Restoration?," *Ecological Restoration* 22, no. 4 (2004): 281–86.

38. I have discussed this in more detail in Celia Deane-Drummond, "Wisdom Remembered: Recovering a Theological Vision for Wisdom in the Academe," in *Wisdom in the University*, ed. Ronald Barnett and Nicholas Maxwell (London: Routledge, 2008), 77–88; and "The Amnesia of Modern Universities: An Argument for Theological Wisdom in the Academe," in *Educating for Wisdom in the Twenty-First Century*, ed. Darin Davis (Waco, TX: Baylor University Press, 2013).

39. MacIntyre, *Whose Justice, Which Rationality?*

40. C. Keller, "Towards an Emancipatory Wisdom," in *Theology and the University: Essays in Honor of John B. Cobb Jr*, ed. D. R. Griffin and J. C. Hough (Albany: State University of New York Press, 1991), 125–47.

41. Keller, "Towards Emancipatory Wisdom," 143.

42. A full discussion of this is outside the scope of this chapter. For more detail, see C. Deane-Drummond, *Creation through Wisdom: Theology and the New Biology* (Edinburgh: T & T Clark, 2000).

43. Deane-Drummond, *Wonder and Wisdom.*

44. The first letter of Paul to the Corinthians, e.g., esp. 1 Cor. 1:8–2:5.

45. Aquinas, *Summa Theologiae,* vol. 4, *Knowledge in God,* trans. Thomas Gornall (Cambridge: Blackfriars, 1964), 1a Q. 14.1.

ABOUT THE CONTRIBUTORS

FRANCISCO J. AYALA is University Professor and Donald Bren Professor of Biological Sciences and Professor of Philosophy at the University of California, Irvine. His research and teaching focuses on evolution, genetics, and the philosophy of biology. Ayala is a member of the National Academy of Sciences (NAS) and a recipient of the 2001 National Medal of Science. He served as chair of the Authoring Committee of *Science, Evolution, and Creationism*, jointly published in 2008 by the NAS and the Institute of Medicine. He has received numerous awards, including the 2010 Templeton Prize for exceptional contribution to affirming life's spiritual dimension, and twenty honorary degrees from universities in nine countries. He has been president and chairman of the board of the American Association for the Advancement of Science and president of Sigma Xi, the Scientific Research Society of the United States. Ayala is the author of numerous books and articles on the intersection of science and the humanities, including *Darwin's Gift to Science and Religion* (2007) and *Am I a Monkey?* (2010).

CELIA DEANE-DRUMMOND is Professor of Theology at the University of Notre Dame, with a concurrent appointment in the College of Science. She is Fellow of the Eck Institute for Global Health and the John Reilly Center for Science, Technology and Values at Notre Dame. She holds a PhD in plant physiology as well as a PhD in systematic theology. Her research focuses on the engagement of systematic theology and the biological sciences, as well as bioethics and environmental ethics. Before coming to the University of Notre Dame in 2011, Deane-Drummond held a professorial chair in theology and biological sciences at the University of Chester and was director of the Centre for Religion and the Biosciences, launched in 2002. In addition to more than thirty scientific articles, she is the author or editor of twenty-two books, as well as thirty-three contributions to books and forty-three articles in areas relating to theology or ethics. Among her most recent books are *Creation through Wisdom* (2000); *Brave New World*, ed. (2003); coeditor, *Re-Ordering Nature* (2003); *The Ethics of Nature* (2004); *Wonder and Wisdom* (2006); *Genetics and Christian Ethics* (2006); coeditor, *Future Perfect* (2006; 2d ed., 2010); *Ecotheology* (2008); *Christ and Evolution* (2009); coeditor, *Creaturely Theology* (2009); *Seeds of Hope* (2010); editor, *Rising to Life* (2011); coeditor, *Religion and Ecology in the Public Sphere* (2011); coeditor, *Animals as Religious Subjects* (2013); *The Wisdom of the Liminal* (2014). Deane-Drummond served as chair of the European Forum for the Study of Religion and Environment from 2011 to 2015. She was editor of the international journal *Ecotheology* (2000–2006), and she was seconded to the spirituality team at the Catholic Fund for Overseas Development, working in the area of environmental justice and climate change (2009–10). She is also co-editor of the journal *Philosophy, Theology and the Sciences*, launched in 2014.

Nicola Di Cosmo is the Henry Luce Foundation Professor of East Asian History in the School of Historical Studies at the Institute for Advanced Study. His main areas of research are relations between China and Central Asia from ancient times to the modern period, the history of foreign dynasties in China, and, more generally, frontier relations seen from archaeological, anthropological, and historical perspectives. Di Cosmo taught at Harvard University and at the University of Canterbury (New Zealand) before joining the faculty of the School of Historical Studies in 2003. He has written on Inner Asian history, Chinese historiography, and military history, and he is the author of several books, including *Ancient China and Its Enemies: The Rise of Nomadic Power in East Asian History* (2002), *A Documentary History of Manchu-Mongol Relations (1616–1626)* (2003), and *Diary of a Manchu Soldier in Seventeenth-Century China* (2006). Di Cosmo has also edited or coedited books, including *Political Frontiers, Ethnic Boundaries and Human Geographies in Chinese History* (2001), *Warfare in Inner Asian History, 500–1800* (2002), *The Cambridge History of Inner Asia: The Chinggisid Age* (2009), and *Military Culture in Imperial China* (2009). He has written numerous book chapters as well as articles in such publications as the *Journal of World History*, *International History Review*, and *Central Asiatic Journal*. He is on the advisory or editorial boards of the *Journal of East Asian Archaeology*, *Asia Major*, and *Inner Asia*. Di Cosmo has received fellowships from the New Zealand Royal Society, Harvard University's Milton Fund, the Chiang Ching-kuo Foundation, the Center for Chinese Studies in Taipei, the Institute of Asian and Middle Eastern Studies in Rome, and the Italian Ministry of Education. In addition, he leads Smithsonian Study Tours to Mongolia.

CARSTEN DUTT is Assistant Professor of German at the University of Notre Dame. His research focuses on the intersection of literary criticism and philosophy. The author or coeditor of several books, Dutt has published in the fields of hermeneutics (*Hermeneutik, Ästhetik, Praktische Philosophie*, 2000, English translation 2001; *Gadamers philosophische Hermeneutik und die Literaturwissenschaft*, 2012), the theory and methodology of conceptual history (*Herausforderungen der Begriffsgeschichte*, 2003; *Zwischen Sprache und Geschichte*, 2013), and modern German literature (*Figurationen der literarischen Moderne*, 2007; *Die Schuldfrage*, 2010; *Zur Lyrik Gottfried Benns*, 2014). He is also coeditor of Karl Jaspers's correspondence (2014, 3 vols.). His current book project focuses on the epistemology of literary interpretation. He received fellowships from the Center for Literary and Cultural Studies in Berlin, the Collegium Budapest, and the Notre Dame Institute for Advanced Study.

ALLAN GIBBARD is Richard B. Brandt Distinguished University Professor of Philosophy at the University of Michigan, Ann Arbor, where he has taught for three decades. His research focuses on ethical theory, social choice theory and decision theory, evolutionary moral psychology, philosophy of language, metaphysics, and epistemology. He is the author of *Wise Choices, Apt Feelings* (1990), *Thinking How to Live* (2003), *Reconciling Our Aims* (2008), and *Meaning and Normativity* (2012). Gibbard is also the author of numerous articles in journals such as *Philosophical Studies*, *Journal of Philosophical Logic*, *Econo-*

metrica, Journal of Philosophy, Social Theory and Practice, Philosophia, Ethics, and *Theory and Decision.* He has served as president of the Central Division of the American Philosophical Association, and he is a member of the National Academy of Sciences, a fellow of the American Academy of Arts and Sciences, a member of the American Philosophical Society, a fellow of the Econometric Society, and a *membre titulaire* of the Institut International de Philosophie. He has held research fellowships from the National Endowment for the Humanities, the Guggenheim Foundation, the Rockefeller Foundation, and the American Council of Learned Societies.

Robert Hanna is Professor of Philosophy at the University of Colorado at Boulder. He is a philosophical generalist whose areas of research include Kant's philosophy and Kantian themes in contemporary philosophy; the history of analytic philosophy; philosophical logic; the philosophy of mind, cognition, and action; and ethics. Hanna is the author of *Kant and the Foundations of Analytic Philosophy* (2001); *Kant, Science, and Human Nature* (2006); *Rationality and Logic* (2006); with Michelle Maiese, *Embodied Minds in Action* (2009); with A. Chapman, A. Ellis, T. Hildebrand, and H. Pickford, *In Defense of Intuitions: A New Rationalist Manifesto* (2013); and *Cognition, Content, and the A Priori* (forthcoming). His current book project, *The Rational Human Condition*, is an attempt to work out a general theory of human rationality in a fully natural and desperately nonideal world.

Vittorio Hösle is Paul Kimball Professor of Arts and Letters in the Department of German and Russian Languages and Literatures and Concurrent Professor of Philosophy and of Political Science at the University of Notre Dame, where he served as founding director of the NDIAS from 2008 to 2013. In 2013, he was appointed to the Pontifical Academy of Social Sciences by Pope Francis. Hösle's scholarly interests include systematic philosophy (metaphysics, ethics, aesthetics, and political theory) and history of philosophy (mainly ancient and modern). He is the author, editor, or coeditor of more than forty books, which have appeared in twenty languages, including *Morals and Politics* (2004) and *God as Reason* (2011), and more than 140 articles. His most widely published work (translated into fourteen languages) is *The*

Dead Philosopher's Café (2000), an exchange of letters with a young girl that offers an imaginative introduction to the world of philosophy.

LAURENT LAFFORGUE is Professeur Permanent at the Institut des Hautes Études Scientifiques in Bures-sur-Yvette, France. His research focuses on number theory and analysis. Lafforgue is the recipient of numerous awards and honors, including the Clay Research Prize in 2000 and the Grand Prix Jacques Herbrand de l'Académie des Sciences in 2001. In 2002, he was awarded the prestigious Fields Medal, the equivalent of a Nobel Prize in the field of mathematics, at the International Congress of Mathematicians in Beijing for his work related to the Langlands Program in number theory. Lafforgue established the Langlands conjectures for a much wider class of cases than previously known by proving the global Langlands correspondence for function fields. In 2003, he was named a member of the French Academy of Sciences and became Chevalier de la Légion d'Honneur. In addition to his accomplishments in mathematics, Lafforgue is actively engaged in the preservation of the French school system from ill-advised reforms. His efforts include significant support for the teaching of humanities in French secondary schools. In May 2011, he received an honorary Doctor of Science degree from the University of Notre Dame.

KEITH LEHRER is Regent's Professor Emeritus of Philosophy at the University of Arizona. His research focuses on autonomy, epistemology, consensus, Thomas Reid, and self-trust. He is the author of *Knowledge* (1974), *Rational Consensus in Science and Society: A Philosophical and Mathematical Study* (1981, with Carl Wagner), *Thomas Reid* (1989), *Metamind* (1990), *Theory of Knowledge* (1990), *Philosophical Problems and Arguments: An Introduction* (1992, 4th ed., with James Cornman and George Pappas), and *Self Trust: A Study of Reason, Knowledge and Autonomy* (1997). His most recent book, *Art, Self and Knowledge* (2012), focuses on the philosophy of art. He is also the editor of nine books and numerous journal articles. Lehrer, also a painter, has an interest in choreography and has begun to use one art form to interpret the other. His most recent research objective is to achieve a new unity of art and epistemology. Lehrer is the recipient of numerous honors and awards, including his election in 2005 as fellow of the American

Academy of Arts and Sciences and his election as fellow at the Center for Advanced Study in Behavioral Sciences, Stanford (2007–8). He has also taught at the University of Miami, Santa Clara University, Stanford University, and University of Graz in Austria.

MICHAEL LYKOUDIS is Professor of Architecture and the Francis and Kathleen Rooney Dean of the School of Architecture at the University of Notre Dame. His research focuses on traditional architecture and urbanism, and he has sought to link architectural tradition and classicism to urbanism and environmental issues. Lykoudis is coeditor of two publications, *Building Cities* (1999) and *The Other Modern* (exhibition catalogue) (2000) and the author of *Modernity, Modernism, and the Other Modern* (forthcoming). He is also the author of numerous articles that have appeared in journals such as *Traditional Building*. Prior to joining the Notre Dame faculty, he was a project designer and architect for firms in Connecticut, Florida, New York, and Greece. He has directed his own practice since 1983 in Athens, Greece, and Stamford, Connecticut, and now has a practice in South Bend, Indiana. Lykoudis has organized several major international conferences in collaboration with the Classical Architecture League, the Institute of Classical Architecture and Classical America, A Vision of Europe, and the Congress for New Urbanism. The conference and exhibition titled "The Art of Building Cities" took place in 1995 at the Art Institute of Chicago and was the first event in the United States to link the practice of contemporary classicism with the new traditional urbanism. An exhibition and conference titled "The Other Modern," took place in Bologna, Italy, in 2000, and a conference titled "Three Generations of Classical Architects: The Renewal of Modern Architecture" was held in October 2005 at Notre Dame.

THOMAS NOWAK is Professor Emeritus of Chemistry and Biochemistry at the University of Notre Dame. He specializes in structural biology and biophysics. A former researcher at the Institute for Cancer Research, Nowak came to Notre Dame in 1972. His research group is currently focusing on enzymes involved in metabolic energy utilization and energy storage and enzyme mechanisms, their regulation and structure, how they are interrelated, and their roles in the regulatory

and catalytic processes. His research has appeared in numerous jour-
nals, including *Journal of the American Chemical Society, Biochemistry, Journal of Biological Chemistry*, and *Archives of Biochemistry and Bio-physics*. Nowak is the recipient of a National Institutes of Health Re-search Career Development Award. He has served as a visiting pro-fessor at the University of Groningen in the Netherlands and at the Pontifical Catholic University of Chile in Santiago. Nowak received the Peter A. Burns, C.S.C. graduate school award in 2001 and the Grenville Clark Award in 2008 from the University of Notre Dame.

ZYGMUNT PIZLO is Professor of Psychology and of Electrical and Computer Engineering at Purdue University. His research interests in-clude visual perception, motor control, and problem solving. Pizlo earned PhD degrees in electronic engineering (1982) and psychology (1991). Testing his theories in a robot, he formulated the first psycho-logically plausible theories of how humans perceive 3D shapes, solve combinatorial optimization problems, and trade speed for accuracy in perception and motor control. In 1994, Pizlo received the New Inves-tigator Award from the Society for Mathematical Psychology. He has over one hundred publications, including papers in *Computer Vision and Image Understanding; Memory and Cognition; Journal of Prob-lem Solving, Perception and Psychophysics; Journal of Vision; Vision Research; Journal of Imaging Science and Technology; Pattern Recog-nition Letters, Electroencephalography and Clinical Neurophysiology;* and *Journal of Mathematical Psychology*. Pizlo is also the author of *3D Shape: Its Unique Place in Visual Perception* (2008), the first mono-graph on human perception of three-dimensional shapes, as well as a coauthor of *Making a Machine That Sees Like Us*, which tells the story of a machine built by the authors that solves the computationally difficult problem of seeing the way humans do. He served on the edito-rial boards of *Behavior Research Methods, Instruments, and Com-puters* (1995–98) and the *Journal of Mathematical Psychology* (2003–9) and was president and vice president of the Society for Mathematical Psychology (2008–10). He was the founding editor and currently serves as editor in chief of the *Journal of Problem Solving*. Pizlo's research has been supported by the National Science Foundation, the National Institutes for Health, the Department of Defense, the Department of

Energy, Hewlett-Packard, Sandia National Laboratories, and the Air Force Office of Scientific Research.

AVIEZER TUCKER is Assistant Director of the Energy Institute at the University of Texas in Austin. He specializes in philosophies of historiography and history, with a particular interest in the epistemic aspects of scientific knowledge of the past and the problem of inference of common causes or origins. His more recent work includes topics in political philosophy and theory. He is the author of *Our Knowledge of the Past: A Philosophy of Historiography* (2004) and *The Legacies of Totalitarianism* (forthcoming). He is editor of *The Blackwell Companion to the Philosophy of History and Historiography* (2009). His numerous articles have appeared in journals that include *History and Theory*, *British Journal for the Philosophy of Science*, *Studies in the History and Philosophy of Science*, *Philosophy*, *Inquiry*, and *Erkenntnis*. He is the recipient of numerous research fellowships, including those held at the University of Cologne, the Max Planck Institute, the Gvirtzman Memorial Foundation in Prague, the Australian National University, New York University, Columbia University, and the Central European University in Prague.

OSBORNE WIGGINS is Professor in the Department of Philosophy and Associate Faculty in the Institute for Bioethics, Health Policy, and Law at the University of Louisville. His areas of interest are phenomenology and philosophical anthropology (especially as they apply to psychiatry), the history of ideas, and the philosophy of medicine. With coauthor Michael Alan Schwartz, M.D., Wiggins has published numerous articles on phenomenological psychiatry, addressing classification in psychiatry, the lifeworld-science relationship, schizophrenic experience, and other topics. For this work and his contributions to phenomenological psychiatry, in 1998 Wiggins received the Margrit Egner Award. He is a member of the core faculty of the M.A. program in Bioethics and Medical Humanities at the University of Louisville. With Annette C. Allen, he edited *Clinical Ethics and the Necessity of Stories: Essays in Honor of Richard M. Zaner* (2010).

INDEX

evolution (*cont.*)
    of religion, 304–5, 317
    spandrels in, 24, 304, 320n.11
    and theology, 23–24, 303–5
    thresholds in, 152
    See also cultural evolution; natural
    selection
Ewing, A. C., 213n.1
exaptation, 23–24, 304, 320n.10
exemplar representation, 6, 83–87
experimental data, 10, 162–63,
    186–87, 196, 238, 240–42
    from observation, 9, 15, 31, 115–17
expertise in self-reflection, 14
expressivism, 16, 207–9, 211–12, 213n4

faith, 41, 115, 116, 300, 310, 321n.26
Fan Ye: *History of the Later Han
    Dynasty (Hou Hanshu)*, 269–70
Fechner, Gustav, 12, 159–60
Fei-Fei, L., 168
Field, Hartry, 100n.6
    on inferential principles, 95
figure-ground organization (FGO),
    167, 168, 170, 172
Fischer, J. M., 151
Five Agents theory, 280
Fleming, A., 118–19
Fodor, J. A., 82, 87
foundational disciplines, 2–3
foundationalism, 5–6, 74–76
Four Horsemen of the Apocalypse
    (video), 321n.24
free will
    and inference, 7, 90, 92, 98–99,
    101n.17
    Kant on, 89
    relationship to morality, 151–52
Frege, Gottlob, 4, 59
    The Thought, 57
French Enlightenment, 49

French imperialism, 32
French Revolution, 238, 241
fructose-1,6-diphosphate (FBP),
    125–26, 127, 129, 130, 132, 133,
    134–35

Gadamer, Hans-Georg, 16
Galileo Galilei, 47, 118, 233
Gallagher, Shaun, 186
Gazzaniga, M. S., 153, 156
gene-culture coevolution, 152–53
Genesis 3:17, 40
genetics, 119–20, 305
    genomes, 247
Gentz, Joachim, 266
geography, 31, 63, 275
geology, 54, 59, 251
German Idealism, 4
germ theory of disease, 118–19
Gestalt psychology, 13, 170, 171, 186
Gettier, Edmund, 230n.17
Gibson, E., 165
Gillett, Grant, 181
givenness
    direct givenness in self-awareness,
    14, 183, 185, 187–88, 190, 191–92
    vs. interpretation, 187–88, 225, 227
    Sellars on myth of the given, 6,
    76–77, 84–85
glycolysis, 9–10, 120–39
God
    as creator, 40, 309–10, 316, 321n.21
    existence of, 24, 321n.26
    goodness of, 24, 309, 310
    and laws of nature, 308
    and mathematics, 24, 111
    perfect knowledge possessed by,
    318
    providence of, 314–15
    as reason, 58
    as trinity, 40